A Guide to Scottish Trusts 2002/2003

Dave Griffiths

Tom Traynor

Louise Walker

Sarah Wiggins

Published by
Directory of Social Change
24 Stephenson Way
London NW1 2DP
Tel. 020 7209 5151; Fax 020 7391 4804
e-mail books@dsc.org.uk
www.dsc.org.uk
from whom further copies and a full publications list are available.

Directory of Social Change is a Registered Charity no. 800517

ISBN 1 903991 08 0

British Library Cataloguing in Publication Data
A catalogue record for this book is available from the British Library

Text designed by Lenn Darroux
Cover design by Keith Shaw
Typeset by Directory of Social Change, Liverpool
Printed and bound by Antony Rowe, Chippenham

Other Directory of Social Change departments in London:
Courses and conferences 020 7209 4949
Charity Centre 020 7209 1015
Charityfair 020 7209 1015
Publicity 020 7391 4900
Research 020 7391 4880

Directory of Social Change Northern Office:
Federation House, Hope Street, Liverpool L1 9BW
Courses and conferences 0151 708 0117
Research 0151 708 0136

Contents

Foreword

The grant-making trust world can often be quite inaccessible to those seeking support and therefore I very much welcome this splendid new guide to Scottish trusts.

It is a firmly held conviction of the trustees of Lloyds TSB Foundation for Scotland that we can only begin to properly serve our customers by being fully transparent in both criteria and working practices. Through this publication a wide range of trusts and foundations have grasped the opportunity to set out their information in a clear and helpful way.

Voluntary organisations throughout Scotland face many challenges, not least finding adequate resources to deliver services that are so vital to communities throughout the country. It is the duty of grantmakers not to act as gatekeepers to resources but to see themselves as facilitators easing the interface between available monies and people who can put it to good use. There is a great deal of time and effort expended by staff and volunteers in fundraising activities and this is especially the case when attempting to secure funds from trusts and foundations. This guide is most comprehensive and the information it offers will make it much easier to deploy time efficiently in pursuit of funding goals.

The major strength of trusts and foundations is that each is unique in terms of criteria and funding priorities. This allows for a wide spectrum of activity to be embraced by the organisations which go to make use of this publication. In recognising this strength one must also recognise that, as a consequence, voluntary organisations must devote a significant amount of time to researching each funder, to identify those which support their type of work and feel inclined towards their area of the country. If there is one aspect which is common to all grantmakers it is their warm appreciation of a well-researched, accurately-targeted, submission.

In setting the above challenge to voluntary organisations of researching potential sources, I must share the experience of Lloyds TSB Foundation for Scotland as clear evidence of how far the sector has advanced in this regard over recent years. In 1996 more than 50% of all submissions received by the foundation were outside criteria. That figure now sits at less than 20%.

The voluntary sector in Scotland stands at an exciting threshold. The growth in awareness generally of the need for greater social inclusion has resulted in the work of the sector gaining a higher place on business and political agendas. We look forward to the recent Charity Law Review giving way to a new framework for charities in Scotland, one which improves the voluntary sector's access to support, advice and guidance. Also, one hopes for a regulatory framework which is both user friendly and at the same time enhances the already excellent reputation enjoyed by charities in the country at large.

The grant-making scene has been greatly improved in recent years through the work of the Scottish Grant Making Trust Group. Around 19 of this country's largest funders work together in areas of common interest, including strengthening links to black and minority ethnic groups, reaching remote rural communities and building relationships with charitable trusts outside Scotland.

This publication seeks to bring funders and grantseekers closer together. As funders we must never lose sight of the fact that we all rely on the enthusiasm and endeavours of those who work, often in a voluntary capacity, for the good of their communities throughout Scotland. We have a first-class social movement in this country, a force for tremendous good, which deserves the sort of supportive grant-making environment this book helps to engender.

Andrew S Muirhead, Chief Executive
Lloyds TSB Foundation for Scotland

Introduction

Welcome to *A Guide to Scottish Trusts 2002/2003*. This guide contains 350 Scottish trusts with an overall grant total of £53 million: 100 more trusts and £16 million more in grants than the Scottish trusts previously detailed in the first edition of *A Guide to the Major Trusts Volume 3*. Most of the increase in grant total is accounted for by previous grantmakers increasing their giving, rather than by new grantmakers emerging: The Shetland Islands Council Charitable Trust alone grew from a £5.6 million grant total in 1998/99, to £12 million in 1999/2000.

This book arrives in a climate of change for the whole of the voluntary sector in Scotland. Devolution, and the recommendations for reform in *The Report of the Scottish Charity Law Commission*, are significant developments in Scotland. Devolution already shows some signs of giving greater political and economic recognition to the role of Scottish charities, and of bringing them together to focus on a developing policy agenda.

The recommendations for a new regulator of, and support structure for, charities could, for example, lead to greater transparency of, and more effective spending by, charities. Within this context there is all the more reason for charities to review their funding structures and plan for sustainability.

We therefore hope that this guide proves beneficial both to fundraisers, who can use the information to better target appropriate trusts, and to funders, who will receive suitable applications that meet their criteria and policies.

Which trusts are in this guide?

Trusts are included in this guide which:

- have a preference for, or stated interest in, Scotland or part of Scotland

- make grants totalling £1,000 or more to organisations in Scotland

- give to organisations, not just to individuals.

Top 25 trusts in Scotland

The top 25 trusts in this guide account for 80% of the grant total (see *The Top 25 Scottish Grant-making Trusts*, on page 9). The Shetland Islands Council Charitable Trust has overtaken The Gannochy Trust and The Robertson Trust to become the largest Scottish trust. This is the result of an increase in spending, rather than a higher income. The geographical restrictions result in a staggering £500 per person being available in the Shetland Islands from this trust alone. To put this in perspective, in the rest of Scotland as a whole, about £8 per person is available from the trusts in this guide. No other unitary authority area, or region in Scotland (or indeed England), comes anywhere near the Shetland Islands in this respect, as the following table indicates.

GEOGRAPHICAL DISTRIBUTION OF GRANTS			
Chapter	Grant total	No. trusts	£ per person
Scotland – general	£36,000,000	212	£7.00
Regions			
Aberdeen & Perthshire	£610,000	31	£0.70
Central Scotland	£119,000	8	£0.19
Edinburgh, the Lothians & the Borders	£840,000	25	£0.87
Glasgow & the West of Scotland	£2,600,00	58	£1.07
Highlands & Islands*	£12,300,000	14	£44.00

*includes Shetlands, which alone has grants of £500 per person.

The Lloyds TSB Foundation for Scotland is the second largest grantmaker in the country, and continues to be a very significant Scottish trust – not least because applications can be made from anywhere in Scotland. Its grant total increased by almost £1 million between 1999 and 2000. It remains an example to other grantmakers, with one of the most transparent, focused grant-making programmes in the UK.

Of the top 25 trusts, a further six have some geographical preference in their grant-making criteria. Central Scotland is the only region of Scotland not represented with a larger trust.

'Buildings of the Church of Scotland' is the most specific cause to be supported by any of the top 25 trusts, with grants from the Baird Trust. Otherwise a range of causes are supported, although a preference for medical care or research appears the most common.

Is Scotland getting a fair share?

The table below shows that Scotland does relatively well for money from locally-oriented trusts.

Charities Aid Foundation research for *Dimensions 2000: Patterns of Independent Grant-making in the UK* also took into consideration trusts with a UK-wide focus. Scotland came out in third position, with £11 per person, behind London (£30 per person), and the south west of England (£12 per person).

SCOTTISH & LOCAL TRUST GUIDES' MONEY AVAILABLE

Area	£ per person
Scotland	£10.35
London	£ 8.00
North of England	£ 4.50
Midlands	£ 3.50
South of England	£ 2.80

This table uses data from this guide and the four *Guides to Local Trusts* for England. The figures reflect the amount of money available per person from trusts that state local preferences only, and do not include grant money from trusts that give UK-wide and internationally.

It is encouraging that some major trusts have taken steps to distribute grants more fairly to those areas that need them the most. The Esmée Fairbairn Charitable Trust (see *A Guide to the Major Trusts Volume 1*), for instance, gives about £2 million a year to Scottish causes a year, which in 1999 worked out at 40p per person, compared with 50p per person in the Greater London Boroughs. This differential had already flattened out considerably by 2000, when in Scotland 42p

per person was donated, compared with 45p in London. The greatest difference was for Northern Ireland, which rose from 18p per person to 42p per person.

Getting the most from this guide – a first stop in Scotland

The Directory of Social Change publishes a number of directories of grant-making trusts. We recommend this guide as the first-stop guide for every organisation carrying out fundraising in Scotland. Our experience shows that fundraisers will have more success if they tap into local money before competing for money which does not have the same geographical restrictions on it. Applicants are more likely to have success with local trusts, whose support can also give credibility to small organisations who are applying to national bodies.

Other ports of call

Of the total income of the voluntary sector in Scotland, 13% is received from grant-making trusts. This is the fourth highest source of income for Scottish charities, after self-generated income (trading, rents, investments, etc.), donations from the general public and other public sector grants. About a quarter of this money is accounted for by trusts in this book, with the rest received from UK-wide and international trusts.

Details of many of these other trusts and sources of income are also available in Directory of Social Change guides, along with information about how to make successful applications.

A complete booklist is available from our London office (020 7209 5151; e-mail: books@dsc.org.uk) and Liverpool office (0151 708 0117; e-mail: north@dsc.org.uk) or via our website: www.dsc.org.uk

How to apply to trusts

For guidance on making applications, please see *How to make an application* by Susan Robinson of Institute of Charity Fundraising Managers Scotland, on page 15. We would like to make just a few points here.

The competition for grants is high, and most trusts get many more applications than they can possibly fund. The Ellis Campbell Charitable Foundation, for instance, received 308

THE TOP 25 SCOTTISH GRANT-MAKING TRUSTS

£12,000,000	**The Shetland Islands Council Charitable Trust**	General in Shetland
£5,700,000	**The Lloyds TSB Foundation for Scotland**	Social and community needs, education and training, scientific, medical and social research in Scotland
£4,800,000	**The Robertson Trust**	Care, education, medical, drugs prevention and treatment, general in Scotland
£4,200,000	**The Gannochy Trust**	General in Scotland, with a preference for Perth and its environs
£2,800,000	**The Scottish Community Foundation**	Community in Scotland
£2,600,000	**BBC Children in Need Appeal**	Disadvantaged children in the UK with a proportion of grants made in Scotland
£1,200,000	**The Dunard Fund**	Arts and music, mainly in Scotland
£1,200,000	**The Hugh Fraser Foundation**	General in the UK, especially western or deprived areas of Scotland
£924,000	**The Northwood Charitable Trust**	Health, general in Scotland, especially Dundee and Tayside
£800,000	**The North British Hotel Trust**	Welfare, health in the UK, but mainly Scotland
£795,000	**The Unemployed Voluntary Action Fund**	Voluntary projects engaging unemployed people as volunteers in Scotland
£700,000	**The MacRobert Trust**	General in the UK, mainly Scotland
£700,000	**The Souter Charitable Trust**	Social welfare, Christianity in the UK, but with a strong preference for Scotland, and overseas
£600,000	**The Scottish Hospital Endowments Research Trust**	Medical research in Scotland
£507,000	**Radio Clyde – Cash for Kids at Christmas**	Children in the Radio Clyde transmission area i.e. west central Scotland
£350,000	**The Carnegie Trust for the Universities of Scotland**	Scottish universities
£314,000	**The Priory of Scotland of the Order of St John of Jerusalem**	Health, welfare, disability in Scotland
£310,000	**The R S MacDonald Charitable Trust**	Visual impairment, cerebral palsy, children, animal welfare in Scotland
£307,000	**The Northern Rock Foundation**	Disadvantaged people in the north east of England, also Scotland, Cumbria, Yorkshire and north west England under certain programmes
£297,000	**The Baird Trust**	Maintenance and repair of churches and halls of the Church of Scotland
£295,000	**City of Edinburgh Charitable Trusts**	General in Edinburgh
£270,000	**The Cunningham Trust**	Medical research projects in Scotland
£268,000	**The D W T Cargill Fund**	General in the UK, with a preference for the West of Scotland
£230,000	**The W A Cargill Fund**	General in Glasgow and the West of Scotland
£229,000	**Mathew Trust**	General in Dundee and district

Please note: The above figures are for the amount given by the trusts in Scotland and not their overall grant total. Sometimes this is an estimation, as precise geographical breakdowns were not available.

applications from people across the UK in 2000, and made
85 grants in total, with 15 in Scotland. However, it is likely that many of these unsuccessful applications did not fit in with the trusts' criteria.

Research which leads to relevant and targeted applications is never wasted. In any case, it is bad practice to apply for grants if you do not fit the eligibility criteria. It only serves to annoy trustees, potentially causing problems for eligible applicants. It is also a waste of your time, paper and stamps.

The layout of this book

The layout of entries, illustrated on page 13, is similar to the pattern established in other Directory of Social Change guides. Please also see page 12 for other information on how to use this guide.

Please note that in this guide we have used the term chair in preference to chairman or chairwoman, unless specifically requested otherwise by the trust.

Unsolicited applications

A number of trusts did not wish to be included in this guide and several reasons were given for this. The most common were that the trusts said they receive too many irrelevant applications (see above) and that they are a 'private' trust. No registered charity is private and, in our opinion, trustees and administrators of trusts should not resent applications for grants, but be committed to finding the most eligible cases for assistance.

Some trusts are established to support the same organisations each year, or target organisations they have found through their own research, and therefore do not consider unsolicited applications. In these cases it is understandable that they do not wish to advertise their grantmaking. However, we continue to include all trusts since our research acts as a survey of all grant money available in the region.

Several trusts state that they will not consider unsolicited applications. It can be the case that this is stated simply as a deterrent to applicants. We therefore suggest that any applications to these trusts should be made with caution as there may be valid reasons for asking organisations not to apply. We advise you state in your letter that if your application cannot be considered the trust

should not feel obliged to reply to your request – do not enclose an sae. If you do not receive a reply, do not chase them.

For best results, we encourage fundraisers to try to establish links between what the trust seems to be interested in and what their organisation is trying to do. Fundraisers are increasingly being advised to take a personal approach, with some trusts preferring to have a lot of contact with charities. Many trusts in this guide consider themselves too small to take such an interest in applicants. Undoubtedly there are restrictions on the voluntary time many trustees can give to their trust's work, but The Lintel Trust is one example of a trust in this guide that shows an openness to discussing with potential applicants how they may approach the trust.

Availability of information

The ethos underpinning our directories is that trusts are public institutions, not private ones, and as such they benefit from being in the light of public scrutiny. They should be publicly accountable and give information about what they do with their money.

Most of the trusts were extremely helpful and efficient in providing us with information. Several actually came to us asking to be included. In carrying out our research, however, we occasionally came across trusts which refused to provide us with accounts or other information. Trusts are legally obliged to send an annual report and accounts, although they can charge a 'reasonable' amount for this. If trusts registered in Scotland do not fulfil the requirement to send information on request, there is no alternative source of information. In these cases it can be very difficult to uncover the work of the trust. One administrator in this guide, for instance, requested £20 per set of accounts for 10, probably all small, trusts. The company would not provide us with any other information on these trusts and in this instance, since we did not think this charge was reasonable or within our budget, we were unfortunately unable to compile more useful entries.

Some trusts administered by councils continue to be difficult to find, following the reorganisation of regional councils in 1996. Councils often administer many local trusts. The Highland Council, for instance, is new to our guides (with an entry under 'Highland Council Charities') and runs a number of funds which can award grants to support local community projects. By contacting your local council you may discover a small local trust which supports your cause.

Training

The Directory of Social Change runs training courses, aiming to equip the voluntary sector to effectively carry out their work. We run an annual Scotland conference, covering topics such as fundraising, management and organisational development. We also deliver workshops in Scotland about how to make successful Community Fund applications. For further information on these and our courses in England, please contact the London or Liverpool offices (see under *Other ports of call*, page 8).

Finally...

The research for this guide has been done as fully and carefully as possible. We are grateful to the many trust officers, trustees and others who have helped us in this. Although draft entries were sent to all the charities concerned, and any comments noted, the text and any mistakes remain ours rather than theirs.

We are aware that some of the information in this guide is incomplete and will become out of date. We are equally sure that we have missed some relevant charities. We regret such imperfections and are always looking to improve our work. If you find mistakes or omissions in this guide, please let us know so they can be rectified in the future. A telephone call to the Liverpool Office Research Department of the Directory of Social Change (0151 708 0136) – or an e-mail to north@dsc.org.uk – is all that is needed.

We intend to update this guide every two years, as during this time many of the trusts move, some change their policy and others cease to exist. For this reason it is worth visiting the errata page on our website (www.dsc.org.uk), which contains corrections to information received since the publication of our guides. Sometimes trusts change addresses, in which case the Scottish Charity Index keeps an up-to-date record of trust contact names and addresses (tel. 0131 777 4040).

To end on a positive note, there are more potential funders than you may think, some of which do not even receive enough applications. Several trusts had large, unspent surpluses, one of which totalled £130,000. There are also a number of trusts whose expenditure has rocketed in recent years. We hope this gives you extra encouragement in fundraising and we wish you success.

How to use this guide

The contents
The guide contains 350 trusts, which are listed alphabetically in six sections as follows:

The first section is general. It includes trusts which can give throughout the country or in more than one regional area. The other sections are regional areas and include trusts which are restricted to these areas.

Finding the trusts you need
1. Within the regional section, look to see if there are any trusts for your particular town and that give to your type of work.

2. Also within the regional section see if there are any trusts which give across the region or wider parts of the region, for which you meet the criteria.

3. Turn to the *Scotland – General* section and check the criteria for those trusts to see whether you are eligible.

Sending off applications which show that the available information has not been read antagonises trusts and brings charities into disrepute within the trust world. Carefully targeted applications, on the other hand, are welcomed by most trusts and usually have a reasonably high rate of success.

A typical trust entry

The Fictitious Trust

£45,000 (2000/01)
Welfare

Beneficial area Scotland, with a preference for New town

The Old Barn, Main Street
New Town ZC48 2QQ

Correspondent Ms A Grant, Secretary

Trustees *Lord Great; Lady Good.*

Information available Full accounts were provided by the trust.

General The trust supports a wide range of causes in Scotland. The trustees will support both capital and revenue projects. 'Specific projects are prefered to general running costs.'

In 2000/01 the trust had assets of £1.5 million and an income of £50,000. About 20 grants were given totalling £45,000. Grants ranged from £100 to £10,000, with about half given in New Town. The largest grants were to: New Town Disability Group (£10,000), Animal Welfare Scotland (£5,000) and Asian Family Support (£4,000). There were 10 grants of £1,000 each, including those to Charity Workers Benevolent Society, Children Without Families, New Town CAB and Refugee Support Group.

Smaller grants were given to a variety of local charities.

Exclusions No grants to individuals or religious organisations.

Applications In writing to the correspondent. Trustees meet in March and September each year. Applications should be received by the end of January and the end of July respectively.

Name of the charity

Grant total (not income) for the most recent year available.

Summary of main activities
What the trust will do in practice rather than what its trust deed allows it to do.

Geographical area
of grantgiving.

Contact address; telephone, fax and minicom numbers; e-mail and website addresses if available.

Contact person

Trustees

Sources of information we used and which are available to the applicant.

Background/summary of activities
A quick indicator of the policy to show whether it is worth reading the rest of the entry.

Financial information We try to note the assets, ordinary income and grant total, and comment on unusual figures.

Grants information The grants range and examples of beneficiaries give an indication of what a successful applicant might expect to receive. We also say whether the trust gives one-off or recurrent grants.

Exclusions – listing any area, subjects or types of grant the trust will not consider.

Applications including how to apply and when to submit an application.

How to make an application

Applying to trusts

Here in Scotland, grants from charitable trusts and foundations play a significant role in the funding of the voluntary sector. Making applications can be tricky, but by following this plan of action, you should manage to avoid most of the common pitfalls.

Take your first step

The first step in a successful application is to clearly define the 'problem' which needs to be solved. This could be a new service which is urgently needed; a gap in your revenue which needs to be filled; the director's latest grand plan; a new building, or other capital need. I am going to use the term project, or problem, to describe the gap which you have identified. This is the first point at which your application can begin to fail. Some questions that you need to be able to answer, before you go much further, are:

- what, **exactly**, is the 'problem'?
- why has the problem occurred?
- is there any clear evidence to support this?
- how do you plan to solve the problem?
- who will benefit?
- where will it take place, and when?
- how much will it cost?
- who else is involved?
- how does this project fit in with your organisation's business or strategic plan?

It can be a lengthy process to try to gather all the information that you need but, unless you have a clear understanding of what the money is needed for, then it can be incredibly difficult to convince potential funders. This stage is often an opportunity for you to get out of the office and go see the need! Talk to service users who will benefit from the changes which your new funding will bring; talk to staff, volunteers, family members, or anyone who will be involved; build up a picture of what the project will look like. Try to get 'stories' from people that you can either build in to the application, or you can use in conversations with funders or assessors.

Research

Identify your potential funders. Use this book wisely. It contains most of the information that you need to know. Please don't use it as a source of names and addresses to 'blanket mail' trusts. Be selective, read through each trust's entry to make sure that your need fits the trust's grant-making priorities. It is also worth looking around your organisation to see whether any members of staff, directors, trustees, clients or volunteers are connected with, or know, anyone in a position to support your application. Did your chair of trustees go to school with the chair of a local trust? Does the director live next door to Lady Bountiful? A personal endorsement of your work is well worth having!

Think about why each particular funder might want to fund your cause. Trusts and foundations exist solely to give money away, but often have very clear criteria, usually set by the founder of the trust.

If the potential funder has an application form

This can make the process much easier, but there are pitfalls.

- Be careful that you meet the funder's objectives – although this information may not be built in to a specific question on the application form. If the funder's aim is 'to decrease social isolation within disadvantaged communities', you can almost guarantee that there won't be a specific question which asks how your project will 'decrease…'. You have to ensure that this information is within the answers that you offer to their questions.
- Try to use language that the funder will understand.
- Remember that there are 'fads' in funding; for example, 'social inclusion' is a priority at the moment, while 'innovative' is out through complete over-use.

- Not wishing to overstate the obvious, but it does happen: don't forget to answer every question! Be clear and concise, but don't be frightened to use all of the space available if you need to.
- Make sure that you enclose your most recent annual report and accounts, but try not to add much more unless it adds real value to your application. For example, if you are applying for a new building, then an architect's drawing can help.
- Try to make sure that your application, and its enclosures, are 'photocopiable' because it is probably only a photocopy which will go to the committee!

If the funder does not have an application form

If there isn't a prescribed format for the application, one style which works successfully is a simple covering letter, a detailed paper on the project, with your latest annual report and accounts.

The usual rules apply:

- KISS – **k**eep **i**t **s**imple, **s**tupid
- AIDA – **a**ttract the reader's attention; create **i**nterest in your problem; make the reader **d**esire to help; inspire **a**ction
- use a plain font of a reasonable size, usually 12 point
- lay out your information clearly and legibly
- try to use no more than two sides of A4 – ideally you should be able to put all the detail on one side!

The covering letter

The covering letter should contain:

- A paragraph of background on your organisation. In no more than 100 words, try to establish the credibility of your organisation: What do you do? Why? Where? To whom? When were you established? Who else is involved? Are you international, national or local?
- A brief summary of the problem that has been identified and your proposed solution.
- A concluding sentence offering to send further information, an invitation to visit, or whatever else you feel is appropriate.
- Your charity number.

- Accurate details of the person to be contacted for further information.

The application
The problem

- What is the problem?
- How has it arisen?
- Why and where is it occurring?
- Who is affected by it?
- How many people are involved?
- What evidence do you have? Have you conducted research, or has anyone else? Are there any statistics?

The solution

This is where you should show the objectives of the project and the specific, measurable outcomes you expect to achieve.

Measure

How will you know if the project is successful? What monitoring processes and procedures will you put in place?

Budget

- How much will it cost?
- When do you need the money?
- Who else is contributing, either in cash, or in kind?

Future funding

- Is this a pilot project, a one-off piece of work, or an ongoing activity?
- How will you continue to fund the project?

This is the standard information that most funders require. However, you should obey any specific instructions given by the funder.

Some additional dos and don'ts
Do:

- research, research, research
- **answer** all the questions on the application form concisely and accurately
- remember that funders want to **solve a problem**
- complete your application in plain English
- give your charity number
- ask for **exactly** what you need

- demonstrate that you have put specific measurement criteria in place
- show your organisation's commitment to equal opportunities
- include your most recent annual report and accounts.

Don't:

- ignore the funder's application criteria
- **assume** that the funder knows your work and will automatically fund you
- attach too much additional information
- use jargon
- use 'mail merge' without checking the details of each application are correct
- put 'refer to Annual Report', or 'see attached leaflet', in sections where funders are asking for specific information – answer the question fully.

Follow up

So, you have thought through your problem; come up with a fantastic solution; researched your potential funders; designed the most spectacular application that it is possible to submit, then sent it off … now four things can happen:

- you don't hear anything at all, ever
- you receive a standard letter telling you that your application didn't meet the funder's criteria
- you get a request for further information, or a visit
- you receive a cheque.

Sadly, even though you have spent hours, days, weeks putting an application together that, as far as you can establish, exactly meets the funder's published criteria … you might still get a 'no'. It is worth trying to contact the funder to seek clarification on why the application was unsuccessful. This can help you to discover whether there is something fundamentally flawed in the application, or whether it failed for reasons completely beyond your control. Sometimes, particularly at the moment, funders seem to be inundated with good projects, but there just isn't enough money in the pot for them to give grants to everyone.

If you receive a request for further information, supply it promptly and accurately. If you get a telephone assessment, make sure that the person receiving the call is well briefed and has a clear understanding of the project, and your organisation. If you receive a visit, it is not like having royalty coming to visit, but ensure that staff know what is happening, and who is visiting.

When you receive a grant, make sure that you get a thank-you letter off to the funder immediately. Be careful of mail merge, do make sure that the letter has the correct funder's name and amount on it … believe me, people do get this wrong! Keep the funder up-to-date with developments during the life of the project. It is worth letting them know the good news, and about things that aren't working as you had predicted. To really be part of your 'team', funders want to build a relationship with you that is based on honesty and integrity.

Acknowledge the support of the funder in your annual report, if the funder wishes (some don't). Make sure that you invite them to any important functions, or events. Do not inundate them with information, but make them part of your network. Please treat your funders well. Then, when you next need some help, financial or otherwise, the first place to look is from within your existing network.

Susan Robinson FICFM
Institute of Charity Fundraising
Managers Scotland

Scotland – General

The 1970 Trust

Disadvantaged minorities

£70,000 (2001)

Beneficial area UK, with an interest in Scotland

Messrs Pagan Osborne, 12 St Catherine Street, Cupar, Fife KY15 4HN

Tel. 01334 653777 **Fax** 01334 655063

e-mail enquiries@pagan.co.uk

Website www.pagan.co.uk

Correspondent c/o C W Pagan, Trustee

Trustees *David Rennie.*

Inland Revenue no. SC008788

Information available Information was supplied by the trust.

General The trust states it supports small UK charities 'doing innovative, educational, or experimental work in the following fields:

- civil liberties (e.g. freedom of information; constitutional reform; humanising work; children's welfare)
- the public interest in the face of vested interest groups (such as the advertising, alcohol, road, war, pharmaceuticals, and tobacco industries)
- disadvantaged minorities, multiracial work, prison reform
- new economics ('as if people mattered' – Schumacher) and intermediate technology
- public transport, pedestrians, bicycling, road crash prevention, traffic-calming, low-energy lifestyles
- preventative health'.

Grants are usually of between £300 and £2,000 and for between one and three years, but they can sometimes cover longer periods. In 2001 the trust's assets totalled £1.5 million, its income was £50,000 and grants were made totalling £70,000. A list of grants for this year was not available.

In 1998/99 a total of £18,000 was given in 24 grants, usually ranging from £300 to £1,000. The largest grant of £3,000 went to Forum for the Future. Other large grants included £1,000 each to MIND, Public Interest Research, Religious Society of Friends in Britain, Welfare and Wildlife, Say Women and Shelter & Winter Nights Appeal. Smaller grants included those to Parent to Parent Adoption Service, Prisoners Wives Project, Scottish Women's Aid and Young Woman's Projects.

Exclusions No support for larger charities, those with religious connections, or individuals (except in rare cases – and then only through registered charities or educational bodies). No support to central or local government agencies.

Applications In writing to the correspondent. Please summarise your proposal on one page and add one or two more pages of supporting information. The trust states that it regrettably only has time to reply to the few applications it is able to fund.

The 3i Charitable Trust

General

£492,000 (1999/2000)

Beneficial area Only in those areas where 3i has an area office: Aberdeen, Birmingham, Bristol, Cambridge, Cardiff, Edinburgh, Glasgow, Leeds, Leicester, Liverpool, London, Manchester, Newcastle upon Tyne, Nottingham, Reading, Southampton and Watford

3i plc, 91 Waterloo Road, London SE1 8XP

Tel. 020 7928 3131 **Fax** 020 7928 0058

Website www.3i.com

Correspondent Sabina Dawson, Assistant
Company Secretary

Trustees *3i Trustee Company Limited.*

Charity Commission no. 1014277

Information available Full accounts were
provided by the trust.

General The 1999/2000 accounts stated:
'The policy adopted by the trustees has not
changed. The trust continues to favour charitable
initiatives with which members of staff are
personally involved. During the year support was
given to UK charities local to 3i's offices. The
trust devotes resources each year to business
educational establishments and initiatives and to
the community.

'Over the financial year donations ranged from
£20 to £100,000 to 239 charities. Over 50% of the
donations made were to support local
community initiatives and educational causes.'

It also matches donations made by 3i employees
under the Give As You Earn scheme.

In 1999/2000 it had assets of £73,000 and an
income of £471,000, mostly from donations but
including a high bank interest income of £11,000.
Grants totalled £492,000, including £62,000 in
matching staff donations. Over 70% of the
donations were for less than £1,000 each.

The largest grants were £100,000 to INSEAD
Trust for European Management Education,
£50,000 each to Prince's Trust and Royal Opera
House for their development appeal and £25,000
to Understanding Industry Trust. Other grants
included £1,000 each to Aberdeen International
Youth Festival, Braemar Mountain Rescue
Association and Gordon Highlanders Museum
Campaign Fund.

Exclusions No grants to individuals.

Applications In writing to the correspondent.
The meetings of the board of directors of
3i Trustee Company Limited are held
approximately every three months.

Aberbrothock Charitable Trust

General

£60,000 (2000)

Beneficial area East of Scotland, north of the
firth of Tay, and exceptionally the Edinburgh
area

Messrs Thorntons, Brothockbank House,
Arbroath, Angus DD11 1NJ

Trustees *G Mcnicol; J G Mathieson;
Mrs A T L Grant; G N J Smart.*

Inland Revenue no. SC003110

Information available Information was provided
by the trust.

General The trust gives grants for the benefit of
the community. It will consider the following
causes: children/young people, disability,
environment/conservation, hospitals/hospices
and medical research.

In 2000 it had assets of £2.2 million and an
income of only £74,000. It gave grants totalling
£60,000. Grants are one-off and range from
£1,000 to £5,000. £5,000 each was given to
Erskine Hospital and Christian Aid for flood
relief work in Mozambique. The Governors of
Dollar Academy were given £4,000 for an
individual, and New School Butterstone Building
and Royal Zoological Society of Scotland both
received £3,000. Other grants went to a range of
organisations including Angus Independent
Advocacy Services, Arbroath and District Athletic
Club, National Youth Orchestra of Scotland and
Scottish Downs Syndrome Association.

Exclusions The only exclusions are
geographical restrictions.

Applications In writing to the correspondent.
Trustees meet to consider grants in March, July
and November.

The Aberdeen Endowments Trust

Education

About £4,700 to organisations (2000)

Beneficial area Aberdeen, Grampian

19 Albert Street, Aberdeen AB9 1QF

Tel. 01224 640194 **Fax** 01224 643918

Correspondent William Russell, Clerk

Trustees *Three persons elected by Aberdeen City Council; one by the Senatus Academicus of the University of Aberdeen; two by the governors of Robert Gordon's College, Aberdeen; two by the Church of Scotland Presbytery of Aberdeen; one by the churches of Aberdeen other than the Church of Scotland; one by the Society of Advocates in Aberdeen; one by the Convener Court of the Seven Incorporated Trades of Aberdeen; one by the trade unions having branches in Aberdeen; one by the Aberdeen Local Association of the Educational Institute of Scotland; plus not less than two and not more than four co-optees.*

Inland Revenue no. SC010507

Information available Guidance notes and annual report (on payment of administration fee) are available on request.

General The main purpose of the trust is to give financial assistance to individuals for educational puposes. The beneficial area is the City and Royal Burgh of Aberdeen as it was prior to 1975. A few grants are given in the former Grampian region under one category. In 2000 the trust had assets of £13.3 million. Its revenue is mainly derived from agricultural land and properties, supported with income from a modest investment portfolio. Costs of running the trust and the upkeep of the land and properties totalled £233,000 in 2000; financial awards made totalled £430,000.

The majority of financial assistance is given to pupils attending Robert Gordon's College, Aberdeen – £409,000 in 2000. Bursaries are also given to pupils at secondary schools in the former Grampian region – £5,700 in 2000.

Under the category 'Plan Expenditure' both individuals and organisations from Aberdeen can be supported and £14,000 was awarded in 2000. Awards are given towards the costs of 'certain aspects of adult education' (£12,000 in 2000), or for 'certain types of group activities and educational travel for children' (£2,000 in 2000). The trust also supports activities in the fields of music, visual arts and drama (£1,900 in 2000). Awards tend to average around £200. The amount to organisations varies from year to year (just over £4,700 in 2000).

Exclusions No grants to people or organisations from outside the former City and Royal Burgh of Aberdeen.

Applications Application forms are available from the correspondent. The Benefactions Committee of the trust, which makes financial awards, normally meets ten times a year.

Miss Agnes Gilchrist Adamson's Trust

Children who are disabled

£43,000 (2000)

Beneficial area UK

Messrs Miller Hendry, 14 Comrie Street, Crieff, Perthshire PH7 4AZ

Tel. 01764 655151

Correspondent Messrs Miller Hendry

Trustees *A R Muir. Another trustee to be appointed.*

Inland Revenue no. SC016517

Information available Information was available from the trust.

General The trust gives grants to organisations providing holidays for children under 16 who are mentally or physically disabled. Grants are usually one-off. In 2000 the trust had assets of £805,000, an income of £67,000 and gave grants totalling £43,000. Donations were given to organisations including Lake District Calvert Trust (£5,500) and Sense Scotland and Uphill Ski Club (£2,000 each).

Applications In writing to the correspondent, including details about the organisation, the number of children who would benefit and the proposed holiday.

The ADAPT Trust

Access for people who are disabled and older to arts and heritage venues

£137,000 (2000)

Beneficial area UK

8 Hampton Terrace, Edinburgh EH12 5JD

Tel. 0131 346 1999 **Fax** 0131 346 1991

e-mail adapt.trust@virgin.net

Website www.adapttrust.co.uk

Correspondent Stewart Coulter

Trustees *Dr Gillian A Burrington, Chair; Michael Cassidy; Elizabeth Fairbairn; Gary Flather; John C Griffiths; Alison Heath; Trevan Hingston; Robin Hyman; C Wycliffe Noble; Maurice Paterson; Rita Tushingham.*

Inland Revenue no. SC020814

Information available A detailed annual report, including full accounts, was provided by the trust.

General The ADAPT (Access for Disabled People to Arts Premises Today) Trust aims to improve accessibility for people who are disabled and older to arts and heritage venues. It does this in several ways. It encourages broader consideration of access at the planning stage of buildings by providing a consultancy service and carrying out disability awareness training. It gives grants to adapt existing facilities through a number of schemes, and awards for excellence, described below. It also seeks to influence government policies and regulations by contributing to relevant committees and commenting on new strategies.

In 2000 the trust had assets of £379,000 and an income of £190,000. It gave grants totalling £137,000, with direct charitable expenditure broken down as follows:

	2000	(1999)
ADAPT – general	–	(£2,500)
Scottish grants scheme	£1,500	(£9,800)
Capital access	£5,000	(£6,600)
Sightline millennial grants	£43,000	(£39,000)
Railtrack museum grants	£63,000	(£39,000)
Millennial awards	–	(£21,000)
Hugh Fraser Foundation	–	(£2,500)
Total	£120,000	(£149,000)

The only exclusively Scottish scheme – Scottish Grants Scheme, only paid out one grant in the year, £1,500 to Gibson Community Centre, Gairlochead. The previous year, three grants were made: £5,000 to Glasgow Film Theatre; £3,000 to Projectability, Glasgow; and £1,800 to Castle House Museum, Dunoon.

In addition to the grants listed above, £6,000 was given in two grants from Scottish Hydro-Electric; £4,000 to Inverness Museum & Art Gallery and £2,000 to Culloden Battlefield, Inverness.

Exclusions No grants to: stately homes, heritage centres and crafts centres; halls designed and used for other purposes such as church halls, hospitals or educational establishments even though they sometimes house the arts; or festivals, unless at a permanent arts venue.

Applications Guidelines and application details are available from the ADAPT office. Applicants for grants have to demonstrate that all aspects of access have been considered, including parking, publicity and staff training.

The Age Concern Scotland Enterprise Fund

Older people

£48,000 (1999/2000)

Beneficial area Scotland

Suite 1C1, Templeton Business Centre, Templeton Street, Glasgow G40 1DA

Tel. 0141 554 2211 **Fax** 0141 554 1564

Correspondent The Membership Unit

Trustees *Members of Age Concern Scotland's Assembly.*

Inland Revenue no. SC010100

Information available Guidelines for applicants and a general leaflet are available.

General The trust gives grants to voluntary and charitable groups working with older people in Scotland. Grants can be for up to £300 for equipment and materials for small local groups or up to £1,000 to establish new projects or services.

A few larger grants, of up to £5,000 are given to members of Age Concern Scotland to start significant new projects.

In 1999/2000 grants totalled £48,000. They included £5,600 to Cumbernuald Action for the Care of the Elderly for a welfare rights outreach service, £4,800 to Talk Lochaber to establish a talking newspaper service, £1,000 each to Age Concern Orkney for fundraising development, Alzheimer's Scotland Action on Dementia to provide information materials in community languages, Anderson Mel-milaap Centre for development of a day care centre, Tranent Day Care Centre for its development, St Mungo's Day Centre for furniture and Ross of Mull Historial Centre for reminisence work with older people and Dunoon Senior Citizens Club for the set-up costs of a lunch club and £970 to Age Concern Glenrothes for equipment for a day centre.

Exclusions No grants to statutory authorities, commercial organisations and individuals. No grants are awarded for minibuses, holidays/outings, dinners/parties, running costs, major building costs and general appeals.

Applications An application form and further details are available from the correspondent. Applications are considered every two months, except for the larger grants to Age Concern member organisations which are given in January.

The Sylvia Aitken Charitable Trust

Medical research, general

£112,000 (1999/2000)

Beneficial area UK, with a preference for Scotland

24 Woodside, Houston, Renfrewshire PA6 7DD

Tel. 01505 610412 **Fax** 01505 614944

Correspondent Jim Ferguson, Trust Administrator

Trustees *Mrs S M Aitken; Mrs M Harkis; J Ferguson.*

Inland Revenue no. SC010556

Information available Full accounts were provided by the trust.

General The trustees' 1999/2000 review states: 'although the focus of grant giving remained the funding of medical projects, the trust made donations to a much wider range of charitable applicants during the year and many smaller charities benefited from a small donation'.

The assets of the trust stood at £4.1 million and the income was £192,000. Grants paid during the year totalled £22,000 with around £90,000 approved but not paid. The following examples of grants were all commitments. The largest were £40,000 to Glasgow University/Royal Infirmary Teleomeres Project and £22,000 to Association for International Cancer Research. There were two grants of £2,500, to Rainbow Trust and Variety Club, and six of £2,000. The remainder ranged from £100 to £1,500 and included those to Chest, Heart and Stroke (£1,500), British Neurological Research Trust (£1,000), Sense Scotland (£750), AbilityNet (£500) and NCH Action for Children and Rape Crisis Centre (each £100).

The trust states that while small local charities are of interest, all applications from registered UK charities are considered on their merits rather than on their geographical location.

Exclusions No grants to individuals: the trust can only support organisations.

Applications In writing to the correspondent. Applicants should outline the charity's objectives and current projects for which funding may be required. The trustees meet at least twice a year, usually in March/April and October/November.

The AMW Charitable Trust

General

About £220,000

Beneficial area Scotland only, with a priority for the West of Scotland

24 Blythswood Square, Glasgow G2 4QS

Tel. 0141 226 5511

Correspondent Campbell Denholm, Trustee

Trustees *R W Speirs; C Denholm; Prof. R B Jack.*

Inland Revenue no. SC006959

Information available Information was provided by the trust.

General The trust supports charities in Scotland with a priority given to the west of Scotland. There is some preference for organisations concerned with young people or education. About £220,000 is available for distribution. Grants usually range from £3,000 to £7,500 and about 15 charities are supported each year. Beneficiaries in 2000 included Arthritis Care Scotland, Christian Aid, The Dystonia Society, Greater Glasgow Scout Council, Kelvin School, Glasgow, Scottish Dyslexia Association, Scottish Motor Neurone Disease Association and University of Glasgow.

Exclusions No grants for individuals, or to organisations outside Scotland.

Applications In writing to the correspondent. Appeals are not acknowledged and the trust only advises successful applications.

James and Grace Anderson Trust

Cerebral palsy

£19,000 (1999/2000)

Beneficial area Scotland

c/o Scott-Moncrieff, 17 Melville Street, Edinburgh EH3 7PH

Tel. 0131 473 3500   **Fax** 0131 473 3535

e-mail tim.straton@scott-moncrieff.com

Correspondent T D Straton, Trustee

Trustees *W A Souter, Chair; J Donald; J D M Urquhart; T D Straton.*

Inland Revenue no. SC004172

Information available Information was supplied by the trust.

General The trust was established in 1974 and currently funds research with a view to alleviating conditions arising from cerebral palsy. In 1999/2000 the trust had assets amounting to £619,000 and an income of £26,000. During the year the trust made two grants totalling £19,000. It continued to support gait analysis, in line with the research described above, and also made a grant to the Sequal Trust.

Applications In writing to the correspondent. Trustees meet in May and October. Applications should be received by the previous month.

Mary Andrew Charitable Trust

General

£22,000 (2000/01)

Beneficial area UK, with a preference for Scotland

Mitchells Roberton Solicitors, George House, 36 North Hanover Street, Glasgow G1 2AD

Tel. 0141 552 3422

Correspondent The Trustees

Trustees *E H Webster; D A R Ballantine; A J Campbell.*

Inland Revenue no. SC021977

Information available Information was provided by the trust.

General The trust makes grants to a wide variety of causes. Areas of interest include churches; health and welfare; education and training; children and young people; and heritage. There is a preference for Scotland. In 2000/01 it had an income of £30,000 and gave grants totalling £22,000.

Applications In writing to the correspondent.

The Anne Duchess of Westminster's Charity

General

£19,000 (1998/99)

Beneficial area UK, with preference for Cheshire, Scotland and Ireland

The Grosvenor Estate, Eaton Estate Office, Eccleston, Chester CH4 9ET

Tel. 01244 684400

Correspondent Miss A Stubbs, Secretary

Trustees *J M Marshall; T J Marshall; D Ridley.*

Charity Commission no. 245177

Information available Full accounts were on file at the Charity Commission.

General Although giving throughout the UK, this trust shows a preference for Scotland. In 1998/99 it had assets of £696,000 and an income of £37,000. Grants, ranging from £10 to £2,700, totalled £19,000. The largest were £2,700 to Riding for the Disabled Association, £1,100 to People's Dispensary for Sick Animals, £1,000 each to Royal British Legion and West Sutherland Fisheries Trust, £750 to Eccleston & Pulford PCC, £700 to Blue Cross, and £500 each to Anchor Housing Trust, Clwyd Special Riding Centre, NSPCC and Royal National Mission to Deep Sea Fishermen. Half of the grants were for £100 or less.

Applications In writing to the correspondent.

The John M Archer Charitable Trust

General

£24,000 (2000/01)

Beneficial area Unrestricted

12 Broughton Place, Edinburgh EH1 3RX

Tel. 0131 556 4518

Correspondent Mrs Ruth L Lothian, Secretary

Trustees *G B Archer; Mrs I Morrison; Mrs A Morgan; Mrs W Grant; Mrs C Fraser; Mrs I C Smith.*

Inland Revenue no. SC010583

Information available Full accounts were available from the trust.

General The trust supports local, national and international organisations, in particular those concerned with:

- prevention or relief of human suffering
- welfare of sick, distressed or afflicted people
- alleviation of need
- advancement of education
- advancement of religious or missionary work
- advancement of medical or scientific research and discovery
- preservation of Scottish heritage and the advancement of associated cultural activities.

During 2000/01 it made 131 grants totalling £23,900. The only donations exceeding £1,000 included in the total were £3,000 to the British Red Cross (general appeals overseas), £1,500 to the Castlebrae School Scholarship Fund and £2,500 to Liverpool University Hospital (Muscular Degeneration Research) which is the first instalment of a five year commitment. Total income for the year was £63,000, of which £35,000 was a donation from Tods of Orkney Ltd and added to the assets. The assets at the end of the year had risen to £628,000.

Applications In writing to the correspondent at the above address.

The BAA 21st Century Communities Trust

Local community

£600,000 (2000/01)

Beneficial area Mainly south east England and Scotland (local communities around the following airports: Heathrow, Gatwick, Stansted, Southampton, Edinburgh, Glasgow and Aberdeen. Also the area immediately surrounding BAA's head office in London SW1)

130 Wilton Road, London SW1V 1LQ

Tel. 01293 503056 **Fax** 01293 503794

e-mail Andrew_Currie@baa.com

Correspondent A B Currie, Community Relations Director

Trustees *T Ward; C Green; Ms J Bradley; Miss V Gooding; A B Currie*

Charity Commission no. 1058617

Information available Information was provided by the trust.

General BAA plc established this trust in 1996/97. It was set up to channel the company's donations to help local communities 'face the challenges of the new millennium, particularly in the areas of the three E's – education, economic regeneration and the environment'. The trust will help local communities in three ways:

- assist projects which are developing educational opportunities including those for people who are disadvantaged

- help groups nurture the physical environment

- assist those whose work is helping to develop employment opportunities.

Generally, grants to UK organisations range up to £20,000 and to local organisations from £50 to £2,500. Projects are mostly recommended by airport staff. Examples of projects supported since the trust was established include: Slough Foyer Appeal which received £50,000 from Heathrow Airport; Springboard Charitable Trust (which funds decoration and repairs for elderly residents in their own homes) which received £12,000 from Stansted Airport; Horley, Crawley Countryside Management Project which received support from Gatwick Airport towards the running cost of a Land Rover; Waverley Care Trust which received support from Edinburgh Airport for its education programme supporting relatives and carers of people with HIV or AIDS; and Dyslexia Institute which received support from Aberdeen Airport to introduce into the region dedicated teachers, trained to help dyslexic people. Support has also been given to the Media Trust and special schools.

In 2000/01 the trust gave grants totalling £600,000. These included those to Stanstead Youth 2000 Gatton Park Education (£15,000), The Crawley Foyer (£14,000) and Educational Youth Project – Mole Valley (£11,000). Other beneficiaries included Carr-Gomm drop-in centre – Hove, 1st Thorley Scout Group, Magna Carta School – Runneymede and Harlow Town Associated Schools Specialist Initiative.

Exclusions No support is given to circular appeals, fundraising events, individuals, purely denominational (religious) appeals, advertising in charity brochures, animal welfare charities, the arts, overseas projects, social welfare or sickness/disability charities. 'Grants are generally not made to nationally-based organisations except in cases where the direct benefit will be felt locally.'

Applications Applicants are advised to write to the community relations manager at Gatwick, Heathrow, Southampton and Stansted airports. For Scotland: Head of Public Affairs, Scottish Airports Ltd, St Andrew's Drive, Paisley, Renfrewshire PA3 2ST.

Dr James and Dr Bozena Bain Memorial Trust Fund

Religion, education

£3,000 (1999/2000)

Beneficial area UK, with a strong preference for Scotland

Eshwood Hall, New Brancepeth, Durham DH7 7HG

Tel. 0191 373 4221 **Fax** 0191 373 0843

Correspondent T B Patterson, Trustee

Trustees *T B Patterson; M N Patterson.*

Charity Commission no. 328356

Information available Full accounts were on file at the Charity Commission.

General This trust supports:

- a place for a student at Edinburgh University Faculty of Medicine who is Polish, or suitable in other ways

- the advancement of religion and religious education for training priests at Ampleforth College in York.

In 1999/2000 the trust's assets totalled £550,000 and its income was £66,000. Grants totalled £3,000, a lot lower than usual. Beneficiaries included St Andrews Church Youth Centre (£900), Ardrossan Academy (£800), West Kilbride War Memorial Trust (£500) and West Kilbride Primary School and Boys Brigade (£400 each).

Applications In writing to the correspondent.

The Baird Trust

Maintenance and repair of churches and halls of the Church of Scotland

£297,000 (2000)

Beneficial area Scotland

182 Bath Street, Glasgow G2 4HG

Tel. 0141 332 0476

Correspondent Ronald D Oakes, Secretary

Trustees *Alexander W Barbour; Miss Marianne Baird; Lieut Cmdr Edward F B Spragge; Col. Hon. W D Arbuthnott; Hon. Mrs Coltman; Maj. J Henry Callander; Maj. J M K Erskine; Revd J R McKay.*

Inland Revenue no. SC016549

Information available Full accounts were provided by the trust.

General 'The principal object of the trust, founded in 1873, is the provision of grants for the maintenance and repair of church buildings although it may also provide grant aid to other activities of the church, especially in the field of

education. Under its Act of Parliament, the trust can assist only the Church of Scotland, of which church the nine trustees must be members.'

In 2000 it had assets of £7.3 million which generated an income of £316,000. Grants totalled £297,000, excluding donations cancelled from previous years.

57 grants voted totalled £244,000. The largest were £10,000 each to Airdrie Flowerhill Parish and Holy Trinity Church. Other grants ranged from £1,000 to £8,000.

The accounts also listed 14 sundry grants totalling £62,000. The largest were £10,000 each to Boys Brigade – Carronvale Centre and Church of Scotland for widows of ministers and £9,000 to Lodging House Mission for a joint chaplaincy. Other beneficiaries included Solid Rock Youth Development Project (£5,000), Church House for its holiday fund (£4,000), Colston Milton Children's Project (£3,000), The Stewartry of Strathearn (£2,000) and Licentiates Book Tokens (£1,000).

Applications In writing to the correspondent at any time.

The Balcraig Foundation

Welfare, particularly children

About £2.5 million

Beneficial area Scotland and Africa

Balcraig House, Scone, Perth PH2 7PG

Tel. 01738 552303   **Fax** 01738 552101

Correspondent David McCleary, Secretary

Trustees *Ann Gloag; David McCleary.*

Inland Revenue no. SC020037

Information available The trust has a policy of not providing its accounts, despite its statutory obligation to do so.

General This trust, which formerly gave towards child welfare in Scotland and Africa, made a decision in 1999 to give most of its annual income to Mercy Ships, with the residue given as standing orders to a number of organisations including Prince's Trust and various hospitals. In 1995/96 under the previous criteria, it made grants totalling £2.5 million and its assets totalled £8 million including shares in Stagecoach Holdings plc which were donated by a trustee and a residential property in Blantyre, Malawi. Further information was not available.

Applications As the trust only supports long-time beneficiaries, unsolicited applications will not be considered.

Barfil Charitable Trust

General

£13,000 (2000/01)

Beneficial area Scotland, with preference for Dumfries

Barfil, Crocketford, Dumfries DG2 8RW

Tel. 01556 690682 **Fax** 01556 690231

Correspondent The Trustees

Trustees *Bob Lee; Maggie Gordon; John Whittaker; Bill Lee; Bill Gordon.*

Inland Revenue no. SC018293

Information available Full accounts were provided by the trust.

General The trust supports causes recommended by the trustees and local appeals in the Dumfries area. In 2000/01 it had an income of £8,200, and gave grants totalling £13,000. The assets at the year end stood at £190,000.

12 grants were made with the largest being £5,500 to Turning Point Scotland to fund a landscaping project at the charity's house in Dumfries, and £3,000 to National Museums of Scotland for a project in the Department of History and Applied Art at the New Museum in Edinburgh. Amnesty International received £1,000, with £750 going to both Grindleford Primary School and The Pink Party. The remaining grants ranged from £50 to £500 with recipients including Borders Forest Trust, Bio-Dynamic Agricultural Association (the only organisation to also receive a grant in the previous year), Castle Douglas Judo

Club (for new mats) and Scottish Spina Bifida Association (for a local group).

Applications In writing to the correspondent.

The Kenneth Barge Memorial Trust

Local charities, disaster funds, the Third World, environment, military, religion

£10,000 (1994/95)

Beneficial area Worldwide, UK, Scotland

c/o Messrs Raeburn Hope, Solicitors, 77 Sinclair Street, Helensburgh G84 8TG

Tel. 01436 671221 **Fax** 01436 675888

e-mail swh@raeburnhope.co.uk

Correspondent Sharon Halliday

Inland Revenue no. SC006063

Information available The entry was compiled from the 1994/95 accounts provided by the trust.

General The trust supports local charitable organisations, Third World charities, military organisations and charities concerned with the environment and religion. Unfortunately up-to-date financial information was not available.

In 1994/95 the trust had assets totalling £29,000. Grants totalled £10,000, including £1,000 each to British Red Cross Society, Christian Aid, CRMF Macmillan Nurse Teacher Project, Kilfinnan Church, Princess Louise Hospital, Thistle Foundation and World Society for the Protection of Animals. Grants of £500 each were made to Scottish Scripture Union, Friends of Loch Lomond and Royal Commonwealth Society for the Blind.

It gives many annual grants and only a few new beneficiaries are supported each year. The trust states that it receives many more applications than it is able to support.

Applications In writing to the correspondent but please note the above.

Bartholomew Christian Trust

Christian organisations, poverty

£4,000 (2001)

Beneficial area Worldwide, but mainly UK

Calgary, Isle of Mull, Argyll PA75 6QT

Tel. 01688 400240

Correspondent J E G Bartholomew

Trustees *Commander I M Bartholomew; Mrs A Bartholomew; D G Bartholomew; A J Bartholomew.*

Inland Revenue no. SC012390

Information available Accounts were provided by the trust.

General The trust awards grants to Christian organisations which promote the Christian faith, provide Christian education and work for the relief of poverty. Grants usually range from £100 to £500. Funds are not usually awarded to pay for building work.

In 2001 the trust had assets totalling £25,000, generating an income of £4,500. Grants totalled £4,000.

Exclusions Grants are only awarded to registered charitable organisations.

Applications In writing to the correspondent at the above address. Unsuccessful applications are not acknowledged.

BBC Children in Need Appeal

Disadvantaged children

£2.6 million in Scotland (1999/2000)

Beneficial area UK with a proportion of grants made in Scotland

Broadcasting House, 5 Queen Street, Edinburgh EH2 1JF

Tel. 0131 469 4225

Correspondent Fraser Falconer

Trustees *Sir Robert Andrew; Jane Asher; Colin Browne; David Carrington; Revd Norman Drummond; Christopher Graham; Andrew Greensmith; Alison Reed; Angela Sarkis; Peter Salmon.*

Charity Commission no. 802052

Information available Guidelines for applicants are available from the correspondent.

General The BBC Children in Need Appeal distributes the funds raised by the BBC's annual broadcast appeal which total between £15 million to £20 million every year. Administration costs are taken from the interest earned on banked donations.

The money raised is used to help disadvantaged children throughout the UK. Of the £19 million given by the appeal through 1,900 grants across the UK in 1999/2000, £2.6 million was given in 283 grants to Scotland causes.

There are four main areas targeted (figures refer to the whole of the UK for the year 1999/2000):

Children with mental and physical disabilities (£4.5 million)
'Some children may need just an extra bit of help to join in with chosen activities; others are very profoundly disabled from birth or from an accident (often a road accident) and therefore totally dependent upon the constant care of others.'

Children with behavioural and psychological disorders (£692,000)
'These are the children in our society who are often labelled "difficult"; the children who from birth or background do not know how to behave and cannot fit in; who are often rejected and desperately unhappy.'

Children experiencing poverty, deprivation or homelessness (£8.7 million)
'These children live in families that struggle each day to be like "normal" families; many spend their childhood in run-down homes or housing estates in a drab and hopeless environment; some experiencing temporary homelessness and insecurity; all of them more disadvantaged than the average child.'

Children suffering through illness, abuse or neglect (£4.9 million)
'Many of these children are "invisible"; some because they are confined to home or hospital

because of illness; some because they are in care; others because they have become quiet and withdrawn through grief, neglect or abuse.'

Most of the money pays for about 200 grants of £30,000 to £100,000, usually payable over three years. However, most grants are for less than £5,000. About half of all applications get a grant (though not always the amount requested).

Grant guidelines

These read as follows:

'We welcome applications for good quality projects which show a clear focus on children and careful planning in order to bring a positive difference or change their lives.

'The children we help are aged 18 years and under in the United Kingdom. Their disadvantages include:

- any kind of disability
- behavioural or psychological problems
- living in poverty or situations of deprivation
- illness, distress, abuse or neglect.

'Please do not apply for a grant to benefit children who do not fall within the above categories. We appreciate the good work which is done for the average child or young person in average circumstances but we are unable to make a financial contribution.

How we work

'BBC Children in Need distributes between £10 and £20 million a year to help children in need in the UK. The trustees, appointed by the BBC's board of governors, are advised by regional committees whose members have knowledge of child welfare issues and the voluntary sector.

'We receive around 6,000 applications each year and most applicants are contacted by our freelance assessors who work from home. An assessor may phone you or your referee to clarify the information provided on your application or to ask you to send additional information. If they cannot reach you during normal working business hours they may phone in the evening. Assessors report to our advisory committees but have no decision-making powers.

Who can apply

'We welcome applications from properly constituted not-for-profit groups. These may be:

- self-help groups
- voluntary organisations
- registered charities.

'We give low priority to applications from statutory (public) bodies and local authorities for schools, hospitals, social services, etc. Such grants are rarely over a few thousand pounds and most are for much smaller amounts.

'We regret that we cannot accept applications from private individuals or parents, nor from social workers or other welfare professionals on behalf of their clients.

'However, we do allocate funds to the Family Welfare Association to make grants to individual children on our behalf. Applications must be made by a qualified social worker or other welfare professional and forms can be obtained from the FWA at 501–505 Kingsland Road, Dalston, London E8 4AU.

One, two or three year funding?

'We give salary and revenue grants for one, two and three years except for the following, to which we give grants for one year only:

- capital projects
- seasonal projects, e.g. holiday playschemes
- holidays and outings
- equipment and welfare funds.

'Organisations may hold only one grant at a time from the BBC Children in Need Appeal.

Salaries

'If you are applying for staff salaries we will be looking at your experience as an employer or your plans to acquire the management skills you need. In the interests of equal opportunities all new posts funded by BBC Children in Need should be publicly advertised, unless for short term or sessional staff. Please would you:

- state whether a salary is for a new post or for an existing one
- make sure your costs include all the extras involved in employing staff (for example: recruitment costs, inflation, and increments, employers costs and any other on-costs)
- enclose a job description, person specification and a first year plan with your application.

Monitoring and evaluation

'When we give grants to staff salaries we ask organisations to take responsibility for monitoring and evaluating their work. This is particularly important when organisations want us to fund their work for more than one year.

'Monitoring and evaluating is about measuring what you have achieved, and comparing it to what you hoped to achieve. So you need to set clear and realistic targets before you write your application.

'The kind of answers we are looking for here are to do with keeping records, doing surveys, getting feedback from your users, or anything else you think gives us an indication of your progress.

'We ask for this information so we can spend our money as wisely as possible, but we do understand that progress isn't problem free, so please be as clear and honest as you can.

Children with disabilities

'We wish to use our funds appropriately to help children with physical, sensory and/or learning disabilities. We recognise that each child with a disability is an individual to be considered as a child first, sharing the same needs and aspirations as all children and equally entitled to respect and dignity.

'Children with disabilities are disadvantaged not only by the effect of their disabilities but also by the attitudes of others towards them and towards their participation in society. They may also experience other disadvantages such as poverty, isolation, illness and restricted opportunities.

'We require applicants to demonstrate a sensitive appreciation of the needs and aspirations of the children to benefit and we want our funds to support children with disabilities in ways that:

- improve their choice and opportunity
- enhance their disabilities
- encourage independence
- build their confidence and self esteem
- involve disabled young people and adults as role models
- counter negative attitudes and barriers to participation
- recognise the needs of families and carers.

Child protection

'As an organisation working with children, you have a responsibility to protect them from any harm, including the possibility of abuse, while they are in your care. We would ask you to think carefully and take any relevant action or advice.

What we are looking for
A focus on children and quality

'We are looking for quality work and projects which show a clear focus on children:

- your project should be about changing the lives of children for the better
- it should be for children (rather than their parents or for the needs of your organisation)
- where possible and appropriate it should take account of children's views and involve them in the decision making.

A thoughtful and honest application

'A thoughtful and honest application always stands out in the crowd. Tell us clearly what the problem is, and how your project will do something about it. Give us relevant facts and figures, please don't use jargon, and don't be vague. You don't need to promise us the moon, just tell us what you can realistically achieve.

'Your budget should show that you've done your homework and know what things cost. A thoughtful and honest application isn't a hurried and last minute dash to meet our deadlines with something dreamed up overnight. It is a serious and sincere attempt by your organisation to use its experience and skill to make a positive difference where it is needed.'

In 1999/2000 the top 50 grants in Scotland included: £75,000 for two years to ISEA Scotland for various support and information services; £74,000 for three years to Stepping Stones in Scotland for the running costs of a children's project including salary for a development worker and administration costs; and £67,000 for three years to YMCA Perth & District for the full-time salary of a project worker for the mobile youth drop-in centre for 12- to 17-year-olds.

Exclusions Grants are not made for trips or projects abroad, medical treatment or medical research, unspecified expenditure, deficit funding or the repayment of loans, projects which take place before applications can be processed, projects which are unable to start within 12 months or the relief of statutory responsibility.

Applications Straightforward application forms and guidelines are available from the appeal at the address above.

There are two closing dates for applications – November 30 and March 30. Organisations may submit only one application and may apply to only one of these dates. Applicants should allow up to five months from each closing date for notification of a decision. (For summer projects applications must be submitted by the November closing date or they will be rejected because they cannot be processed in time.)

Bell's Nautical Trust

Maritime education

£14,000 (2000/01)

Beneficial area Scotland, with a preference for Leith

11 Corrennie Gardens, Edinburgh EH10 6DG

Tel. 0131 447 9859

Website www.bellstrust.org.uk

Correspondent W H G Mathison

Trustees *R S Salvesen; S J Boyd; C W Davidson; J MacNeill; J W Sellars; N C Souter; Capt. A H F Wilks; W McDonald; Capt. J W O Simpson; Capt. R M Logan; J A G Lowe; E Gillespie; G J Hughes; J Taylor.*

Inland Revenue no. SC017199

Information available Information was provided by the trust.

General The trust supports maritime education. An average grant is £1,000, the largest is usually £2,500. Grants are often given for equipment or towards travel/accommodation costs. Several grants are recurrent and about half the grants are given to Sea Cadets groups. The removal of the Advance Corporation Tax Credit, which is being phased out by the government over a number of years, has unfortunately led to a reduction in the trust's income. In 2000/01 grants totalled £14,000. In 1999/2000 it had an income of £18,000, £16,000 of which was given in grants. Recent beneficiaries have included sailing clubs, Sea Cadets groups, Sea Scouts, the Tall Ships, Jewel and Esk Valley College.

Exclusions No grants to individuals.

Applications An application form and guidelines are available from the correspondent. Trustees meet once a year to consider grants. Applications should be received by the end of November, grants are distributed in February.

The Bethesda Charitable Trust Fund

Christian, churches, welfare, general

nil (2000/01)

Beneficial area Preference for Scotland

6 Albert Place, Aberdeen AB25 1RG

Tel. 01224 626090

Correspondent Jim Wilson, Trustee

Trustees *J Wilson; B Wilson; Mrs A R P Wilson.*

Inland Revenue no. SC007968

Information available Information was provided by the trust.

General The trust supports Christian charities and churches for education and outreach. It will also give grants for general charitable purposes. Grants are usually one-off for capital projects, and can be for buildings. They rarely exceed £1,000.

It receives its income from the profits of a company. In 2000/01 it did not receive this income so no grants were made. It anticipated in January 2002 making grants during 2002.

In 1997/98 it had an income of £39,000 and gave grants totalling £26,000. Beneficiaries were Deeside Christian Fellowship Church which received £19,000 for building work, Doulos Trust (£6,000) and SIM United Kingdom (£1,000).

Exclusions Grants are not given for expeditions, scholarships, individuals, housing or animal charities.

Applications In writing to the correspondent, including an sae. A trustee usually visits a charity considered for support.

The Birnie Trust

General

£13,000 a year

Beneficial area Worldwide with a preference for Scotland

Turcan Connell, Princes Exchange,
1 Earl Grey Street, Edinburgh EH3 9EE

Correspondent G W R Scott

Trustees *Lt Col. E F Gordon; D A Connell; Mrs E A G Gordon; Dr L J King; N C Gordon; Mrs R E Simpson.*

Inland Revenue no. SC005509

Information available Information was provided by the trust.

General The trust was set up in 1986 to award grants to Scottish charities and some international projects.

The assets of the trust are about £300,000 producing an income of about £13,000 a year, all of which is given in grants. These range from £150 to £1,000 and are given for specific projects rather than general appeals. There is a preference for supporting causes concerned with disadvantaged people.

Exclusions No grants to individuals, to other grant-making bodies or for buildings.

Applications In writing to the correspondent, preferably including an sae. The trust stated that it receives 20 to 30 applications a week, only 1 or 2 of which will be successful.

Kenneth Blackwood Charitable Trust

General

Not known

Beneficial area Scotland

Wylie & Bisset, 135 Wellington Street, Glasgow G2 2XE

Tel. 0141 248 3904 **Fax** 0141 226 5074

Inland Revenue no. SC006726

Information available Limited information was available on this trust.

General This trust has general charitable purposes in Scotland. Further information was not available.

Applications In writing to the correspondent.

The Bourne-May Charitable Trust

Medical research, military, conservation, animal welfare

£5,400 (1998/99)

Beneficial area UK, but with a preference for central and south west Scotland and Rutland

Murray Beith Murray WS, 39 Castle Street, Edinburgh EH2 3BH

Fax 0131 225 4412

Correspondent The Trustees

Trustees *J J S Bourne-May; J K Scott Moncrieff; Mrs J J Bourne-May; G G Bourne-May.*

Charity Commission no. 286195

Information available Information was provided by the trust.

General Funding is awarded mainly to UK charities – in particular to those concerned with medical research, the military, conservation and animal welfare. Local organisations based in central and south west Scotland and Rutland are also considered. Grants rarely exceed £350.

In 1998/99 it had assets of £119,000 and an income of £22,000. Grants to 19 charities totalled £5,400, the same as the administration costs.

Beneficiaries included 1st Battalion Coldsteam Guards (£750), Naomi House Children's Hospice (£500), Kirkandrews Kirk – Borgue (£400), with £200 each to Arthritis Care, Coldsteam Guards Association, Fairbridge in Scotland, Hollyfield Wild Bird Hospital and Animal Sanctuary, LOROS, PDSA, Redwings Horse Sanctuary and Tixover Church.

Exclusions No grants to individuals. Local charities are only considered if they are based in central and south west Scotland or Rutland.

Applications In writing to the correspondent. Telephone enquiries are not welcome.

James Boyle's Trust

Relief of human suffering

£8,000 (1994)

Beneficial area Scotland

34 Albyn Place, Aberdeen AB9 1FW

Tel. 01224 643573

Correspondent Stronachs, Administrators

Trustees *G Cunningham; J E F Thomson; G W Stevenson.*

Inland Revenue no. SC021125

Information available Information was supplied by the trust.

General This trust was set up with funds of £116,000 on the death of James Boyle. Organisations are funded at the discretion of the trustees and grants are awarded 'for general or specific purposes of the charities named by the settlor'. No further information was available.

Applications The trust states that there is no application procedure. Contact the correspondent at the above address for details.

Miss Marion Broughton's Charitable Trust

Older people, medical, disability, churches

£40,000 (1999/2000)

Beneficial area Scotland, with a preference for the Lothians

Brodies Solicitors, 15 Atholl Crescent, Edinburgh EH3 8HA

Tel. 0131 228 3777

Correspondent A M C Dalgleish, Trustee

Trustees *E J Cuthbertson; A M C Dalgleish.*

Inland Revenue no. SC009781

Information available Information was provided by the trust.

General This trust supports Scottish organisations working with children, older people and people who are disabled. It has a preference for the Lothians. Special emphasis is given to infirm and older people and also for exceptional work on the fabric of churches. In 1999/2000 it had assets of £900,000 and an income of £40,000, all of which was given in grants. No further information was available for this year.

In 1998/99 it had assets of £1.1 million and an income of £48,000. A total of £46,000 was given to 30 organisations. Grants ranged from £500 to £10,000. The largest grants were £10,000 to Marie Curie Cancer Care and £5,000 to Cancer Research Campaign. Grants of £1,500 were given to 12 organisations including Alzheimer's Scotland, Capability Scotland, Drum Riding, Edinburgh & Leith Age Concern and St Mary's Cathedral. Eight grants of £1,000 were given, including those to Acredale House, Clackmannanshire Care & Repair, Enable and Scottish Motor Neurone Association. Smaller grants of £500 included those to Brainwave, Edzell Lethnot Church Project 2000, DIG Scotland and REMAP Scotland.

Applications In writing to the correspondent but please note the trust states it is 'overburdened with applications' and not looking for more.

Colonel T R Broughton's Charitable Trust

Older people, people who are infirm, ex-servicemen

£6,000 (1999/2000)

Beneficial area Preference for Scotland

Messrs Brodies WS, 15 Atholl Crescent, Edinburgh EH3 8HA

Tel. 0131 228 3777 **Fax** 0131 228 3878

Correspondent Andrew M C Dalgleish

Trustees *C S R Stroyan; E J Cuthbertson; Brodies & Co (Trustees) Ltd.*

Inland Revenue no. SC003782

Information available Information was provided by the trust.

General The trust supports people who are elderly or infirm, with special reference to ex-servicemen. In 1999/2000 it had assets of £280,000 and an income of £10,000. Grants totalled £6,000. Six grants of £1,000 each went to Cancer Research Campaign – Edinburgh, Leith Age Concern, Ex-Services Mental Welfare Society, Lord Robert's Workshop, National Benevolent Fund and Scottish Veterans' Residences.

Exclusions No grants to individuals.

Applications In writing to the correspondent.

The Callander Charitable Trust

General

Not known

Beneficial area Falkirk, other parts of central Scotland and Galloway

Messrs A J & A Graham, 105 West George Street, Glasgow G2 1QA

Tel. 0141 204 4225 **Fax** 0141 204 4511

Correspondent J A Aitkenhead

Inland Revenue no. SC016609

Information available Limited information was available on this trust.

General Donations are awarded to various charitable organisations for general charitable purposes. Principal donations are given for work in Falkirk, other parts of central Scotland and Galloway. Unfortunately we were unable to obtain further infomation about the trust.

Applications Contact the correspondent for further details.

The W A Cargill Charitable Trust

General

£83,000 (1999/2000)

Beneficial area Scotland

190 St Vincent Street, Glasgow G2 5SP

Tel. 0141 204 2833

Correspondent Norman A Fyfe, Trustee

Trustees *A C Fyfe; W G Peacock; N A Fyfe; Mirren E Graham.*

Inland Revenue no. SC012076

Information available Accounts were provided by the trust at the cost of £23.

General The trust supports a wide variety of organisations, as follows: welfare, local projects, hospices and medical research, recreational organisations for young people, schools, people with visual impairments, animals and wildlife and lifeboat services. It has the same address and trustees as two other trusts, The DWT Cargill Fund and The WA Cargill Fund, although they all operate independently (see separate entries for this trust in this guide).

In 1999/2000 it had assets of £3 million which generated an income of £97,000. Grants totalled £83,000, listed as annual grants and appeals.

Annual – 27 grants totalling £68,000
Church of Scotland received three grants, £5,000 for aged and infirm ministers and £2,000 for both maintenance of the ministry and home missions. Other larger grants were £7,000 to Crossroads (Scotland) Care Attendant Scheme and £6,000 to City of Glasgow Social Services. Other beneficiaries included Glasgow Braendam Link and Trefoil House (£3,000 each), Cornerstone Community Centre and Scottish Conservation Projects (£2,000 each), National Asthma Campaign (£1,500) and Leonard Cheshire Foundation and Sighthill Youth Centre (£1,000 each).

Appeals – 14 grants totalling £15,000
These included £2,000 each to Glasgow Braendam Link, Possil & Milton Forum on Disability and Stobhill Kidney Patients Association, £1,000 each to Cue & Review Recording Services, Dalmarnock Centre,

St George & St Peter's Community Association and The Towersey Foundation, £500 to Reality at Work – Scotland and £300 to National Children's Society.

Exclusions No grants are given to individuals or organisations which have been 'nationalised or taken over by state/local authorities'.

Applications In writing to the correspondent.

Caring for Kids (Radio Tay Charity Auction Trust)

Children and young people

£84,000 to individuals and organisations (1999/2000)

Beneficial area Tayside, Angus and north east Fife

Radio Tay Ltd, 6 North Isla Street, Dundee DD3 7JQ

Tel. 01382 200800

Correspondent The Coordinator

Trustees *Moira Naulty, Chair; Arthur Ballingall; Margaret Laird; Kathleen Codognato; Lorraine Stevenson.*

Inland Revenue no. SC008440

Information available Full accounts were provided by the trust.

General The trust's fundraising appeal starts in October and continues until Christmas. The main event is the station's charity auction, for which gifts are donated by local businesses and individuals. All the money raised is distributed within the community covered by the radio service.

The trust's objects are to support children who are disabled, disadvantaged, deprived or otherwise in need, in Tayside, Angus and north east Fife. It aims to support those children who need assistance most.

In 1999/2000 it had assets of £50,000 and an income of £95,000, of which £92,000 came from donations received. After administration and

fundraising expenses of £17,000, grants totalled £84,000.

Grants were given to individuals and organisations and ranged from £30 to £2,500. Around 11,000 children benefitted from grants. Seven grants of £1,000 or more were made to organisations as follows: £2,000 to PA Charity Fund for New Life, £1,500 to Alyth Youth Partnership, £1,100 to Rainbow House Publications and £1,000 each to Blairgowrie Guide and Scout Hut Committee, CAFE Project – Arbroath, Perth Action on Autism and Playfield House at Stratheden Hospital – Cupar.

Applications Application forms are available from the correspondent from early December. They must be returned by the end of January for consideration for the distribution in March. Applications from individuals must be recommended from a third party such as a social worker, doctor, headteacher, Children 1st etc.

The Carnegie Trust for the Universities of Scotland

Scottish universities

£350,000 to organisations (2000/01)

Beneficial area Scotland

Cameron House, Abbey Park Place, Dunfermline, Fife KY12 7PZ

Tel. 01383 622148 **Fax** 01383 622149

e-mail jgray@carnegie-trust.org

Website www.carnegie-trust.org

Correspondent Sir John P Arbuthnott, Secretary and Treasurer

Trustees *There are 14 appointed trustees. Ex-officio trustees comprise the principals of the Scottish universities, the Lord Provosts of Edinburgh and Glasgow and the Secretary of State for Scotland.*

Inland Revenue no. SC015600

Information available Detailed guidance notes and application forms for both personal research grants and for assistance with fees are available from the trust.

General The Carnegie Trust for the Universities of Scotland was established by Andrew Carnegie to improve and expand Scottish universities, to help pay tuition fees for students of Scottish 'birth or extraction', and to provide research and similar grants.

The original endowment was of US $10,000,000 (a then unprecedented sum: at the time, total government assistance to all four Scottish universities was about £50,000 a year). The demands on the trust have changed greatly and there are now 13 Scottish universities in place of the original 4 in 1901. The trust assists the universities primarily by making capital grants (but see below) and block travel grants, and grants for research.

By its royal charter, one half of the net income of the trust is to be applied to the improvement and expansion of the universities of Scotland and one half to the payment of fees of students of Scottish 'birth or extraction' in respect of courses leading to a degree of a Scottish university.

In 2000/01 the trust had assets of £50 million and an income of £2 million. A total of £1.6 million was given in grants. Capital grants to universities amounted to £350,000. Awards for advanced research and study totalled £875,000. Grants to students totalled £156,000.

The research grants have a maximum value of £2,000. They are intended to support low-cost research, for example to help with the costs of accessing archives, art galleries, libraries and museums and for travel and subsistence costs when field trips are conducted. In 2000/01, 234 research grants were given out of 262 applications, two-thirds of which were given to existing or retired members of staff and the remainder to postgraduates studying for PhD at a Scottish university.

A category of larger grants has been introduced to assist projects which involve and are of benefit to Scottish universities as a whole. Grants awarded range from £8,000 to £30,000. These grants are not for individuals. Examples of projects approved for support were available for 1999/2000 and included development of an Institute for the Languages of Scotland, Lacuna Project aimed at enhancing the use of ethographic film in teaching and learning and Scottish Screen – a pilot project over three years in support of an annual event, Scottish Students on Screen. Out of 15 applications received in 2000/01, nine were successful.

The Carnegie Scholarships are made for the support of full-time research extending over three years at a university in the UK. In 2000/01 12 new awards were made from 89 applications. Applicants must be nominated by a professor, reader or lecturer in a Scottish university.

To mark the centenary of the founder's benefaction, the trust has created the centenary fund. The initial purpose of this fund is to support the presence each year in Scottish universities of one or two outstanding scholars. The selection of these centenary professors is made from nominations by the universities. Two such professorships were to be held in 2002.

The number of awards given for fee assistance for undergraduates in the year was 89 (from 111 applications). The trust also awards Vacation Scholarships designed to 'enable undergraduates of high academic merit to undertake a piece of research, usually in the summer vacation between their second and third years'. These are competitive awards, and names are submitted by deans of faculties by 1 April. 71 such awards were made in the year, from 97 applications.

Exclusions Research grants can be made only to members of staff and graduates of Scottish universities; costs of equipment, consumables, bench fees, radiocarbon dating and secretarial, technical and other assistance are specifically excluded. The trust does not give grants to individuals for attendance at conferences, participation in expeditions, travel (other than for research) or attendance at institutions other than Scottish universities. Assistance is not given for the fees for first degree or postgraduate diploma courses at Scottish universities.

Only those born in Scotland, with a parent born in Scotland or with at least two years secondary education in Scotland, are eligible to apply to the trust and awards made by other bodies will not be supplemented.

Carnegie Scholarships are open only to those holding a degree with first-class honours from a Scottish university and nominated by a member of staff, although final year students who are expected to get first-class honours may also apply.

Applications Regulations and application forms can be obtained from the secretary. Preliminary telephone enquiries are welcome. Trustees meet in February, June, and November to consider research grants.

Fee assistance is considered from April to 1 October for the coming session. Scholarships close on 15 March.

The Cattanach Charitable Trust

Homelessness, disability

£134,000 (1998/99)

Beneficial area UK, with a preference for Scotland

Royal Bank of Scotland plc, Private Trust and Taxation, 2 Festival Square, Edinburgh EH3 9SU

Tel. 0131 523 2648 **Fax** 0131 228 9889

Correspondent Don Henderson

Trustees *Royal Bank of Scotland plc; Colette Douglas Home; Lord MacLay; F W Fletcher; Adam Thomson; William Syson.*

Inland Revenue no. SC020902

Information available Information was provided by the trust.

General The trust's objects are the relief of poverty, advancement of education and religion and other purposes which benefit the community. Preference is given to organisations with a Scottish connection.

However, the trust has two current themes which will be in operation until December 2002, these are homelessness (with a focus on young homeless people under 30) and assisting people who are disabled to achieve their full potential.

In addition, the trust will consider any appeals from charities named in the trust deed and any appeals they consider extraordinary. An appeal is regarded as extraordinary if it is urgent, addresses an especially compelling need and is of direct benefit to those the trust seeks to help.

The trust prefers to fund specific projects either entirely, or with a significant contribution, rather than make small contributions to large projects.

It prefers not to commit to permanent funding of long-term projects. Grants usually range from £2,000 to £10,000, but occasionally larger grants are given.

In 1998/99 the trust had assets of £6.4 million, with over £500,000 added to the capital during the year. The income was £240,000. A total of £134,000 was given in 30 grants. The largest grant was £11,000 to ECSH. Three grants of £10,000 went to Ex-Services Mental Welfare, Glasgow Simon Community and LEAD Scotland.

Other grants included those to Barnardos (£7,000), Big Issue and Samaritans (£5,000 each), Pollockshaws After School Service (£4,500), Princes Trust and Thistles Foundation Centre (£3,000), West of Scotland Children's Society (£2,000) and National Blind Children's Society (£1,000). One grant given was under £1,000, £600 to Freespace.

Eight grants were recurrent from the previous year. The trust includes in its report a listing of all grants made since it was established in 1992. In six years, one charity, SSPCA, received grants for five years totalling £63,000 while two charities have received grants for four years: Children 1st and Ex-Services Mental Welfare, totalling £98,000 and £19,000 respectively.

Exclusions Only registered charities can receive support. Grants will not be given to fund salaries of staff already in post. Appeals which do not fall into the current themes will only be considered if they are urgent and directly benefit those the trust seeks to help.

Applications In writing to the correspondent. It would be helpful to the trust if the following details are included:

- the exact purpose of the grant
- how much is required and how the budget has been worked out
- how the project will be monitored and evaluated
- what other money has been raised and applied for
- a short history of the organisation's aims and functions
- the charity registration number and tax exemption number if one is available

- a copy of the most recent annual report and financial statement. Please also advise if the charity is subject to any investigation by the Charity Commission, Scottish Charities Office or Inland Revenue.

Trustees meet at the end of June and December each year, applications should be sent three months prior to these meetings. Appeals after this deadline will only be considered if they are extraordinary.

Celtic Charity Fund

Children, drug-related projects, promotion of ethnic and racial harmony

£100,000 available (1999/2000)

Beneficial area Preference for Scotland and Northern Ireland

Celtic Football Club, Celtic Park, Glasgow G40 3RE

Tel. 0141 556 2611 **Fax** 0141 551 8106

Website www.celticfc.co.uk

Correspondent The Public Relations Department

Trustees *Eric Riley; Kevin Sweeney; John Maguire.*

Information available Information was provided by the trust.

General The fund raises its income through donations from Celtic supporters, staff and directors, the players, corporate clients, the general public and club funds. In addition to cash grants, hundreds of signed footballs, other items and complimentary tickets are also given away for charitable purposes.

The policy was originally to raise money to provide food for the poor of the East End of Glasgow and to encourage positive social integration between the Scottish and Irish people living in Glasgow. Today's policy reflects these original aims, the three main areas of support are as follows:

- children
- drug-related projects
- promoting religious and ethnic harmony.

It also supports three subsidiary areas which are:

- homelessness
- unemployment
- alleviation of suffering caused by illness and famine and to aid innocent families within areas of war.

During 1999/2000 the fund raised over £100,000 from which grants were made, including those described below.

Children's needs
A hospital unit for seriously ill children was supported at Glasgow's Yorkhill Hospital.

Religious and ethnic harmony
'Celtic's concentrated effort to combat bigotry and encourage social integration continued … .' A grant was made to the Equality Goal conference, which focused on issues of racism and discrimination within sport.

Homeless
Glasgow Simon Community received a grant towards its annual Christmas party for 300 homeless people.

International aid
Beneficiaries included Dhaka Orphanage in Bangladesh, Express Aid International for orphans in Romania and Tickety Boo Tea to support disadvantaged children in India.

Applications An application form should be requested in writing from the trust. Trustees meet to consider grants in July each year.

John Christie Trust

Religion, missions, welfare of orphans

£84,000 (2001)

Beneficial area Scotland

c/o Tods Murray, 66 Queen Street, Edinburgh EH2 4NE

Tel. 0131 226 4771 **Fax** 0131 225 3676

Correspondent The Trustees

Trustees *J D Lennie; D W McLetchie; Ina Rankin; Katherine M B Severn; M J R Simpson; Margaret K Watt; R York.*

Inland Revenue no. SC005291

Information available Information was provided by the trust.

General This trust supports the same organisations each year, most of which are concerned with religion, missionary work or the welfare of orphans. They are listed in the trust deed and receive the income in fixed, but not equal, proportions. If any of the charities change their activities substantially, the trustees can remove them from the list and decide how the resulting funds are distributed. Aside from these unexpected and unforeseeable circumstances, the trustees do not have the freedom to influence how the funds are spent. In 2001 the trust's income was £84,000, all of which was given in grants.

Applications Due to the nature of this trust unsolicited applications cannot be considered.

The Claremont Trust

Christian work, social welfare

£9,200 (2000)

Beneficial area Scotland and overseas

13a Hill Street, Broughty Ferry, Dundee DD5 2JP

Tel. 01382 778636

e-mail ag_gammack@yahoo.co.uk

Correspondent Ann Gammack, Secretary

Trustees *Mrs J Craig; Mrs C Davis; Mrs A Gammack; D McHenry; Mrs H Mein; K Pattison; P Robinson; Mrs M A Ure.*

Inland Revenue no. SC002721

Information available The trust produces a set of guidelines for applicants and a leaflet about its work, as well as an annual report.

General The trust was set up in 1948 to assist small innovative projects involved in Christian witness, renewal and social action within and outside the church, in Scotland and overseas. It is ecumenical and states that it welcomes applications from inter-church and secular groups. Grants totalled £9,200 in 2000.

Grants usually range between £250 and £750, although larger grants are occasionally made. The average grant during 2000 was around £485. Two longer-term grants were made which would be

repeated for a second year, provided satisfactory reports are received. The trustees are keen to extend the scope of the trust through a larger number of longer-term grants, but so far comparatively few applications for such grants have been received.

Beneficiaries in 2000 included Enact for Women for a women's festival, HOPE towards basic skills training for prisoners, Mains Child and Family Centre for a multi-sensory garden, Newfields Primary School for an outdoor activity weekend, and Ruchill Parish Church for a summer outreach programme.

Exclusions Large building appeals, general appeals from well-established charities and applications from individuals for study or travel, whether in Scotland or abroad, are not considered.

Applications On a form available from the correspondent.

Clyde Marine plc Charitable Trust

General, social welfare, medical/health

£15,000 (2000)

Beneficial area UK, with a preference for Scotland

Cumbrae House, 15 Carlton Court, Glasgow G5 9JP

Tel. 0141 429 2181 **Fax** 0141 429 4348

e-mail ach@clyde-marine.com

Website www.clyde-marine.com

Correspondent Angela Hemphill, Trust Secretary

Inland Revenue no. SC001402

Information available Information was supplied by the trust.

General The trust gives grants to a wide range of causes, especially organisations concerned with social welfare and medical and health causes. In 2000 the trust had an income of £16,000 mostly donations from Clyde Marine plc. It gave 24 grants totalling £15,000. Grants ranged from £100 to £2,000. The largest grants of £2,000 went to Prince & Princess of Wales Hospice, RNLI and Salvation Army. Others included £1,000 each to Macmillan Cancer Relief, TAK Tent and The Scottish Association for Mental Health. Smaller grants included those to Glasgow City Mission, Glasgow Seamen's Friends Society, Glasgow Veteran Seafarers' Association, Princess Louise Scottish Hospital (Erskine Hospital) and Trefoil Holiday and Adventure Centre for the Disabled. 16 of the grants were recurrent from the previous year.

Exclusions Grants are not given to political or religious appeals.

Applications In writing to the correspondent. The trustees meet in August to consider grants. Applications should have been received by July.

Columba Charitable Trust

Health, children, general

£4,000 (2000/01)

Beneficial area Scotland

Bird Semple, 249 West George Street, Glasgow G2 4RD

Tel. 0141 304 3434

Correspondent Norman Alexander

Inland Revenue no. SC021517

Information available Accounts were provided by the trust.

General 'The trust makes donations to organisations, often dealing with health issues or with children.' In 2000/01 it had assets of £57,000 and an income of £970. Four grants of £1,000 each were made, to East Park, Erskine Hospital, RNLI and Shelter Scotland.

Applications In writing to the correspondent.

Columba Trust

Catholic buildings, education, homelessness

£18,000 (1998/99)

Beneficial area Scotland

Grant Thornton, 95 Bothwell Street, Glasgow G2 7SZ

Tel. 0141 223 0000

Correspondent The Trustees

Inland Revenue no. SC008586

Information available Information was provided by the trust.

General The trust's main aims are to support the following:

* students studying theology or related subjects
* charities working with people who are homeless
* projects associated with significant Catholic properties.

In the past the trust gave grants for Catholic educational purposes. It has since broadened its area of work to include the above categories. It has also decided to support a smaller number of charities each year and offer longer term funding of three to five years. In 1998/99 it gave grants totalling £18,000. Grants ranged between £500 and £8,000. Beneficiaries have included St Mary's Cathedral which received a commitment of £8,000 a year for three years towards the costs of a new organ. One-off grants of £5,000 each went to Lifeline (Pregnancy Counselling and Care) and St Mary's Church in Greenock for building work while Family House of Prayer received a one-off grant of £500 for educational materials.

Applications In writing to the correspondent. Trustees meet twice a year to consider grants in May and November.

The Martin Connell Charitable Trust

General

£140,000 (2000)

Beneficial area Scotland

Messrs Maclay Murray & Spens,
151 St Vincent Street, Glasgow G2 5NJ

Tel. 0141 248 5011

Correspondent The Trustees

Inland Revenue no. SC009842

Information available Information was provided by the trust.

General The trust supports general charitable purposes in Scotland. In 2000 it had an income of £150,000 and gave £140,000 in grants. Further information was not available.

Exclusions No grants to individuals.

Applications In writing to the correspondent. The trustees meet in June and December.

Gordon Cook Foundation

Education and training

£214,000 (1999/2000)

Beneficial area UK

Hilton Place, Aberdeen AB24 4FA

Tel. 01224 283704 **Fax** 01224 485457

e-mail i.b.brown@norcol.ac.uk

Correspondent Irene B Brown, Administrative Officer

Trustees *D A Adams, Chair; Prof. B J McGettrick; Dr P Clarke; Dr W Gatherer; J Marshall; C P Skene; D S C Levie.*

Inland Revenue no. SC017455

Information available Full accounts and guidelines were provided by the trust.

General This foundation was set up in 1974 and is dedicated to the advancement and promotion of all aspects of education and training which are likely to promote 'character development' and 'citizenship'. The following information was taken from the foundation's leaflet.

'In recent years, the foundation has adopted the term "Values Education" to denote the wide range of activity it seeks to support. This includes:

- the promotion of good citizenship in its widest terms, including aspects of moral, ethical and aesthetic education, youth work, cooperation between home and school, and coordinating work in school with leisure-time pursuits

- the promotion of health education as it relates to values education

- supporting relevant aspects of moral and religious education

- helping parents, teachers and others to enhance the personal development of pupils and young people

- supporting developments in school curriculum subjects which relate to values education

- helping pupils and young people to develop commitment to the value of work, industry and enterprise generally

- disseminating the significant results of relevant research and development.

'The view of the trustees is that the work of the foundation should:

- invest in people and in effective organisations

- have an optimum impact on the educational and training system, and consequently on children and young people in life and work.'

In 1999/2000 assets stood at £9.3 million, up over £400,000 on the previous year but generating an income of only £285,000.

Grants totalling £214,000 were made to 28 different projects and ranged from £1,000 to £30,000. The larger grants went to the Norham Foundation (£30,000), Health Education Board for Scotland (£20,000), Institute for Global Ethics – UK Trust (£16,000), Western Isles Education and Society of Education Officers (£15,000 each) and Citizenship Foundation (£14,000). At least half the grants appeared to be to Scottish organisations including four for projects at University of Glasgow (ranging from £2,000 to £10,000). Other smaller grants included those to North Lanarkshire Council (£10,000), Scottish

Office Education & Industry Department (£8,000) and Association of Head Teachers in Scotland (£2,300).

Exclusions Individuals are unlikely to be funded.

Applications In accordance with announced programmes and invitations to tender, the trust welcomes applications. Forms may be obtained from the correspondent.

The Craignish Trust

Arts, education, environment, general

£82,000 (2000/01)

Beneficial area UK, with a preference for Scotland

Messrs Geoghegan & Co., 6 St Colme Street, Edinburgh EH3 6AD

Tel. 0131 225 4681

Correspondent The Secretaries

Trustees *Clifford Hastings; Mrs Caroline Hobhouse; Ms Margaret Matheson.*

Inland Revenue no. SC016882

Information available Full accounts were provided by the trust.

General Established in 1961 by the late Sir William McEwan Younger, the 2000/01 accounts summarised the funding criteria as follows:

- no large national charities
- Scottish bias, but not exclusively
- arts, particularly where innovative and/or involved in the community
- education
- environment
- of particular interest to a trustee.

In 2000/01 it had assets of £4.1 million which generated an income of £151,000. From a total expenditure of £117,000, grants were given to 48 organisations totalling £82,000. Nine of the beneficiaries were also supported in the previous year.

The largest grants were £5,000 each to Henley Symphony Orchestra and Institute of Economic Affairs, £4,000 to Autonomic Disorders Association and £3,500 to John Muir Trust Appeal. Other grants included £2,500 each to Boilerhouse Theatre Group, Drug Prevention Group, Edinburgh Common Purpose and Friends of the Earth Scotland, £2,000 each to Edinburgh Cyrenians and Sustrans, £1,500 to Cannongate Youth Project, £1,000 each to Braendam Link, ChildLine Scotland, Edinburgh Youth Orchestra Society, Reality at Work in Scotland and Visible Fictions Theatre Company, £500 each to Edinburgh Sitters and Working for Environmental Community Action and £250 to Orcadia Creative Learning Centre.

Exclusions Running costs are not normally supported.

Applications There is no formal application form; applicants should write to the correspondent. Details of the project should be included together with a copy of the most recent annual report and accounts.

The Cray Trust

Young people, animals, disadvantaged areas

£52,000 (2000/01)

Beneficial area Mainly the east of Scotland

c/o Springfords, Dundas House, Westfield Park, Eskbank, Midlothian EH22 3FB

Correspondent The Trustees

Trustees *Mrs S P B Gammell; P R Gammell; J E B Gammell.*

Inland Revenue no. SC005592

Information available The trust provided some information for this entry.

General The trust's income for 2000/01 amounted to £53,000 after expenses. Assets totalled £1.1 million. Grants totalling £52,000 were awarded to 74 organisations whose work was of concern to the trustees.

Grants ranged between £100 and £20,000 with the vast majority being in the £200 to £500 range. The only information provided on the types of beneficiaries was that the trust made a large number of grants to charities supporting young people on GAP years such as BSES, Raleigh International, Project Trust, VSO and Link Overseas.

Exclusions No political appeals are considered. No grants to individuals.

Applications In writing to the correspondent. The trust stated: 'applications should be short and to the point. Grants are aimed to make a difference and so will seldom be made to large national charities unless for specific projects in east Scotland.'

Hamish and Doris Crichton's Charitable Trust

Animal welfare, conservation

£15,000 (1999)

Beneficial area Scotland, with a preference for Berwickshire/East Lothian

Turcan Connell WS, Princes Exchange, 1 Earl Grey Street, Edinburgh EH3 9EE

Tel. 0131 228 8111 **Fax** 0131 228 8118

Correspondent Hubert Ross, Secretary

Trustees *G M Menzies; H J Ross.*

Inland Revenue no. SC000347

Information available Information was provided by the trust.

General This trust was established in 1999 and is the amalgamation of two trusts: The Hamish Crichton Charitable Trust and The Doris Crichton Charitable Trust. In June 1999 the trust had funds totalling £300,000 after providing a capital donation of £15,000 to the Royal School of Veterinary Studies. More recent information was not available.

Applications The trust does not solicit applications and is proactive in finding its beneficiaries.

The Cross Trust

Young people, music, drama, education

£158,000 to individuals and organisations (2000)

Beneficial area Scotland

25 South Methven Street, Perth PH1 5ES

Tel. 01738 620451 **Fax** 01738 631155

Correspondent Mrs Dorothy Shaw, Assistant Secretary

Trustees *Revd Hon R D Buchanan-Smith; Dr R H MacDougall; Dr A R MacGregor; Mrs Clair Orr; Dougal Philip; Mark Webster.*

Inland Revenue no. SC008620

Information available Information was provided by the trust.

General In 2000 the trust had an income of £215,000 and gave grants totalling £158,000. About 80% of the grants are given to individuals for educational purposes (including travel for their courses). Applicants must be of Scottish birth or parentage. Grants to organisations are normally made for music, drama or outdoor activities to benefit young people. Grants range from £150 to £1,500.

Exclusions No retrospective applications will be considered.

Applications Application forms and guidance notes are available from the correspondent.

Cruden Foundation Ltd

General

£83,000 (1999/2000)

Beneficial area Mainly Scotland

c/o Cruden Group, Baberton House, Juniper Green, Edinburgh EH14 3HN

Correspondent M R A Matthews, Secretary

Inland Revenue no. SC004987

Information available Full accounts were available from the trust.

General In 1999/2000 the trust had assets of £798,000 and an income of £93,000. Grants totalled £82,500. A wide variety of causes were supported with an emphasis on health and welfare. Grants ranged from £100 to £7,500 and were given to 120 beneficiaries. Many of these grants were recurrent from the previous year. A grant of £7,500 was given to Scottish Hospital Endowments Research Trust, and one of £6,000 to Scottish Agricultural College Scholarship. Grants ranging from £1,000 to £5,000 were given to 19 organisations including Dementia Services Development Centre, Edinburgh Headway Group, Indigent Old Women's Society, and the Talbot Rice Gallery, University of Edinburgh. 47 grants were given ranging from £300 to £750 and included those to Craigmillar Festival Society, Glasgow & South West Scotland Federation of Boys' and Girls' Clubs, Lothian Marriage Counselling Service, Marriage Counselling Scotland, Scottish Adoption Association, Scottish Opera and The Scottish Society for Autism.

Smaller grants included those to Leith School of Art, One Parent Families Scotland, and the Scottish Wildlife Trust.

Applications In writing to the correspondent.

The Cunningham Trust

Medical research projects

£270,000 (1999/2000)

Beneficial area Scotland

Murray Donald & Caithness, Solicitors, Kinburn Castle, St Andrews, Fife KY16 9DR

Tel. 01334 477107 **Fax** 01334 476862

Inland Revenue no. SC013499

Information available Accounts were provided by the trust.

General This trust is a Scottish charity established in 1984 whose main purpose is the encouragement of medical research and the relief of suffering. Since it was set up, the income has been committed to medical research, mainly at Scottish university medical departments. It supports specific projects rather than giving general funding to research bodies.

In 1999/2000 the trust's assets totalled £5 million, generating an income of £268,000. Grants totalled £270,000 and were made to 11 recipients. Five new grants were approved during the year.

The grants included three for projects at Edinburgh University, five for various projects at Glasgow University and two for projects at St Andrews University. The trust has commitments totalling £451,000 to projects at five universities, including the three named above.

It is unlikely that applications from non-regular beneficiaries will be supported.

Applications Current information about dates and procedures for submitting applications is supplied to the Deans of Faculty of Medicine of the Scottish universities. Applications need to be received by May and trustees meet in June and November. All applications must be submitted on the standard form, and early admission is advisable. Please not the comments under General.

Robert O Curle Charitable Trust

Medical, health, medical research, environment and conservation

£10,000 (2001)

Beneficial area UK, but mainly Scotland

c/o Lindsays WS, 11 Atholl Crescent, Edinburgh EH3 8HE

Tel. 0131 477 8713 **Fax** 0131 229 5611

e-mail wbr@lindsays.co.uk

Correspondent W Brian Robertson, Administrator

Inland Revenue no. SC018939

Information available Information was provided by the trust.

General The trust supports medical or health charities and medical research. Charities concerned with the environment and conservation are also considered. It prefers to support specific projects or a 'shopping list' of items required by an organisation.

In 2001 it gave £10,000 in grants. Beneficiaries included Edinburgh and Leith Age Concern, Deafblind Scotland, Plantlife, Seagull Trust, University of Edinburgh Development Trust for a brain campaign and Water of Leith Conservation Trust.

Exclusions No grants to individuals. The trust will not fund organisations involved in the following areas: the arts, children/young people, education/training, overseas projects, political appeals, religious appeals, sports/recreation and social welfare.

Applications In writing to the correspondent. Applications should be sent in October for consideration in December.

Miss Edith Findlay Currie Charitable Trust

General

About £1,500

Beneficial area Scotland

Messrs Mitchells Robertson Solicitors, George House, 36 North Hanover Street, Glasgow G1 2AD

Tel. 0141 552 3422 **Fax** 0141 552 2935

e-mail jamc@mitchels-robertson.co.uk

Correspondent J A M Cuthbert

Inland Revenue no. SC027244

Information available Limited information was available on this trust.

General The trust makes grants totalling about £1,500 a year to general causes.

Applications In writing to the correspondent.

Alex Deas Charitable Trust

Education, women's rights, disability, international aid

About £500,000 a year to individuals and organisations

Beneficial area UK and overseas

5th Floor, 68–70 George Street, Edinburgh EH22 2NB

Correspondent Dr Alex Deas

Inland Revenue no. SC027244

Information available Limited information was available on this trust.

General The trust gives money for individuals to go and work in other countries in fields such as education, human rights, and helping people who are disabled. The trust also funds other charities working in these areas. Grants to individuals and organisations total about £500,000 a year.

Exclusions This trust does not fund political activity, genetic or medical research, and cannot fund a charity where any officer earns higher than the average wage in their own country.

Applications In writing to the correspondent.

The Demigryphon Trust

Medical, education, children, general

£27,000 (1999/2000)

Beneficial area UK, with a preference for Scotland

Pollen House, 10–12 Cork Street, London W1S 3LW

Tel. 020 7439 9061

Correspondent Alan Winborn, Secretary

Trustees *The Cowdray Trust Ltd.*

Charity Commission no. 275821

Information available Full accounts are on file at the Charity Commission.

General In 1999/2000 the trust had assets of £2.8 million and an income of £90,400. The trust will support a wide range of organisations and appears to have a preference for education, medical, children and Scottish organisations. During the year, 21 grants were given totalling £26,900 and 3 of the organisations had received a grant in the previous year.

Grants ranged from £100 to £10,000. The largest grant of £10,000 went to Lonach Village Hall. Other grants included CHASE (£5,000), The Game Conservancy (£3,000), Tommy's Campaign (£2,000) and Helen Rollason Cancer Care Centre (£1,000). Recipients of smaller grants included Aboyne and Deeside Festival, Gordon Group – Riding for the Disabled Association, and Royal Scottish Agricultural Benevolent Institution.

In addition, payments totalling £31,000 were made to 30 pensioners.

Exclusions No grants to individuals; registered charities only.

Applications In writing to the correspondent including an sae. No application forms or guidelines are issued and there is no deadline. Acknowledgements are not sent to unsuccessful applicants.

John Furguson Denholm Charitable Trust

General

£5,600 (2000/01)

Beneficial area Scotland

Newton of Belltrees, Lochwinnoch PA12 4JL

Tel. 01505 842406

Correspondent Sir Ian Denholm

Inland Revenue no. SC002503

Information available Information was provided by the trust.

General The trust supports selected recognised Scottish charities only. In 2000/01 it had an income of £6,600 and made 30 grants totalling £5,600.

The only grants over £250 both went to The Treasurer Paisley Abbey (£1,400 and £650). Recipients of smaller grants (£25 to £250) included Children's Music Foundation, Erskine Hospital, Save the Children and Scotland & Newcastle Lymphoma Group.

Applications In writing to the correspondent.

The Douglas Charitable Trust

General

About £34,000 each year

Beneficial area Scotland

Turcan Connell, Princes Exchange, 1 Earl Grey Street, Edinburgh EH3 9EE

Tel. 0131 228 8111 **Fax** 0131 228 8118

Trustees *Revd Prof. D Shaw; D Connell; E Cameron.*

Inland Revenue no. SC019840

Information available This trust is one of 10, probably all small, trusts administered by Turcan Connell. The company would not provide us with any information on these trusts, only agreeing to send each trust's accounts for the cost of £20 each. We did not think this was reasonable for such small trusts.

General The trust supports general charitable purposes in Scotland. It gives about £34,000 each year in grants. Preference is given to the universities of Edinburgh and St Andrews and church restoration projects in Edinburgh and St Andrews.

Grants range between £1,000 and £2,000. Past beneficiaries have included Law for All, Oxfam, the Parish Church of the Holy Trinity in St Andrews and Shelter.

Applications In writing to the correspondent. Apply at any time.

The Drummond Trust

Evangelical Christian publications

£18,000 (2000)

Beneficial area UK and worldwide, with a preference for Scotland

Messrs Hill & Rob, 3 Pitt Terrace, Stirling FK8 2EY

Tel. 01786 450985 **Fax** 01786 451360

Correspondent Douglas S Whyte

Trustees *J F Sinclair; Revd B W Dunsmore; Revd A Sheila Blount; D B Cannon; Miss M J S Henderson; Revd G Richards; J K Sinclair, A J Skilling; Revd A A S Reid.*

Inland Revenue no. SC011077

Information available Information was provided by the trust.

General The trust supports Christian publications which should be 'of sound Christian doctrine and evangelical purpose'. In 2000 its assets amounted to £500,000, generating an income of £24,000. Grants totalled £18,000 and ranged between £250 and £1,250. Beneficiaries included the St Andrew Press and Christians in Sport. The trust also runs a series of lectures in partnership with University of Stirling.

Exclusions Scholarships are not awarded.

Applications Application forms are available from the correspondent at the above address. Trustees meet twice a year in March and September. Completed forms must be returned by 31 January or 31 July of each year.

The Dunard Fund

Arts and music

£1.3 million (1999/2000)

Beneficial area Mainly Scotland

4 Royal Terrace, Edinburgh EH7 5AB

Tel. 0131 556 4043

Correspondent Mrs C Høgel, Trustee

Trustees *Carol Høgel; Elisabeth Høgel; Catherine Høgel; Colin Liddell.*

Charity Commission no. 295790

Information available 1999/2000 accounts were provided by the trust (at a cost of £10), but included no information on the size or beneficiaries of the grants.

General The trust supports a few charities chosen by the trustees and is not open to applications. It states that this policy is unlikely to change.

The funds are committed principally to the training for and performance of classical music at the highest standard and to education and display of the visual arts, also at international standard. A small percentage of the fund is dedicated to environmental projects.

The assets at the year end stood at £1.5 million. The total income for the year was £1,832,000 of which £1.8 million came from donations received. Grants totalled £1,325,000. No further information on the grants was included in the accounts.

Exclusions Grants are only given to charities recognised in Scotland or charities registered in England and Wales.

Applications Unsolicited applications and applications on behalf of individuals are not considered.

Mrs J C Dunn's Trust

General

About £8,000

Beneficial area UK, with a preference for Scotland

16 Walker Street, Edinburgh EH3 7NN

Tel. 0131 225 4001

Correspondent J H MacFie, Trustee

Trustees *J H MacFie; J S F MacGregor; E M Paget.*

Inland Revenue no. SC009243

Information available Information was provided by the trust.

General The trust has a net annual income of about £8,000, all of which is given in grants. Beneficiaries were the Salvation Army and the Royal Society for the Relief of Indigent Gentlewomen of Scotland. The trustees prefer to support charities in which the settlor was interested.

Applications Unsolicited applications are not invited.

W J & Mrs C G Dunnachie's Charitable Trust

World war two veterans

£50,000 a year to individuals and organisations

Beneficial area Preference for Scotland

Low Beaton Richmond, 20 Renfields Street, Glasgow G2 5AP

Tel. 0141 221 8931

Correspondent The Trustees

Inland Revenue no. SC015981

Information available Information was provided by the trust.

General The trust supports world war two charities which assist people who are experiencing sickness, infirmity or other disadvantages as a result of the war. Individuals are also supported. There is a preference for assisting organisations connected with Scotland. Grants to individuals and organisations total about £50,000 a year.

Applications In writing to the correspondent at any time.

Endrick Trust

General

About £9,000

Beneficial area UK

30 George Square, Glasgow G2 1LH

Tel. 0141 221 5562 **Fax** 0141 221 5024

Correspondent A O Robertson

Inland Revenue no. SC012043

Information available Limited information was available on this trust.

General The trust makes grants to a range of causes in the UK. Further information was not available.

Applications In writing to the correspondent.

The Erskine Cunningham Hill Trust

Church of Scotland, General

£52,000 (2000)

Beneficial area UK, with priority given to Scottish registered charities and projects/appeals

121 George Street, Edinburgh EH2 4YN

Tel. 0131 225 5722

e-mail fmarsh@cofscotland.org.uk

Correspondent Fred Marsh, Secretary

Trustees *G W Burnett; H Cole; A C E Hill; Very Revd Dr W B Johnston; R M Maiden; D F Ross; D F Stewart.*

Inland Revenue no. SC001853

Information available Full accounts were provided by the trust.

General The object of the trust is stated as making grants in approximately equal proportions to Church of Scotland schemes and recognised charities, particularly those largely administered by voluntary or honorary officials.

In awarding grants to the schemes of the Church of Scotland, the trustees usually make these to the central funds of the church, rather than to individual congregations.

In making grants to non-Church of Scotland charities, the trustees normally give priority to the following areas of charitable work:

- older people
- young people
- ex-service personnel
- seafarers.

In 2000 it had assets of £1.3 million and an income of £53,000. Grants totalled £52,000, with half of this given to Church of Scotland funds. The other half was given in 26 grants of £1,000 to a range of charities.

Exclusions No grants to individuals.

Applications In writing to the correspondent at the above address. There is a two-year time bar on repeat grants.

Exclusive Charity Haggerston Owners

Hospitals, special schools

£15,000 (1999/2000)

Beneficial area Scotland and north east England

Haggerston Castle Holiday Park, Haggerston, Berwick-upon-Tweed TD15 2PA

Tel. 01289 381419

Correspondent Sean Quilty

Trustees *James Kirkwood, Chair; John Brown; John Shaw; Pamela Brown.*

Charity Commission no. 1064455

Information available Full accounts were on file at the Charity Commission.

General This inventive trust is based at a holiday home in Berwick and raises funds by running raffles, bowls marathons, border marches and gala days for holidaymakers and holiday-homeowners. The trust uses the funds generated to purchase items for organisations benefiting disabled people, mostly in Northumberland, although it also supports organisations in the areas where guests have travelled from.

In 1999/2000 this produced an income of £19,000. Grants were given to hospitals and special schools totalling £15,000.

Beneficiaries included Scotland Yard Adventure Camp – Edinburgh for a ball cone (£2,900), Falrkirk and District Royal Infirmary for a portable suction machine (£540) and St John's Hospital – Livingstone for three PC review stations for the eye department.

Exclusions No cash grants are given, only items bought by the trust. No grants to individuals.

Applications In writing to the correspondent.

The Ferguson Bequest Fund

Churches

£163,000 (2000)

Beneficial area South west Scotland

182 Bath Street, Glasgow G2 4HG

Tel. 0141 332 0476

Correspondent Ronald D Oakes, Secretary

Trustees *D L M McNicol, Chair; R B Copleton; W S Carswell; S Bell; Revd R W M Johnston; I F Mackay; A D Maclaurin; J Boyle; T G Fielding; D Macrae; Revd D Kay.*

Inland Revenue no. SC009305

Information available Full accounts were provided by the trust.

General 'The principle objective of the fund, established by an Act of Parliament in 1869, is the provision of grants for the maintenance and

THE FERGUSON BEQUEST FUND – GRANTS APPROVED TO CHURCHES

	ministers' stipend	gifts to retired ministers and deaconesses	church repairs	other
Church of Scotland	–	£22,000	£117,000	£2,000
Free Church	–	£500	–	£1,300
Reformed Presbyterian	£9,000	–	£1,000	–
United Reformed Church	–	£1,300	–	1,300
United Free Church	–	£800	£5,000	£1,300

repair of church buildings although it may also grant aid other activities of the churches, especially in the field of education. Under the Act of Parliament, the fund can assist only certain Scottish churches. As a rule, the operations are limited to the south west of Scotland.'

In 2000 it had assets of £4 million and an income of £171,000. Grants to churches totalled £163,000. It also paid £3,200 in grants through Mortification (Irvine) Scheme 1931 and £7,000 through the scholarship fund.

Grants to churches were broken down as shown in the table.

Applications Written requests for application forms should be sent to the correspondent. Applications can be considered at any time.

Elizabeth Hardie Ferguson Charitable Trust Fund

Children, medical research, health, hospices

£46,000 (1998/99)

Beneficial area UK, with some interest in Scotland

c/o 11a Craig Street, Peterborough PE1 2EJ

Correspondent Ted Way, Secretary

Trustees *Sir Alex Ferguson; Cathy Ferguson; Huw Roberts; Ted Way; Les Dalgarno.*

Inland Revenue no. SC026240

Information available Information was provided by the trust.

General This trust was created by Sir Alex Ferguson in 1998 in memory of his mother. It supports a range of children's and medical charities. In 1998/99 the trust gave £46,000 to children's charities, medical research and hospices. Grants range from £250 to £10,000 and can be recurrent. Various high profile events, including concerts by Simply Red, premieres of Spiceworld the Movie in Glasgow and Manchester and a dinner hosted by Chinese chef Ken Hom have contributed to the trust's income. Grants are distributed in the areas where the income is raised. Charities supported by the founder in his home town of Govan will continue to be supported through the trust. Recent beneficiaries have included The Govan Initiative and The Harmony Row Boys' Club in Govan.

Exclusions Non-registered charities and individuals are not supported. The trust does not make grants overseas.

Applications An application form and guidelines should be requested in writing to the correspondent. The committee meets to consider grants at the end of January and July. Applications should be received by December and June respectively.

The J & C Fleming Trust

Religion, medical research, refugees, older people

£10,000 (1997)

Beneficial area Scotland

1 Doune Crescent, Newton Mearns, Glasgow G77 5NR

Correspondent The Trustees

Inland Revenue no. SC010026

Information available Limited information was available from the trust.

General The trust supports religious causes, medical research and the welfare of refugees and older people in Scotland.

In 1997 the trust had an income of £20,000 and gave grants totalling £10,000.

Applications In writing to the correspondent.

The trust declined to confirm the entry and stated that the address was incorrect. However, the address was correct according to the Scottish Charities Index.

The Row Fogo Charitable Trust

Medical research, older people

£96,000 (1999/2000)

Beneficial area Edinburgh, Lothians and Dunblane

Messrs Brodies WS, 15 Atholl Crescent, Edinburgh EH3 8HA

Tel. 0131 228 3777

Correspondent Andrew M C Dalgleish

Trustees *E J Cuthbertson; A W Waddell; Dr C Brough.*

Inland Revenue no. SC009685

Information available Annual report and accounts were provided by the trust.

General This trust makes grants for medical research projects, with particular emphasis on the neurosciences, smaller local charitable projects and care of the elderly.

In 1999/2000 the assets stood at £3.5 million generating an income of £182,000. Grants totalled £96,000. Those donations representing more than 2% of the revenue of the trust were listed in the accounts. They included Meningitis Association Scotland (£18,000), Cancer Relief Fund (£6,000), Abbeyfield Edinburgh Society and Scotland Newcastle Lymphona Group (£5,000 each), and Age Concern Scotland, Muscular Dystrophy Campaign and Salvation Army (£4,000 each).

In all, 38 grants were made, of which 33 were for £1,000 or over.

Exclusions No grants are made to individuals.

Applications In writing to the correspondent.

W G Forsyth Fund

Children and young people, disability

£12,000 (1998/99)

Beneficial area UK, with a preference for Scotland

Turcan Connell, Princes Exchange, 1 Earl Grey Street, Edinburgh EH3 9EE

Tel. 0131 228 8111 **Fax** 0131 228 8118

Correspondent Neil Stringer

Inland Revenue no. SC011564

Information available Information was provided by the trust.

General The trust supports children, young people and disability causes. Grants are not given for other causes. In 1998/99 it had assets of £300,000 and an income of £10,000. It gave grants totalling £12,000. Beneficiaries included East Park School and Scottish Society for Autistic Children. One-off or recurrent grants can be given.

Exclusions No grants to individuals.

Applications In writing to the correspondent.

The Emily Fraser Trust

See below

£47,000 to organisations (1999/2000)

Beneficial area Scotland

Turcan Connell, Princes Exchange, 1 Earl Grey Street, Edinburgh EH3 9EE

Tel. 0131 228 8111 **Fax** 0131 228 8118

e-mail lk@turcanconnell.com

Correspondent Lesley Kelly, Trust Administrator

Trustees *Dr Kenneth Chrystie, Chair; Hon. Ann Fraser; Patricia Fraser; Blair Smith.*

Inland Revenue no. SC007288

Information available The information for this entry was supplied by the trust.

General The trust makes grants mainly to people in Scotland and their dependants who were or are engaged in the drapery and allied trades and the printing, publishing, books and stationery, newspaper and allied trades. Preference is given to people who are or were employed by House of Fraser Limited, Scottish Universal Investments Limited and Paisleys.

Grants are also made to Scottish organisations caring for older and infirm people with connections in the fields described above. It prefers to support small, community organisations which find it difficult to raise funds. It also prefers to support organisations in areas where there is little local funding available. The trustees 'consider that grants to large highly publicised national appeals are not likely to be as effective a use of funds as grants to smaller and more focused charitable appeals'.

In 1999/2000 the trust had assets of £2.3 million and an income of £87,000. Grants were made totalling £81,000, of which £47,000 went to organisations. Those grants which exceeded 2% of gross income are listed in the accounts. The largest were £7,000 to Sue Ryder Foundation and £5,000 each to Communicability and Manic Depression Fellowship Scotland. Others included £3,000 to Brainwave, £2,500 to Age Concern Orkney and £2,000 each to Springburn Youth and Community Project (the final one of these

grants), and Govan Society of Weavers (the second one of three). There were 10 smaller grants of £400 to £1,000 and 26 individuals received support.

Applications In writing to the correspondent. The trustees meet quarterly to consider applications. In 2000 the meetings were held at in July/August and the end of January, April and October. The trustees of this trust are the same as the trustees of the Hugh Fraser Foundation and applications are allocated to one or other of the trusts as appears appropriate.

The Gordon Fraser Charitable Trust

Children, young people, environment, arts

£147,000 (2000/01)

Beneficial area UK, with some preference for Scotland

Holmhurst, Westerton Drive, Bridge of Allan, Stirling FK9 4QL

Correspondent Mrs M A Moss, Trustee

Trustees *Mrs M A Moss; W F T Anderson.*

Charity Commission no. 260869

Information available Full accounts were provided by the trust.

General The trustees are particularly interested in supporting children/young people in need, the environment and visual arts (including performance arts). Most grants are given within these categories. The trust states that 'applications from or for Scotland will receive favourable consideration, but not to the exclusion of applications from elsewhere'.

In 2000/01 the trust had assets of £3 million and an income of £119,000. A total of £147,000 was given in almost 200 grants, ranging from £150 to £18,000. The grants list includes several health charities; these may receive grants especially for work with children/young people.

Most grants given were between £300 and £500, with only 29 for £1,000 or more. The largest grant was given to Scottish International Piano

Competition (£18,000), with other larger grants to Ballet West (£12,000), MacRobert Arts Centre (£5,500), Scottish Museums Council (£5,000), Artlink Central (£4,000) and Brendan Family House and Royal Scottish National Orchestra (£3,000 each).

Other recipients of £1,000 or more included Borderline, Church of Scotland, Crossroads (Scotland) Care Attendant Schemes, Eastgate Theatre and Arts Centre, Glasgow University Union, John Muir Trust and Scottish Society for Autism.

Smaller grants were given to a wide range of charities, both national and local, throughout Scotland.

Exclusions No grants are made to organisations which are not recognised charities, or to individuals.

Applications In writing to the correspondent. Applications are considered in January, April, July and October. Grants towards national or international emergencies can be considered at any time. All applicants are acknowledged, an sae would therefore be appreciated.

The Hugh Fraser Foundation

General

£1.6 million (1998/99)

Beneficial area UK, especially western or deprived areas of Scotland

Turcan Connell, Princes Exchange,
1 Earl Grey Street, Edinburgh EH3 9EE

Tel. 0131 228 8111 **Fax** 0131 228 8118

Correspondent Heather Thompson

Trustees *Dr Kenneth Chrystie, Chair; Hon. Mrs Ann Fraser; Miss Patricia Fraser; Blair Smith.*

Inland Revenue no. SC009303

Information available Annual report and accounts are available for £10.

General The foundation was established by Lord Fraser of Allander and endowed by him with shares in House of Fraser and Scottish and

Universal Investments (SUITS); the two companies are based in the west of Scotland and were directed Lord Fraser.

The trust says: 'The trustees' policy is to pay special regard to applications from the West of Scotland and applications from those parts of Scotland where the local economy makes it more difficult to raise funds for charitable purposes. Applications from other parts of Britain and Northern Ireland are considered.

'The trustees consider that grants to large highly publicised national appeals are not likely to be as effective a use of funds as grants to smaller and more focused charitable appeals.

'The trustees also consider that better use of funds can be made by making grants to charitable bodies to assist them with their work, than by making a large number of grants to individuals.

'The trustees are prepared to enter into commitments over a period of time by making grants in successive years, often to assist in new initiatives which can maintain their own momentum once they have been established for a few years.

'The foundation makes donations to charities working in many different sectors, principally hospitals, schools and universities, arts organisations and organisations working with the handicapped, the underprivileged and the aged. The trustees are nevertheless prepared to consider applications from charities working in other fields.'

In 1998/99 it had assets of £30 million generating an high income of £2.5 million. Management and administration costs were low at less than two per cent of the income. Grants were given to 284 organisations totalling £1.6 million.

Only the nine organisations which received grants of two per cent or more of the gross income were listed, the minimum required by Scottish law. These represented 33% of the grants total and were to: The Lighthouse Project Glasgow 1999 (£235,000); Scottish Science Trust (£100,000); Columba 1400 (£40,000); Quarriers and Walter and Joan Gray Home (£30,000 each); and Scottish Motor Neurone Association, The Murray Foundation, The Princess Royal Trust for Carers and Prince & Princess of Wales Hospice (£25,000 each). The remaining 275 grants, all for less than £25,000, averaged £4,000.

Exclusions Grants are not awarded to individuals. Major highly publicised appeals are rarely supported.

Applications In writing to the correspondent. The trustees meet on a quarterly basis to consider applications.

Gaelic Language Promotion Trust

Gaelic language education projects

About £10,000

Beneficial area UK

Birchbrook, Dounerd, Dunblane, Perthshire FK15 9ND

e-mail ian@transcom.ltd.uk

Correspondent Ian Smith

Inland Revenue no. SC004414

Information available Limited information was available on this trust.

General This trust encourages and promotes teaching, learning and use of the Gaelic language, and the study and cultivation of Gaelic literature. Unfortunately no further information on grants or beneficiaries was available.

In February 2002 the trust stated that at their AGM in April they would be appointing a new trust secretary who would then be the correspondent. Contact the correspondent listed in this entry for up-to-date information.

Applications In writing to the correspondent in January, April, August or December.

Agnes Gallagley Bequest

Roman Catholic charities, education, social welfare

Nil (2000/01)

Beneficial area Not known, possible preference for Scotland

Grant Thornton Accountants, 196 Clyde Street, Glasgow G1 4JY

Tel. 0141 223 0000

Correspondent Mrs Patricia Munroe

Inland Revenue no. SC016337

Information available Accounts were available at a cost of £20.

General The trust's main concern appears to be to support Roman Catholic causes and it also supports education and social welfare. In 1998 the trust had an income of £20,000 and no grants were made. In the previous year the trust also had an income of £20,000 and distributed £30,000 in grants. The trust stated that grants are given to organisations it makes contact with itself.

Applications Unsolicited applications are not invited.

The Gamma Trust

General

About £50,000

Beneficial area UK, with a possible preference for Scotland

Clydesdale Bank, Trust & Executry Unit, Brunswick House, 51 Wilson Street, Glasgow G1 1UZ

Tel. 0141 223 2507

Correspondent The Manager

Inland Revenue no. SC004330

Information available Information was provided by the trust.

General This trust has general charitable purposes. It appears that new grants are only given to UK-wide organisations although most grants are ongoing commitments to local organisations in Scotland. It has a grant total of about £50,000 a year. Further information was not available.

Exclusions No grants to individuals.

Applications In writing to the correspondent for consideration quarterly.

The Gannochy Trust

General

£4.3 million (1999/2000)

Beneficial area Scotland, with a preference for Perth and its environs

Kincarrathie House Drive, Pitcullen Crescent, Perth PH2 7HX

Tel. 01738 620653

Correspondent Mrs Jean Gandhi, Secretary

Trustees *Dr Russell Leather, Chair; Mark Webster; James A McCowan; Dr James H F Kynaston; Dr James I Watson.*

Inland Revenue no. SC003133

Information available Annual report and accounts, with a full list of beneficiaries.

General The Gannochy Trust was founded by Arthur Kinmond Bell, a whisky distiller from Perth who built the Gannochy Housing Estate consisting of 150 houses. The trustees maintain this estate and in recent years have enlarged it by providing 69 sheltered houses for older people.

The main objects are the needs of youth and recreation, but the trustees are not restricted to these objects. There is an obligation to show preference for Perth and its environs.

In 2000/01 the trust had assets totalling £127 million and its income totalled £4.7 million. Grants paid and payable totalled £4.2 million. A total of 255 grants were made, of which 138 were of £5,000 or under.

Grants were broken down as follows (previous year figures in brackets):

Arts	15%	(8%)
Education	6%	(9%)
Environment	6%	(6%)
Health	22%	(31%)
Recreation	33%	(18%)
Social welfare	19%	(28%)

The trust continues to make the comment that the interests of youth were amply served within the headings.

The annual report for the year listed the 12 largest donations. Grants of above £100,000 were:

- Perth & Kinross Recreational Facilities Limited received £567,000 for the installation of a new floor and spectators' seating system.

- £250,000 was donated to the University of Stirling towards the establishment of the new National Swimming Academy.

- £190,000 was donated to Kincarrathie Trust for refurbishment and maintenance of a home for older people.

- £150,000 was donated to the Maggie Keswick Jencks Cancer Centre in Dundee, towards the provision of support and comfort for cancer patients and families in the Tayside area.

- £150,000 to Perth & Kinross Recreational Facilities Limited, of which £90,000 was directed to renovation and repair of community facilities in the Perth area, and £60,000 was directed to sports coaching for youth.

- £105,000 to Perth Theatre towards refurbishment and upgrading of the foyer and restaurant areas.

Other grants were made to a range of organisations, and included: £70,000 to Perth Festival of the Arts towards the 2001 Festival; £50,000 to Historic Scotland towards Stanley Mills; £20,000 to Guildtown Hall & Playing Field Association towards an all weather sports surface; £10,000 to General Anderson Trust to upgrade the kitchen and laundry; £7,500 to Hebridean Trust towards lighthouse keepers cottages; £5,000 to L'Arche Edinburgh towards The Skein for people with learning difficulties; and £1,800 to Perth & Kinross Association of Voluntary Service Ltd towards a Christmas Goodwill Gift Scheme.

Exclusions No grants to individuals. Donations are confined to organisations recognised by the Inland Revenue as charitable.

Applications In writing to the correspondent, confined to two pages of A4 including:

- a general statement on the objects of the applicant's charity
- the specific nature of the application
- the estimated cost and how this is arrived at
- the contribution of the applicant's charity towards the cost
- the contributions of others, actual and promised
- estimated shortfall
- details of previous appeals to the trust – whether accepted or rejected
- a copy of the latest audited accounts.

'It is the practice of the trustees to scrutinise accounts before making donations.'

Time rarely permits visits either to the trust office or to the charity concerned.

The trustees meet frequently, generally monthly, to consider appeals.

The G C Gibson Charitable Trust

Churches, health, welfare, general

£620,000 (2000/01)

Beneficial area UK, with interests in East Anglia, Wales and Scotland

Deloitte & Touche, Blenheim House, Fitzalan Court, Newport Road, Cardiff CF24 0TS

Tel. 029 2048 1111

Correspondent Karen Griffin

Trustees *R D Taylor; Mrs J M Gibson; George S C Gibson.*

Charity Commission no. 258710

Information available Inadequate report and accounts, lacking the required analysis and review of grantmaking.

General Beneficiaries of this trust work within a range of charitable fields, but as the trust does not categorise them it is difficult to discern trustees' preferences. Some of the better funded charitable fields are perhaps churches, medical research, hospices/nursing homes, military welfare and youth/education.

The trust's work has previously been reported as follows: 'Although grants are made for one year at a time, once a charity has been awarded a grant the trustees are likely to continue to make grants to that charity provided they are happy with the way the money is being spent. They are very happy that such grants should go towards core running costs. Some organisations have received regular grants from the trust for as long as 20 years. Occasionally grants are made on an explicitly one-off basis, usually for a capital project.

'Grants for statutory bodies such as museums and hospitals will be considered, but these will usually be for a capital project, for example a hospital scanner appeal, or research costs. Co-funding arrangements will also be considered. The trustees have awarded several grants in conjunction with Lottery funding.

'Particularly in the case of lesser-known charities, the trustees tend to look favourably on applications from charities that are recommended by someone they know.'

In 2000/01 the trust had assets of £14.5 million and an income of £565,000. Grants totalling £620,000 were made to 162 organisations. Beneficiaries were frequently well-established UK charities – about 10% had 'royal' or 'national' in their titles. The great majority of grants were in the range of £1,000 to £5,000.

Beneficiaries in Scotland included Cancer Relief – Aberfeldy, Strathtay and District Local Committee (£5,000 each) and Cancer Research Scotland (£5,000). It is possible that Scottish branches of UK charities were supported during the year.

Exclusions Only recognised charities are supported.

Applications In writing to the correspondent in October/November each year. Trustees meet in December/January. Successful applicants will receive their cheques during January.

Organisations that have already received a grant should reapply describing how the previous year's grant was spent and setting out how a further grant would be used. In general, less detailed information is required from national charities with a known track record than from small local charities that are not known to the trustees.

'Due to the volume of applications, it is not possible to acknowledge each application, nor is it possible to inform unsuccessful applicants.'

The Helen and Horace Gillman Trusts

Protection of birds and birds' habitat

£27,000 (1999/2000)

Beneficial area Great Britain and Northern Ireland, with a special interest in Scotland

Drummond Miller, 32 Moray Place, Edinburgh EH3 6BZ

Tel. 0131 226 5151 **Fax** 0131 225 2608

Correspondent Miss Carole Hope

Trustees *J K Burleigh; F Hamilton; I Darling.*

Information available Information was provided by the trust.

General The trusts, which were set up in 1982, are valued at about £620,000. In 1999/2000 their joint income was about £30,000 and they collectively gave grants totalling £27,000.

The trusts support the protection of birds and their habitat. Grants range between £500 and £10,000. In 1999/2000 they included several to support various projects run by RSPB. Other beneficiaries included British Trust for Ornothology, FWAG Wild Birds Project and National Trust for Scotland.

Applications In writing to the correspondent. Trustees meet two or three times a year, usually including January/February time, and September/October time. Applications should be received in the preceding month.

The Gough Charitable Trust

Youth, Episcopal and Church of England, preservation of the countryside, social welfare

£169,000 available (2000/01)

Beneficial area UK, with a possible preference for Scotland

Lloyds TSB Private Banking Ltd, UK Trust Centre, 22–26 Ock Street, Abingdon OX14 5SW

Correspondent Mrs E Osborn-King, Trust Manager

Trustees *Lloyds Bank plc; N de L Harvie.*

Inland Revenue no. 262355

Information available Full accounts were on file at the Charity Commission.

General In 2000/01 the trust had an income of £48,000 and an expenditure of £45,000. The trust says the grant total varies. According to the accounts, the balance available for distribution in 2000 was just under £169,000. Charitable payments of £40,000 were made, leaving over £128,000 carried forward to the following year. The trust has previously shown a preference for Scotland, however it is not clear if this is still the case.

Beneficiaries included St Luke with Holy Trinity Charlton (£15,000), RNLI (£10,000), Wykeham Crown and Manor Trust and 999 Club (£5,000 each). Small grants of £100 to £200 were given to National Army Development Trust, Lifeboat Service, Trinity Hospice, Household Brigade Lodge Benevolent Fund, The Prince of Wales Lodge Benevolent Fund, Irish Guards Fund, Lloyds Benevolent Fund and Lloyds Charities Fund.

Exclusions No support for non-registered charities and individuals including students.

Applications In writing to the correspondent at any time. No application forms are available, no acknowledgements are sent. Applications are considered quarterly.

The trust would not confirm this entry, but the address was correct, and the rest of the entry was updated using information available at the Charity Commission.

William Grant & Sons Ltd Charitable Trust

General

About £40,000 to £50,000 a year

Beneficial area UK, but mainly Scotland

William Grant & Sons Ltd, Phoenix Centre, Strathclyde Business Park, Bells Hill ML4 3AN

Tel. 01698 843843

Correspondent Ewan Henderson

Inland Revenue no. SC000974

Information available Information was provided by the trust.

General The trust gives to a wide range of charities and has a preference for Scotland. It supports organisations mainly, but also individuals. The grant total varies but is usually between £40,000 and £50,000 each year. Grants range from £100 to £4,000.

Applications In writing to the correspondent. The trustees meet once a year in the summer to consider grants. It is advisable to apply before June each year.

Dr Guthrie's Association

Children and young people

£50,000 a year

Beneficial area Scotland

c/o Scott-Moncrieff, 17 Melville Street, Edinburgh EH3 7PH

Tel. 0131 473 3500 **Fax** 0131 473 3535

e-mail smedin@scott-moncrieff.co.uk

Correspondent R Graeme Thom

Inland Revenue no. SC009302

Information available Information was provided by the trust.

General The trust supports children and young people under 21 years of age in Scotland. It prefers to support established groups working with young people. It has assets of £1.5 million and an income of £60,000. It gave grants totalling £50,000. Grants are generally one-off and usually range from £500 to £4,000. It has supported residential weekends for young people and help with running costs of providing outreach services to young people who are disadvantaged or abused.

Applications In writing to the correspondent. Trustees meet to consider grants in February, June and October.

The Susan H Guy Charitable Trust

General, environment, animal welfare

£19,000 (2000)

Beneficial area UK, with a strong preference for Scotland

24 Blythswood Square, Glasgow G2 4QS

Tel. 0141 226 5511

Correspondent KPMG, Factors to the Trustees

Trustees *R W Speirs; G D Caldwell.*

Inland Revenue no. SC000393

Information available Information was provided by the trust.

General The trust has general charitable purposes with some preference for environment, animal welfare and health charities. In 2000 it gave about £19,000 in grants.

Beneficiaries have included Marie Curie Cancer Care, RNLI, RSPB and Salvation Army. It prefers to give to Scottish branches of UK charities. Grants range from £1,000 to £4,000.

Exclusions No grants to individuals.

Applications In writing to the correspondent. Trustees normally meet to consider grants in April and November.

The Harbour Trust

Evangelical Christian work

£6,200 (1998/99)

Beneficial area Unrestricted but with some preference for Scotland

62a Brook Road, Thomashunt Knights, Essex CO5 0RH

Tel. 01621 818416

Correspondent Dr Alan McCormick, Trustee

Trustees *Mrs H McCormick; Dr A H I McCormick; Mrs R McCormick.*

Inland Revenue no. SC002764

Information available Information was supplied by the trust.

General The trust mainly supports evangelical Christian work. It only gives grants to individuals and organisations which are personally known or recommended to the trustees.

In 1998/99 it had an income of £6,500 and gave 28 grants totalling £6,200, including 19 grants that were recurrent from the previous year. Grants ranged from £10 to £1,700. The large grants were given to Fullbridge Evangelical Church, Essex (£1,700) and Abbot Hall, Dunfermline (£740). Other grants were up to £500 and included Operation Mobilisation and Youth with a Mission – Mercy Ships in Guinea (both £500), Scottish Christian Counselling Service (£200), Scottish Crusaders (£50) and National Bible Society for Scotland (£25). Seven individuals were supported and received grants totalling £460.

Applications Applications are not invited and unsolicited appeals do not receive a response.

Mrs D L Harryhausen's 1969 Trust

Animal welfare, the David Livingstone Centre

£27,000 (1998/99)

Beneficial area UK, with an interest in Scotland

Turcan Connell, Princes Exchange, 1 Earl Grey Street, Edinburgh EH3 9EE

Tel. 0131 228 8111

Correspondent S A Mackintosh, Trustee

Trustees *Mrs Vanessa Harryhausen; Simon Mackintosh; George Menzies.*

Inland Revenue no. SC015688

Information available Accounts were available from the trust.

General The trust supports animal welfare and the activities of the David Livingstone Centre. In 1998/99 the trust had assets of £322,000 and an income of £12,000. It gave 11 grants totalling £27,000, ranging from £1,000 to £8,000. The largest grants were £8,000 to David Livingstone Centre, £7,000 to Theatrium Botanica, £3,000 to Flora Brendon Charitable Trust and £2,000 to Jill Hetherington Charity (Tzaba). Grants of £1,000 each included those to Battersea Dogs Home, Rosedell Animal Sanctuary and Worldwide Fund for Nature.

Exclusions Grants are not normally given to individuals.

Applications In writing to the correspondent, however please note the trust states that applications are not invited as the income is fully committed.

The Douglas Hay Trust

Physically disabled children under 18

About £4,000 to organisations
(1999/2000)

Beneficial area Scotland

Whitelaw Wells, 9 Ainslie Place,
Edinburgh EH3 6AT

Tel. 0131 226 5822 **Fax** 0131 220 3949

Website Whitelawwells.co.uk

Correspondent The Secretary

Inland Revenue no. SC014450

Information available Information was supplied by the trust.

General Grants are usually only for individuals and are awarded through local authority social work departments. However, when it has a surplus, grants are also given to organisations concerned with disability. In 1999/2000 it had an income of £35,000, most of which was given in grants. A few grants were given to organisations totalling about £4,000. Beneficiaries included Capability Scotland which received £2,000.

Applications Applications are invited through Social Work Department Medical Advisors.

The Christina Mary Hendrie Trust for Scottish & Canadian Charities

Youth, older people, general

£81,000 (1999)

Beneficial area Scotland and Canada

48 Castle Street, Edinburgh EH2 3LX

Tel. 0131 220 2345

Correspondent George R Russell

Trustees G A S Cox; Mrs A D H Irwin; C R B Cox; J K Scott Moncrieff; Miss C Irwin; Maj. Gen. A S H Irwin; R N Cox; A G Cox.

Inland Revenue no. SC014514

Information available Information was supplied by the trust.

General The trust was established in 1975 following the death in Scotland of Christina Mary Hendrie. The funds constituting the trust originated in Canada. Grants are distributed to charities throughout Scotland and Canada, although the majority is now given in Scotland. There is a preference for charities connected with young or older people, although other groups to receive grants include cancer charities.

Grants in 1999 totalled £81,000. Grants normally range from £1,000 to £5,000. Unfortunately there was no information available on the beneficiaries supported.

Exclusions Grants are not given to individuals.

Applications In writing to the correspondent. The trustees meet twice a year to consider grants, usually in March and November.

The Anne Herd Memorial Trust

Visual impairment

£78,000 (2000/01)

Beneficial area Scotland, with a preference for Tayside, the City of Dundee and Broughty Ferry

Bowman Scottish Lawyers, 27 Bank Street, Dundee DD1 1RP

Tel. 01382 322267

Correspondent The Trustees

Trustees B N Bowman; Mrs P M M Bowman; Mrs E N McGillivray; R W H Hudson; Mrs Elizabeth M Breckon; Robert J Wild.

Inland Revenue no. SC014198

Information available Information was provided by the trust.

General The trust supports both individuals who are visually impaired and organisations working with them in the beneficial area. Most grants to individuals are given through an organisation.

In 2000/01 it had an income of £30,000. The grant total was £78,000, although this was exceptionally high due to the distribution of £56,000 from accumulated funds. The largest grant was £20,000 to Dundee Society for the Visually Impaired for its new Herd building, the first instalment of a total of £100,000 committed over five years. Other beneficiaries included Sense Scotland (£10,000) and RNIB Talking Book Service (£9,000).

Applications In writing to the correspondent. Trustees meet once a year to consider grants, usually in June. Applications should be received by March/April.

The Highgate Charitable Trust

General

£15,000 (2000/01)

Beneficial area Primarily Scotland

Miller, Beckett & Jacksons, Solicitors, 190 St Vincent Street, Glasgow G2 5SP

Tel. 0141 204 2833 **Fax** 0141 248 7185

e-mail mail@millerbj.co.uk

Correspondent George A Maguire, Trustee

Trustees *G A Maguire; N A Fyfe; Mrs E A Thomson; D H Aitken.*

Inland Revenue no. SC008130

Information available Information was provided by the trust.

General The trust will consider supporting:

- education/training
- medical and health, including hospitals/hospices and medical research
- religion
- social welfare.

In 2000/01 the trust had assets of £370,000, an income of £14,000 and gave grants totalling £15,000.

A total of 17 grants were made with four of over £500 each. These went to High School of Glasgow Educational Trust and Highgate Hall (£3,500 each) and Park Church and Uddingston Congregational Church (£2,000 each). Recipients of smaller grants included Dystonia Society, Enable, New Scottish Choir and Orchestra and Salvation Army.

Applications In writing to the correspondent. Trustees meet once a year in November to consider grants. Applications should be received by September.

The L E Hill Memorial Trust

General

£25,000 (1997)

Beneficial area UK, with a preference for Scotland

Turcan Connell, Princes Exchange, 1 Earl Grey Street, Edinburgh EH3 9EE

Tel. 0131 228 8111 **Fax** 0131 228 8118

Correspondent The Secretary

Trustees *Turcan Connell Trustees Ltd; J Ivory; M H H Hill.*

Inland Revenue no. SC003454

Information available This trust is one of 10 trusts, probably all small, administered by Turcan Connell. The company would not provide us with any information on these trusts, only agreeing to send each trust's accounts for the cost of £20 each. We did not think this was reasonable for such small trusts.

General In 1997, the trust had an income of £24,000 and gave grants totalling £25,000. Grants range between £200 and £4,000. Past beneficiaries have included Doon School English Charitable Trust Foundation, Magdalene College, St John's Episcopal Church in Fofar, British Red Cross, Salvation Army in Tayside, Gordonstoun Schools

Ltd, Reswalke Hall Trust and Dundee Heritage Trust.

Exclusions The trust does not support non-registered charities.

Applications In writing to the correspondent.

The Hope Trust

Temperance, reformed protestant churches

£119,000 (2000)

Beneficial area Worldwide, with a preference for Scotland

Drummond Miller, 32 Moray Place, Edinburgh EH3 6BZ

Tel. 0131 226 5151

Correspondent Carole Hope, Secretary

Trustees *Revd Prof. D W D Shaw; Prof. G M Newlands; Prof. D A S Ferguson; Revd G R Barr; Revd Dr Lylal; Carole Hope.*

Inland Revenue no. SC000987

Information available Information was provided by the trust.

General This trust was established to promote the ideals of temperance in the areas of drink and drugs, and protestant church reform through education and the distribution of literature. In 2000 its income was £174,000. Grants towards temperance causes totalled £15,000, and other grants to causes related to the protestant reformed tradition in Scotland and worldwide totalled £104,000. PhD students of theology studying at Scottish universities were also supported.

Larger grants included those to Church of Scotland Priority Areas Fund (£11,000), World Alliance of Reformed Churches (£10,000), National Bible Society for Scotland (£4,000) and Feed the Minds and Waldensian Mission Aid (£3,000 each).

Exclusions No grants to gap year students, scholarship schemes or to any individuals, with the sole exception of PhD students of theology studying at Scottish universities. No grants for the refurbishment of property.

Applications In writing to the correspondent. The trustees meet to consider applications in June and December each year. Applications should be submitted by mid-May or mid-November each year.

The James Thom Howat Charitable Trust

General

£197,000 to organisations (1998/99)

Beneficial area Scotland, in particular Glasgow

Biggart Baillie, Dalmore House, 310 St Vincent Street, Glasgow G2 5QR

Correspondent Mrs Jean Lane

Trustees *Leslie Duncan; James Thom Howat; Russell Howat; Gordon Wyllie; Christine Howat.*

Inland Revenue no. SC000201

Information available Accounts were provided by the trust.

General In 1998/99 the trust stated that it had 'continued to address real needs in the community and it was their policy to maintain this in the future'. Primarily it supports projects which are for the benefit of 'Glasgow and her citizens' but Scottish and UK-wide projects will be considered for small grants if they can be applied locally.

In 1998/99 the trust had assets of £5 million and an income of £241,000. In total £216,000 was given in grants, of which £197,000 was given in general grants and £19,000 in educational grants.

The accounts list those grants which were in excess of 2% of the gross income. The largest grants were of £10,000 and were given to Crossroads (Scotland) Care Attendant Scheme and Eastpark Home for Infirm Children. Three other grants were listed, they were: University of Glasgow and University of Strathclyde (£8,000 each) and Royal Blind Asylum & School (£5,000). All these organisations received the same size grant the previous year.

Educational grants were given to 56 individuals; grants ranged between £100 and £1,000.

Exclusions The following are not usually supported: medical electives, second or further qualifications, payment of school fees or costs incurred at tertiary educational establishments.

Applications In writing to the correspondent. There is no application form for organisations. Applications should contain a summary not longer than one side of A4, backed up as necessary with schedules. A copy of the latest accounts and/or business plan should be included. Costs and financial needs should be broken down where possible. It should be clear what effect the grant will have and details of other grants applied for or awarded should be given. Evidence that the project will enhance the quality of life of the clients and that they are involved in the decision making must be included.

'Applications should include evidence of charitable status, current funding, and the use you are making of that. Projects should be demonstrated to be practical and business-like. It is a condition of any grant given that a report be made as to how the funds have been used. Grants not used for the purposes stated must be returned.'

Successful applicants should not reapply in the following year. Unsuccessful applicants are not acknowledged due to the large number of applications received by the trust. The trustees meet to consider grants in March, June, September and December. Applications should be received in the preceding month.

This entry was not confirmed by the trust.

Howman Charitable Trust

Conservation, medical, education
Not known

Beneficial area Scotland and overseas

William Thomson & Sons, 22 Meadowside, Dundee DD1 1LN

Tel. 01382 201534 **Fax** 01382 227654

Correspondent The Secretary

Trustees *Mrs M J B Howman; K C R Howman; A McDougall.*

Inland Revenue no. SC001387

Information available Unfortunately we have been unable obtain up-to-date information on this trust.

General Mrs M J B Howman set up this trust in 1977 and is still one of the trustees.

The trust mainly makes grants to organisations working in nature conservation. In 1993/94 grant recipients included World Pheasant Association, Salmon and Trout Association Charitable Trust and St Mary's Church of Scotland, Kirriemuir.

Exclusions No grants are made to individuals.

Applications The trust states that no applications will be considered or acknowledged. The trust did not want to appear in this guide but confirmed the address.

Miss Agnes H Hunter's Trust

Social welfare
£254,000 (1999/2000)

Beneficial area UK, with a preference for Scotland

Robson McLean WS, 28 Abercromby Place, Edinburgh EH3 6QF

Correspondent Mrs Jane Paterson, Grants Administrator

Inland Revenue no. SC004843

Information available Information, but with no grants list, was supplied by the trust. An explanatory leaflet was also available from the correspondent.

General The trust was established in 1954. Its main aims are to support:

* charities for people who are blind in Scotland

* people who are disabled

* training and education for people who are disadvantaged

- research on the cause, relief or cure of cancer, tuberculosis or rheumatism.

These aims are currently being pursued in the following areas: children and family support, youth development, older people, homelessness, physical and mental illness and the environment.

The trustees are highly selective and priority is given to Scottish projects. The trustees review their policies periodically and areas of interest may change.

Grants range from £500 to £8,000, although they are usually not higher than £5,000. In 1999/2000 the trust gave 67 grants totalling £254,000. Further information was not available for this year.

Its capital assets in property and investments were valued at £3.4 million in 1997/98. In that year 55 grants totalling £224,000 were approved. A grants list was not provided.

Exclusions No grants to individuals, or to organisations under the control of the UK government.

Applications Applicants should write, in the first instance, to request the trust's guidance notes. The closing dates for final applications are 15 January and 1 September every year.

The Mrs E Y Imries Trust

Older people who are blind or visually impaired

Nil (2000/01)

Beneficial area Scotland

Archibald Campbell & Harley, 37 Queen Street, Edinburgh EH2 1JX

Tel. 0131 220 3000 **Fax** 0131 220 2288

Correspondent Fiona Hutchinson

Trustees *D W Cockburn; K W Dunbar.*

Information available Limited information was provided by the trust.

General The trust makes grants towards older people who are blind or visually impaired.

In 2000/01 the trust's assets totalled £71,000. No grants were made during the year. Typical grants range from £1,000 to £2,000. The trust told us that in 1998/99 grants totalled £6,000. Previous beneficiaries have included Fife Society for the Blind, Royal Blind Asylum and School in Edinburgh and Visual Impairment Services in south east Scotland.

Applications In writing to the correspondent.

The Inchrye Trust

Health, elderly people, medical research

£33,000 (1996/97)

Beneficial area Mainly Scotland

Turcan Connell, Princes Exchange, 1 Earl Grey Street, Edinburgh EH3 9EE

Tel. 0131 228 8111 **Fax** 0131 228 8118

Correspondent The Trustees

Trustees *Miss R Finlay; Mrs J David.*

Inland Revenue no. SC013382

Information available This trust is one of 10, probably all small, trusts administered by Turcan Connell. The company would not provide us with any information on these trusts, only agreeing to send each trust's accounts for the cost of £20 each. We did not think this was reasonable for such small trusts.

General The organisation's charitable objects are wide but it is particularly concerned with relieving ill health and the care of older people, as well as training and research.

In 1996/97 the trust gave £33,000 in grants. Grants were in the range of £100 to £5,000. Beneficiaries included Child Psychotherapy Trust – Scotland (£5,000), Leith School of Art for courses for disadvantaged children (£3,600), 'Milan' Senior Welfare Council (£3,500), Prison Phoenix Trust for yoga and meditation in Scottish prisons (£3,000) and Pain Association Scotland for teaching pain control without drugs (£2,500).

Applications In writing to the correspondent.

Miss P M Ireland's Charitable Trust

General

£9,100 (2001)

Beneficial area Scotland, especially local to Dundee

c/o Messrs Lawson, Coull & Duncan, Solicitors, 136 Nethergate, Dundee DD1 4PA

Tel. 01382 227555 **Fax** 01382 200978

Correspondent Mrs McDonald

Trustees *D G Lawson; H D McKay.*

Inland Revenue no. SC003560

Information available Information was provided by the trust.

General The trust supports general charitable purposes in Scotland, particularly in the Dundee area. In 2001 grants totalled £9,100. Grants were all of £275 and 33 charities were supported. All the grants were recurrent.

Beneficiaries have included Church of Scotland, National Trust for Scotland, Dovedale Enterprises, Dundee Disabled Children's Association, Oxfam and Pestalozzi Children's Village Trust. New charities are not often supported. When new grants are awarded they are added to the list of annual grants, the trust therefore must ensure it will be able to continue to support them.

Exclusions Grants are not made to individuals.

Applications Applications are not encouraged.

The Annie Jack Memorial Trust

Disability, disadvantaged people, heritage

£13,000 (2000/01)

Beneficial area Scotland

Bourne Hill Cottage, Hadlow, Kent TN11 0EX

Tel. 01732 850 357

Correspondent D F Stirling, Trustee

Trustees *D F Stirling; P J Stirling; G D Stirling.*

Charity Commission no. 1026512

Information available Full accounts were on file at the Charity Commission.

General The trust's objects are 'to promote the preservation, restoration and the public display of items which demonstrate the social, industrial and cultural heritage of Scotland and in addition assists other charities, principally in Scotland who care for those who may be physically, mentally or otherwise disadvantaged'.

In 2000/2001 the trust had assets of £28,000 and a net income of just over £13,000, all of which was given in grants. The largest grant of £5,500 went to Sense Scotland to provide holidays for deafblind children and young adults. Strathcarron and St Wilfred's Hospices shared £3,500, Scottish Veterans' Residences received £2,500 while the Royal British Legion Scotland, Hopscotch and The Variety Club received £500 each. The grants were similar to those made in previous years. The trust owns the Beardmore Taxicab built by William Beardmore in Glasgow in 1932, which remains on loan to the Glasgow Transport Museum.

Applications Applications are not considered.

Lady Eda Jardine Charitable Trust

General

£50,000 to £60,000 a year

Beneficial area Scotland

Anderson Strathern, 48 Castle Street, Edinburgh EH2 3LX

Tel. 0131 220 2345

Correspondent Mrs L E Pennell, Trustees

Inland Revenue no. SC011599

Information available Limited information was available on this trust.

General This trust has general charitable purposes in Scotland, with no preferences or exclusions. A total of between £50,000 and

£60,000 is distributed each year. There are no minimum or maximum grants.

Applications In writing to the correspondent by the end of April for consideration in July.

The Jeffrey Charitable Trust

Medical research, disability, children

£53,000 (2000)

Beneficial area Scotland and elsewhere

29 Comrie Street, Crieff, Perthshire PH7 4BD

Tel. 01764 652224 **Fax** 01764 653999

Correspondent R B A Bolton, Trustee

Trustees *R B A Bolton; R S Waddell; Mrs M E Bolton.*

Inland Revenue no. SC015990

Information available Information was provided by the trust.

General In 2000 the trust generated an income of £67,500. Grants to organisations and individuals totalled £53,000, with most of the 31 grants made going to organisations. Grants ranged between £250 and £20,000.

Exclusions Animal-related charities, medical electives and projects eligible for statutory support are not considered.

Applications In writing to the correspondent, although due to continuing support to long-term projects and anticipated repeat grants to other organisations, new requests for assistance are unlikely to be successful in the short to medium term.

The Kinpurnie Charitable Trust

General

£44,000 (1996/97)

Beneficial area Scotland

Kinpurnie Estate, North Street, Newtyle PH12 8TT

Correspondent Sir James Cayzer

Inland Revenue no. SC003986

Information available Although this information was confirmed by the trust, unfortunately it was not updated from 1996/97.

General In 1996/97 the trust had an income of £42,000 and gave grants totalling £43,000. Beneficiaries included Royal Marsden Hospital Cancer Fund (£5,000), Pushkin Prizes (£4,000), National Galleries of Scotland (£3,000), National Symphony Orchestra of Scotland (£1,500) and SSAFA Dundee branch (£1,000).

Exclusions Only registered charities are supported.

Applications In writing to the correspondent.

The Kintore Charitable Trust

Environment, young people, general

£32,000 (1998/99)

Beneficial area Scotland with a preference for Grampian

Turcan Connell, Princes Exchange, 1 Earl Grey Street, Edinburgh EH3 9EE

Tel. 0131 228 8111 **Fax** 0131 228 8118

Correspondent The Trustees

Trustees *The Countess of Kintore; Turcan Connell.*

Inland Revenue no. SC000702

Information available This trust is one of 10 trusts, probably all small, administered by Turcan Connell. The company would not provide us with any information on these trusts, only agreeing to send each trust's accounts for the cost of £20 each. We did not think this was reasonable for such small trusts.

General The trust supports environmental causes, young people and local projects in the Grampian area. In 1998/99 the trust gave grants totalling £32,000. Past beneficiaries have included Council for Music in Hospitals, Crail Museum, Duke of Edinburgh's Award, Edinburgh Book Festival, Mackie Academy for the Earl of Kintore and Museum of Scotland Project.

Applications In writing to the correspondent.

The Fanny and Leo Koerner Charitable Trust

(*formerly the* Kurt and Olga Koerner Charitable Trust)

Conservation, environment, education

£90,000 (1999)

Beneficial area UK, with a strong preference for Scotland and Sussex

39 Sloane Street, London SW1X 9LP

Tel. 020 7235 9560 **Fax** 020 7235 9580

e-mail kok@arcticnet.com

Correspondent Mrs E Owen, Administrator

Trustees *Ms L Koerner; J L Koerner; S Rausing; M Rausing.*

Inland Revenue no. 1067133

Information available Information was provided by the trust, and accounts were on file at the Charity Commission.

General Established in 1997, the trust has no guidelines. It has stated previously: 'donations have broadly been to organisations involved with conservation and care of the environment. The trust has also made some educational donations'. It has a preference for Scotland and Sussex. A list of grants was available for 1999 and showed a strong preference for Scotland and for projects concerned with the environment and education.

In 1999 the trust had assets of £986,000 and an income of £72,000. A total of £90,000 was given in 18 grants. The largest was £30,000 to Francis Holland School Trust. Grants of £10,000 each went to Big Brothers & Sisters UK, The Parnham Trust, Soil Association and Sustrans. Other large grants were £5,000 each to Association of Art Historians and Royal Botanic Garden (Edinburgh) and £2,500 to STIRK.

Smaller grants ranged from £50 to £500, including those to Homes for a Future, Let the Children Play, Kinlochleven Youth Group, Lochaber & District Fisheries Trust, The Pesticides Trust and West Highland Museum. Eight of the grants (mainly the smaller ones) were recurrent from the previous year when they received similar amounts.

In 2000 the trust had an income of £13 million. In February 2002 the trust stated that this money had been given to the Charities Aid Foundation. We were also informed that the trustees were unsure as to the future of the trust.

Exclusions No grants to individuals.

Applications By invitation from the trustees only. Due to the number of applications received, the administrator regrets that it is not possible to send a reply if the application is not successful. Trustees meet twice a year, in April and September.

The Landale Charitable Trust

Churches, hospitals, the arts

£11,000 (1999/2000)

Beneficial area South west Scotland

Chiene & Tait, Cairn House, 61 Dublin Street, Edinburgh EH3 6NL

Tel. 0131 558 5800

Correspondent J Younger

Charity Commission no. 274722

Information available Full accounts were on file at the Charity Commission.

General Grants are mainly given in Scotland, to churches, hospitals and the arts. In 1999/2000 the trust had both an income and an expenditure of £21,000 and made grants totalling £11,000. Assets totalled £393,000. The main beneficiaries were Kirkmahoe Parish Church (£5,500) and Dumfries and Galloway Care Trust(£3,500). Other beneficiaries included National Gallery Patrons (£500), Camphill Village Trust and David Pattie Memorial Fund (£250 each), Dumfries and Galloway Arts Festival (£200) and Not Forgotten Association (£100).

Exclusions No grants to individuals.

Applications In writing to the correspondent.

Russell Lang Charitable Trust

General

About £15,000

Beneficial area UK, with a preference for Scotland

GL, 23 Polwarth Street, Hyndland, Glasgow G12 9UD

Tel. 0141 337 2949

Correspondent Mrs Diana R Crichton, Administrator

Inland Revenue no. SC015665

Information available Information was provided by the trust.

General This trust was originally established with general charitable purposes to support causes of particular interest to the Lang family, such as charities, churches and hospitals. Initially it gave mainly in Scotland but it now gives more generally throughout the UK, giving around 15 grants of £1,000 each a year.

Applications The trust stated that unsolicited applications are not considered.

The R J Larg Family Charitable Trust

Education, health, medical research, arts – particularly music

About £100,000 (1999/2000)

Beneficial area UK but generally Scotland, particularly Tayside

Messrs Thorntons WS, 50 Castle Street, Dundee DD1 3RU

Tel. 01382 229111 **Fax** 01382 202288

Correspondent N Barclay

Inland Revenue no. SC004946

Information available Information was provided by the trust.

General The trust has an annual income of approximately £127,000. Grants, which totalled about £100,000 in 1999/2000, ranged between £250 and £6,000 and were given to a variety of organisations. These include organisations concerned with cancer research and other medical charities, youth organisations, university students' associations and amateur musical groups.

Beneficiaries of larger grants included: High School, Dundee (£6,000 for the cadet force and £5,000 for the Larg Scholarship Fund); Whitehall Theatre Trust (£4,000); Macmillan Cancer Relief – Dundee and Sense Scotland Children's Hospice (£2,500 each); with £2,000 to Rachel House.

Exclusions Grants are not available for individuals.

Applications In writing to the correspondent. Trustees meet to consider grants in February and August.

Rachel & Jack Lass Charities Ltd

Jewish, children, education, medical research

£150,000 (1999/2000)

Beneficial area England, Scotland and Wales

15 Neville Drive, London N2 0QS

Tel. 020 8446 8431 **Fax** 020 8458 4578

Correspondent Leonard Lass, Governor

Trustees *Leonard Lass; Sally Lass.*

Charity Commission no. 256514

Information available Accounts were on file at the Charity Commission.

General The trust gives primarily to Jewish charities, preferring those involved with children, education and medical research. In 1999/2000 the trust had assets of £259,000, an income of £161,000 and an expenditure of £162,000. The majority of the income came from donations received. The largest grant was £40,000 to Ravenswood Foundation. Grants of £20,000 each went to Yeshiva Horomo Talmudical College and Gevurath Ari Torah Academy Trust. Other notable beneficiaries included Craven Walk Charitable Trust (£16,000) and Beth Hamedresh Ponovez (£10,000).

Other grants of less than £600 each totalled almost £13,000.

Exclusions No grants to students.

Applications In writing to the correspondent.

Leng Charitable Trust

General

£140,000 (2000)

Beneficial area UK, with a strong preference for Scotland, especially Tayside

Messrs Thorntons, 50 Castle Street, Dundee DD1 3RU

Tel. 01382 229111 **Fax** 01382 202288

e-mail afmcdonald@thorntonsws.co.uk

Website www.thorntonsws.co.uk

Correspondent A F McDonald, Trustee

Trustees *A F McDonald; J S Fair; Dr J Wood; Thorntons Trustees Ltd.*

Inland Revenue no. SC009285

Information available Information was provided by the trust.

General The trust supports a wide range of causes including the arts, education, health, social welfare and the environment. In 2000 it had assets of £4.8 million and an income of £151,000. Grants totalled £140,000.

Exclusions Grants are not given to individuals, overseas projects, political or religious appeals or for sports or recreation.

Applications In writing to the correspondent. Trustees meet to consider grants in January.

The Lethendy Charitable Trust

General

£49,000 (2001)

Beneficial area Scotland, with a preference for Tayside

Henderson Loggie, Chartered Accountants, Royal Exchange, Panmure Street, Dundee DD1 1DZ

Tel. 01382 200055 **Fax** 01382 221240

e-mail ghay@hendersonloggie.co.uk

Correspondent George Hay

Trustees *N M Sharp, Chair; W R Alexander; D L Laird; I D Rae; D B Thomson.*

Inland Revenue no. SC003428

Information available Accounts are available from the trust.

General The trust was established in 1979 to support general charitable purposes in Dundee. It has since widened its geographical area to include Angus, Perthshire and Fife. The trustees have a preference for education, health, the development of young people and religious organisations. Grants normally range from £100 to £10,000, with the trust preferring to make a small number of larger donations.

In 2001 it had assets of £1.6 million and an income of £49,000. Grants to 6 organisations and 48 individuals totalled £49,000. Beneficiaries were University of Dundee Cancer Treatment Appeal and Game Conservancy Scottish Lowlands Research Project (each £10,000), Links Overseas and Princes Royal Trust for Carers (£5,000 each), The University of St Andrews – Saving the stained glass of St Salvator's Chapel (£1,500) and The Byre Theatre Appeal (£1,000). Grants to individuals ranged from £50 to £350.

Applications In writing to the correspondent. Trustees meet once a year in July to consider grants.

Lindsay's Charitable Trust

Conservation, the environment, arts, medical research

£3,600 (2001)

Beneficial area Scotland

Lindsays WS, 11 Atholl Crescent, Edinburgh EH3 8HE

Tel. 0131 477 8713 **Fax** 0131 229 5611

Correspondent W Brian Roberston

Trustees *Lindsays Trustees Ltd.*

Inland Revenue no. SC002014

Information available Information was provided by the trust.

General The trust supports conservation, the environment, wildlife, the arts and medical research. Preference is given to smaller, less well-known organisations which work in specialist areas.

In 2001 grants totalled £3,600. Beneficiaries were Action Research, Borders Exploration Group, Maggie's Cancer Care Centres, Scottish Community Foundation, Scottish Redundant Churches Trust, University of Edinburgh towards an annual memorial lecture and VISSES for a braille library.

Applications In writing to the correspondent. Applications should arrive by January for consideration in March.

The Lintel Trust

Housing and community projects in Scotland

£100,000 (2001)

Beneficial area Scotland

38 York Place, Edinburgh EH1 3HU

Tel. 0131 556 5777 **Fax** 0131 557 6028

e-mail lintel@sfha.co.uk

Website www.sfha.co.uk

Correspondent Joyce Gegan, Director

Trustees *Andrew Robertson; David Orr; Neil Hall; David Chalmers; Stewart Kinsman; Robert McDowell; Margaret Richards; Eileen Shand; Lynne Carr; Dinesh Joshi; Isabel Moore; Kate Dewar.*

Inland Revenue no. SC024763

Information available The charity produces an application form and guidance notes for applicants.

General The trust's aim is to help people live full and independent lives in their own homes. Originally the Scottish Housing Associations Charitable Trust (SHACT), it has been helping to provide good quality housing and support for people in housing need for over 20 years. It now also supports community projects in urban and rural areas.

The trust funds organisations in Scotland which work with:

- single homeless people
- older people
- people with support needs or disabilities of all kinds
- people of ethnic minorities
- refugees.

It makes grants or interest-free loans, for the following, to:

- provide or promote accommodation and support for people in housing need

- promote volunteering in housing-related projects

- promote participation in housing activities within communies

- help social housing providers with activities which benefit their tenants and local communities

- promote innovative ideas in housing provision.

The trust raises its income from donations from the voluntary housing sector, the corporate sector, individuals, events and it also manages funds on behalf of other charitable trusts. In 2000/01 it gave £100,000 in grants.

The following are areas the trust has been involved in during the past year.

Older people
The Lintel Trust manages a small-scale grants programme for projects for older people on behalf of the Housing Associations Charitable Trust (hact) and has supported, amongst others, a range of care and repair projects, enabling handyperson services to be developed and making a contribution to hardship funds. Grants have also been made to day centres to allow them to develop their services.

Homelessness
Edinburgh Cyrenians received a grant to employ a project worker for an innovative 'Flatmates' project to help homeless young people sustain shared tenancies. Inverness New Start was awarded a grant for volunteer training for their project to give homeless people practical help in their new tenancy. The Greater Easterhouse Foyer Steering Group was given a grant to help develop the first foyer in this part of Glasgow, offering accommodation and training to young homeless people.

Disabilities
A Turning Point project in Dumfries received a grant to purchase interactive computer equipment to help people with learning difficulties manage the change to independent living. A grant for committee training was awarded to the Disabled Persons Housing Service in the Borders. Cornerstone Community Care in Dundee received a grant to develop their services in Dundee for people with disabilities.

Minority Ethnic Groups
Positive Action in Housing was awarded a grant for its work with asylum seekers in Glasgow. The Scottish Council for Minority Rights received a grant for volunteer training for its helpline.

Others
These include Women's Aid projects, Tenants Associations and Govanhill Festival.

Exclusions The trust does not fund individuals, large capital projects, large UK organisations, holidays or vehicles.

Applications On a form available from the correspondent. The trustees meet four times a year. Applicants are encouraged to telephone the administrator beforehand for a general discussion.

The Lloyds TSB Foundation for Scotland

Social and community needs, education and training, scientific, medical and social research

£5.7 million (2000)

Beneficial area Scotland

Henry Duncan House, 120 George Street, Edinburgh EH2 4LH

Tel. 0131 225 4555 **Fax** 0131 260 0381

e-mail karen.l.toughill@lloydstsb.co.uk

Website www.ltsbfoundationforscotland.org.uk

Correspondent Andrew Muirhead, Chief Executive

Trustees *J G Mathieson, Chair; Archie Robb; Prof. Sir Michael Bond; Mrs Sandra E Brydon; Mrs Fiona Crighton; Ms Rani Dhir; Revd Ronald Ferguson; Alistair Findlay; Ms Susan R Moody; John Scott; Mrs Anne Simpson.*

Inland Revenue no. SC009481

Information available Criteria, priorities and principles booklet. Excellent annual reviews and application packs. Full report and accounts.

Comprehensive information is also available on the foundation's website.

General This is Scotland's largest grant-making trust, with £5.7 million distributed in grants in 2000. Most are from £1,000 to £15,000. Higher amounts are given, but rarely for more than £50,000 in a single year and not for periods of more than three years.

'The Lloyds TSB Foundation for Scotland, formerly known as TSB Foundation for Scotland, was formed in 1986 as one of four independent charitable trusts established by the then TSB Group. Collectively the foundations receive 1% of the bank's pre-tax profits for distribution. The Foundation for Scotland receives 19.46% of this amount .... The foundation was originally formed to support local community groups, and to this day is still very much a 'community foundation' with the majority of awards being made to grassroots charities.'

The foundation operates within published criteria, and distributes funds in support of registered charities on the basis of social need and community benefit. Every three years the trustees review the criteria and priorities which guide them. Those for January 2000 to December 2002 are given in a leaflet *Criteria, Priorities and Principles* from which much of the following information was taken.

There are three grant-making schemes: Standard Grant Scheme, Capacity Building Grant Scheme and the Partnership Drugs Initiative.

Standard grant scheme
General criteria
The trustees of the foundation are focused on the needs of disadvantaged and marginalised people in Scottish communities. They allocate funds to charities that enable people to be active members of society and to improve their quality of life. Children, young people, ageing population and minority groups are among those which are of particular interest, and can be assisted through the three main objectives to which the foundation seeks to allocate funds, which are:

- social and community needs

- education and training

- scientific, medical and social research.

Social & community needs
- community activities – elderly people's clubs, family centres, youth clubs, after school clubs, playgroups/nurseries (within areas previously designated as Areas of Priority Treatment by the Scottish Office), self-help groups

- crisis and advice services – homelessness, addictions, family guidance, bereavement, counselling, befriending, money advice

- disabled people – day centres, residential accommodation, carers, advice and support, transport

- health issues – information and advice, mental health, home nursing, hospices, day care for people who are elderly

- civic responsibility – crime prevention, offenders and their families, at risk/hard to reach young people, promotion of good citizenship

- cultural enrichment – access to the arts and national heritage specifically for disadvantaged and disabled people.

Education & training
- motivation – projects which assist individuals to obtain employment, with particular emphasis on guiding young people to develop their potential, improve literacy skills, build self-confidence and self-esteem

- employment – training which will provide disadvantaged and disabled people with employment opportunities

- life skills and independent living – particular interest in young people, the elderly, and people who are mentally or physically disadvantaged.

Scientific, medical & social research
Projects related to underfunded fields of research which are less fashionable and harder to find funding for.

Priorities
Every three years the trustees establish priorities from within the general criteria. Priority support will be considered for projects which include the following:

Children
Projects which:

- provide a safe place where children can talk about their worries/concerns/emotional issues, e.g. children's counsellors or therapeutic services

- create a safe environment for children to have the opportunity to play together

- build self-esteem and self-confidence, which will enhance life chances and experiences for children, broaden their horizons through opportunities which they may not have, e.g. life skills projects/drama/art

- promote peer support and advocacy giving children a voice and encouraging empowerment

- support children as young carers and their siblings, including siblings of special needs children.

Young people
Projects which:

- value young people by listening to them and addressing their problems

- show evidence of young people's involvement by including them in decision making

- work hard to reach young people who do not include themselves in organised youth work

- support detached and outreach work which reaches the most vulnerable young people in our society

- promote accreditation of young people by recognising their contribution through involvement as a volunteer or as a service user, thus building self-esteem.

Ageing population
Projects which:

- represent and promote the needs and wellbeing of older people through advocacy, advice, or support; encourage inclusion and reduce isolation

- support older people who provide direct services, i.e. work done by older people for older people

- support inter-generational projects or themes, which strengthen contact across generations and cultural divides

- help and encourage independence and independent living.

Parenting
Projects which:

- promote parenting skills, which help with understanding and responding to children's social, emotional and developmental needs

- encourage male participation by promoting the importance of the role of fathers, and their active involvement in the lives of their children

- support opportunities which allow families to take part in ordinary family life, e.g. outings/holidays (within the UK).

Rural disadvantage
Projects which:

- promote access to groups and communities through transport, befriending, buddies schemes and volunteering

- encourage social inclusion and improve services in rural communities.

Physical and mental disability
Projects which:

- improve the quality of life for disabled people by promoting independence and raising awareness of disability

- assist people with learning difficulties, sensory impairments and users of mental health services.

Homelessness
Projects which:

- establish support networks to assist homeless people back to mainstream society

- provide information, advice, and raise awareness of available services

- work with people living in supported/temporary accommodation.

Substance misuse
Projects which:

- focus on early intervention, including education, and alternative activities aimed at building awareness and minimising harm

- provide support, advice and information to people whose lives are affected by the misuse of drugs, alcohol or volatile substances, e.g. solvents.

Minority groups
Projects which:

- represent and promote the needs of minority groups through advocacy, advice and awareness raising

- promote anti-racism and provide support for people who suffer from bullying and prejudice.

Infrastructure
To assist with:

- operational efficiencies or improve access to funding for charitable organisations

- development of staff and volunteers, as well as the skills of user groups, for the good of their communities

- provision of training for chief executives and management staff to ensure their professional/ personal development is continued

- training of management committees to equip them with the knowledge of responsibilities required in the role of trustee/director.

Principles
The undernoted principles will apply to all applications, and priority support will be considered for projects demonstrating one or more of the following:

- encourage empowerment by consulting and involving users

- help and encourage independent living and development of life skills

- provide new and continuing opportunities for personal enrichment and quality of life, e.g. skills training across all age bands

- collect information through contacts or research to establish, consolidate and promote good practice and develop policy

- represent and promote the needs of people through advocacy, advice, information and support. In particular for people with mental health problems, physical and learning disabilities and the elderly

- demonstrate a collaborative approach by networking with other agencies/providers to avoid duplication of services

- demonstrate equality of opportunity

- promote anti-racism and discourage anti-social behaviour

- demonstrate good evaluation and monitoring procedures

- adopt preventative measures and stimulate early intervention programmes

- encourage the involvement of volunteers

- recognise cultural diversity and particular needs that may arise.

The trustees are keen to support innovative projects but recognise the value of established services which provide support for vulnerable people. Both approaches are seen as having equal value and will be considered for support on the merit of individual projects.

Within the standard grant programme, the breakdown between the three categories for 2000 was as follows:

social and community needs	75%
education and training	19%
scientific, medical and social research	6%

About £1 million went to education and training, given in 94 grants. Of these, 14 were towards employment training, 13 focused on training for disabled people, 35 were to help promote life skills and 32 to enhance education. Almost £4 million went on social and community needs to 276 charities.

Geographical distribution
The foundation undertakes a great deal of developmental activity. 65 surgeries were scheduled for 2000 throughout the country. The geographical breakdown of grants in 2000 was as follows:

Borders	4%
Central	3%
Dumfries & Galloway	1%
Fife	3%
Grampian	7%
Highlands	7%
Islands	1%
Lothian	14%
Strathclyde	32%
Tayside	8%
Scotland-wide	20%

The capacity-building grants scheme
Following a year-long pilot involving 40 Scottish charities, in October 1999 the foundation launched a grant-making process which provides funding for voluntary organisations to access a

panel of independent consultants. The consultants are experienced in the voluntary sector and can assist in resolving many of today's issues affecting charities. The panel of consultants has skills in areas such as:

- financial management
- fundraising planning
- good governance
- information technology
- marketing
- strategic planning
- staff development.

The foundation issues a separate note for applicants interested in this programme. Some of its contents are as follows:

'[This is] a programme which will support growth and development activities and address short-term skills gaps within the voluntary sector in Scotland … we anticipate considerable interest in this programme and we are unlikely to be able to meet all requests …. Essentially, we have constructed a panel of external specialists with a wide range of skills relevant to the management of voluntary organisations. A member of the panel will make arrangements to meet with you to review your needs and establish the level of input required … and to discuss a plan of action and establish the associated costs …. Assuming you are happy to proceed, your application, now costed, … will go forward to our trustees.'

The foundation has budgeted a substantial £300,000 for this programme in 2001 and expects to make something over 50 grants. Experience suggests that the average grant will cover about 10 days' consultancy. By summer 2000, enquiries about the programme were coming in at the rate of about 300 a year. Of these, about a third would get to the first stage of an initial application and costing, and a majority of these applications were successful.

As is usually found in programmes of this kind, many applicants start off by thinking that what they need is fundraising advice and help, but discussion often suggests that funding difficulties are due, at least in part, to lack of convincing strategies and plans, and that addressing these is the priority.

Fuller details about this new grant programme can be obtained from Geoff Weir, the Capacity Building Grant Coordinator, on 0131 225 4555.

Partnership drugs initiative

During 2000 the foundation embarked on a partnership funding programme with the Scottish Executive to invest in work to reduce harmful drug misuse amongst vulnerable children and young people. Funding is targeted in the following areas:

- children and young people in families in which parents misuse drugs
- pre-teen children who are at higher risk of developing substance misuse
- young people who are developing or have established problem drug use.

Types of grant

Awards are either one-off for capital needs or multi-year grants for revenue costs. The trust states that they 'recognise the demand for ongoing revenue support, however, that must be balanced against the need for funding the many excellent projects which will continue to emerge'.

Multi-year grants

Future year commitments are restricted to 30% of the next year's projected income and 15% of the following year's projected income. Grants given over several years are often tapered i.e. the grant is reduced each year. The trust also states: 'smaller charities that are more fragile, have priority on multi-year awards, as larger more sophisticated applicant groups arguably have the machinery to enable them to make applications on a regular basis, and are consequently better able to win resources'.

Application volumes and allocation of funds

In 2000 over 1,500 applications were considered through the various programmes. 12.5% were rejected as being outside the foundation's criteria; a further 25% were rejected at board level. Of the grants made, 94% were through the standard programme. This includes both new grants and releases made under existing commitments. The average grant was just over £14,000. The other grants were given under:

- the staff matched giving programme, through which £140,000 was given to 496 charities (this is where the charitable fundraising efforts and voluntary time given by staff of Lloyds TSB

Group in Scotland are matched on a pound for pound basis)

- the capacity building grants scheme through which £141,000 was given.

Issues on rejection

The trustees regret that demands made on the foundation's funds always outstrip the funds available and this means that many good applications, whilst meeting criteria, cannot be supported. Owing to the high quality of applications in general, there is often a narrow margin between success and failure.

In assessing past applications, there were a few recurring features in those which were unsuccessful:

- limited completion of application form relying on a range of attachments. Attachments cannot be circulated to trustees. The trustees will only see your application form plus one other A4 sheet containing supporting information. The assessor responsible for your case will only see any other documents

- lack of clear plans for other fundraising

- insufficient detail on potential benefits a project would create

- 'all or nothing' requests for large appeals. (The foundation would prefer to see a part-funding option)

- inadequate explanation about the financial position of an applicant, e.g. policy on reserves, reasons for changes in level of costs year on year, etc.

- no clear strategy on safety/security, particularly important where a group is working with children or vulnerable adults, or engaged in transport.

Multi-year funding:

- lack of strategy for the period beyond which funding was being sought

- vague objectives.

It should be stressed that applications are generally of a very high quality, however applicants may find the above to be a helpful checklist. In particular the foundation emphasises the following, to be remembered when completing the application form:

- keep it simple – be concise and direct

- stress the difference our support will make – facts and figures are important

- always provide a detailed breakdown of costs

- tell us about other fundraising – we will be particularly interested to learn of local community fundraising as well as approaches to other charitable trusts

- it is essential that objectives relating to revenue funding are 'SMART' – Specific, Measurable, Achievable, Realistic and Testing.

The foundation has six full-time assessors and an ongoing grant-awarding process.

Examples of grants in 2000

About half of the grants were for £5,000 or less, and most of those were one-off. Multi-year awards are rarely for less than £3,000 a year.

There were six awards of £50,000 or more, to:

- Hansel Foundation (£54,000 towards furnishing the 4-person accommodation within the courtyard development)

- Christian Aid (£75,000 to aid the logistical and programme support for the relief operations of victims of the Mozambique floods)

- National Museums of Scotland (£50,000 for the Discovery bus project, 3rd of 4 payments)

- University of Dundee (to equip the bacterial culture laboratory, 2nd and 3rd of 3 payments)

- Royal Society of Edinburgh (towards research on the ageing population and masterclasses in science and technology)

- The Donaldson Trust (£50,000 for a pre-school suite, 3rd of 3 payments).

Further examples of multi-year awards: Harmeny Education Trust Ltd (£30,000 to complete the funding of the drama and music facility, 3rd of 3 payments); Stepping Stones in Scotland (£11,000 to fund 50% of the director's salary, 3rd of three payments); Saheliya (£6,500 to fund the Bengali Speaking Support Worker for 10 hours each week); Manic Depression Fellowship Aberdeen (£4,500 towards the office running costs, 2nd of 3 payments); Volunteer Action Dumfries & Galloway (£3,600 to meet the salary costs of a young volunteers development worker, 2nd of 3 payments); Homestart Leith (£2,700 to fund the hall rental and part-time development worker's salary, 3rd of 3 payments); and Skye & Lochalsh

Council on Alcohol (£1,500 to cover the travel costs of the project, 2nd of 3 payments).

Other recipients of one-off grants: Edinburgh Festival Society (£25,000 for the salary of the education programme development manager); Ardgowan Hospice (£23,000 to equip and furnish the relaxation and training rooms); Brainwave (£11,000 to fund the salary of the part-time physiotherapist); Wick Youth Club (£7,600 for sports equipment and furniture); Talk Lochaber (£3,300 to cover the cost of volunteer's expenses and rent for one year); Breadalebane Riding for the Disabled (£1,000 to buy a mounting block and support the maintenance of one pony); and Granton Toddlers Group (£770 to replace the climbing house, easels and play accessories).

Exclusions The trustees regret they cannot support all fields of voluntary and charitable activity. To focus funding on the foundation's priority areas, the following purposes will not be considered:

- organisations which are not recognised as a charity by the Inland Revenue
- individuals, including students
- animal welfare
- environment, e.g. geographic and scenic, conservation and protection of flora and fauna
- mainstream activities of schools, universities and colleges
- hospitals and medical centres
- activities which collect funds for subsequent redistribution to others
- sponsorship or marketing appeals
- endowment funds
- expeditions or overseas travel
- fabric appeals for places of worship, other than where such buildings provide accommodation to community groups
- historic restoration.

Applications On application forms, complete with comprehensive guidance notes, available from the foundation. These can be requested by telephone, by e-mail, or through the website.

Standard grant scheme process
Before submitting an application, information and advice can be assessed through surgeries,

visits, telephone or e-mail contact. Once submitted, applications are allocated to an assessor. The assessor will contact you, either by telephone or personal visit to discuss the application. The assessor's report is then presented to the assessment team which meet weekly. The team puts forward recommendations to the trustees. The trustees consider applications at their board meetings which are held every two months. Dates for the meetings in 2002 will be available from October 2001. Closing dates for applications are usually 12 weeks before each board meeting. Applicants will be notified of the decision withing 14 days of the meeting.

One-off awards: progress reports should be sent within a year of receiving the grant. Review visits will be carried out upon at least 50% of these awards. You can reapply 12 months after the original award date. Multi-year awards: one month before each payment is due, a progress report will be requested. The report should include objectives for the coming year and a copy of the most recent audited accounts. Following receipt of the report, an evaluation visit will take place and if this is satisfactory the next payment will be issued. You can reapply 12 months after the final payment is scheduled.

The capacity-building grant process
The application procedure differs from the standard scheme. Every potential applicant is visited by the programme coordinator for exploratory talks before applications are submitted. Applications are dealt with by a team of consultants before recommendations are given to the trustees. The trustees meet about three times a year. Closing dates for applications are usually 20 weeks prior to board meetings. If successful a consultant will contact you to complete an agreement and action plan; once this has been signed the grant will be given and the consultant will commence the work as agreed. More details on this process can be found the trust's annual review or on the website.

The foundation's literature also includes helpful tips on filling in the application.

Partnership drugs initiative
Applications are invited through drug action teams twice a year in April and October. For further information contact the programme manager, Jackie McRae at the foundation's address.

Low & Bonar Charitable Trust

General

See below

Beneficial area UK, but mostly Tayside and North East Fife

Thornton WS, 50 Castle Street, Dundee DD1 3RU

Correspondent N Barclay

Inland Revenue no. SC010837

Information available Basic information was provided by the trust.

General This trust informed us in January 2002 that it had been created from the assets of Low & Bonar Charitable Fund, a company trust. This new trust is not connected to Low & Bonar plc, which means it will not be receiving the same level of funds as has been available in the past (previously around £65,000 a year). The trust stated that it will concentrate its giving to smaller charities, particularly in Tayside and north east Fife, although other organisations will still be supported.

Exclusions Support is only given to charities registered with the Charity Commission or Inland Revenue.

Applications In writing to the correspondent including your organisation's latest audited report and evidence of charitable status.

Mrs M A Lumsden's Charitable Trust

General

Not known

Beneficial area Scotland

Turcan Connell, Princes Exchange, 1 Earl Grey Street, Edinburgh EH3 9EE

Tel. 0131 228 8111 **Fax** 0131 228 8118

Inland Revenue no. SC005176

Information available This trust is one of 10 trusts, probably all small, administered by Turcan Connell. The company would not provide us with any information on these trusts, only agreeing to send each trust's accounts for the cost of £20 each. We did not think this was reasonable for such small trusts.

General The trust supports general charitable purposes. Further information was unfortunately unavailable.

Applications In writing to the correspondent.

The McCorquodale Charitable Trust

Children, health, heritage, wildlife

£18,000 (1998/99)

Beneficial area UK, particularly Scotland

Coutts & Co., Trustee Department, PO Box 1236, 6 High Street, Chelmsford, Essex CM1 1BQ

Correspondent The Trust Manager

Trustees *C N McCorquodale; Coutts & Co.*

Charity Commission no. 297697

Information available Accounts were on file at the Charity Commission.

General The trust mainly supports charities concerned with children, health and heritage. Wildlife organisations are also supported.

Grants can be given for building costs, core costs, projects and research. They generally range from £100 to £1,000, although most grants were for £200. In 1998/99 the trust had an income of £7,000 and an expenditure of £19,000. Grants totalled £18,000. The largest beneficiary by far was the Scotlands Churches Scheme which received £12,000. Other recipeints included National Trust Scotland (£1,200 in total) and Imperial Cancer Research Campaign (£400). Several UK charities were supported, presumably local Scottish branches. Some grants were recurrent, with some beneficiaries receiving more than one grant during the year.

Applications In writing to the correspondent.

The R S MacDonald Charitable Trust

Visual impairment, cerebral palsy, children, animal welfare

£310,000 (2001)

Beneficial area Scotland

27 Cramond Vale, Edinburgh EH4 6RB

Tel. 0131 312 6766

Correspondent Richard K Austin, Trustee

Trustees *E D Buchanan; D W A MacDonald; Ms Sheila C MacDonald; Donald G Sutherland; Richard K Austin.*

Inland Revenue no. SC012710

Information available Information was supplied by the trust.

General The trust supports charities concerned with the following:

* the care and welfare of people with visual impairment or cerebral palsy

* research into the causes, prevention or treatment of visual impairment and cerebral palsy

* the prevention of cruelty to children

* the prevention of cruelty to animals.

Six organisations are mentioned in the trust deed and these are often, but not always, supported.

The trust is prepared to give very large grants to enable organisations to carry out major projects or develop ideas. Average grants are about £30,000.

In 2001 the trust had assets of over £18 million and an income of £415,000. Grants totalled £310,000. Direct charitable expenditure in 2001 was broken down as follows:

£50,000 to Royal Blind Asylum and School (£50,000 in 2000)
£35,000 each to Sense Scotland and Deafblind Scotland
£34,000 to Children's Fund (£21,000 in 2000)
£33,000 to Capability Scotland (£50,000 in 2000)
£25,000 each to Children 1st and SSPCA (£100,000 and £75,000 respectively in 2000)
£25,000 to Eyeless Trust
£20,000 to RNLI (£20,000 in 2000)

£18,000 to Glasgow & West of Scotland Society for the Blind (£16,000 in 2000)
£10,000 to Visually Impaired Services South East of Scotland.

Also supported in 2000 were St Dunstans (£25,000) and British Council for the Prevention of Blindness (£5,000). Yorkhill NHS Trust on behalf of Visually Impaired appears to be the remaining organisation mentioned in the trust deed, although received no funds during these years.

Exclusions Grants are not given to non-registered charities or individuals.

Applications In writing to the correspondent including a copy of the latest audited accounts and constituting documents. Applications should be received by March/April to be considered in the summer. Trustees usually want to meet new applicants requesting a larger grant. Successful applicants are asked for a follow-up report and are often visited by a trustee.

The N S MacFarlane Charitable Trust

General, see below

Not known

Beneficial area Mainly Scotland

Wright Johnston & Mackenzie, 302 St Vincent Street, Glasgow G2 5RZ

Tel. 0141 248 3434 **Fax** 0141 221 0432

e-mail im@wjm.co.uk

Correspondent Ian Macdonald

Trustees *Lord Macfarlane of Bearsden; Hon. Hamish Macfarlane; Alan M Simpson; Andrew Reekie*

Inland Revenue no. SC010834

Information available Information, but with no financial details, was provided by the trust.

General The trust will support a wide range of organisations. It will consider the following causes:

* animal welfare

* arts

- buildings
- children and young people
- disability
- environment, conservation, heritage
- education/training
- medical/health, including medical research
- older people
- religious appeals.

It gives grants mostly ranging from £100 to £1,000 except for a small number of major awards each year. Unfortunately no financial information was available.

Exclusions Grants are not normally given to individuals. Overseas projects and political appeals are not supported.

Applications In writing to the correspondent, giving details of the organisation or project and financial information. Trustees usually meet quarterly to consider applications.

M L MacIntyre Begonia Trust

Begonias

About £15,000

Beneficial area Scotland

73 Russell Drive, Bearsden, Glasgow G61 3BB

Correspondent Michael Black

Inland Revenue no. SC007597

Information available Limited information was available on this trust.

General Grants given for horticultural and botanical work on begonias.

Applications In writing to the correspondent.

Catherine Mackichan Trust

Scottish history, schools

£1,500 (2000)

Beneficial area Scotland, especially the West Highlands

Aros, Towerside, Whittingham, Alnwick NE66 4RF

Tel. 01665 574335

Correspondent The Honorary Secretary

Inland Revenue no. SC020459

Information available The information for this trust was provided by the trust.

General The trust funds research into various aspects of Scottish history including archaeology, genealogy and language studies. Schools can also receive grants. Individuals who are umemployed, senior citizens or disabled are also supported.

It prioritises the West Highlands, followed by Scotland, and then causes outside Scotland that have connections with Scotland. Grants range from £50 usually up to £600.

Applications Applications are welcome from academic institutions as well as individuals or groups not in the academic field. Application forms are available from Mr I Fraser, Vice Chair, The Catherine Mackichan Trust, School of Scottish Studies, 27–29 George Square, Edinburgh, EH8. Apply between the start of January and 15 April each year. The trust stated in 2001 that its address may be changing in the near future.

The Mackintosh Foundation

Performing arts, general

£756,000 (2000/01)

Beneficial area UK, with an interest in western Scotland, and overseas

1 Bedford Square, London WC1B 3RA

Tel. 020 7637 8866

Correspondent The Appeals Secretary

Trustees *Sir Cameron Mackintosh, Chair; Martin McCallum; Nicholas Allott; D Michael Rose; Patricia Macnaughton; Alain Boublil.*

Charity Commission no. 327751

Information available Good annual report and accounts. Detailed and excellent information available from the foundation.

General The foundation makes around 300 grants a year, up to 90% being for amounts under £10,000 and typically ranging from £1,000 to £5,000, for a wide range of causes. The few large grants, peaking at £150,000, are usually to support the theatre (48% of grants), while those for community projects tend be made in the west of Scotland.

The foundation was established to:

- promote and develop theatrical, musical and dramatic arts

- relieve and promote research into the causes and treatment of AIDS

- provide for medical research generally and the relief of sickness

- provide relief for people who are homeless and living in poverty

- provide for the relief of refugees

- provide funds for any other objects which are exclusively charitable under UK-law.

In 1996 the objects were extended to include the promotion of the conservation, protection and enhancement in the UK of nature and the amenities of the countryside, including areas of natural beauty and areas or buildings of special scientific, historic or architectural interest for the benefit of the public.

The foundation produced information in January 2002, which states that it 'has to date tended not to be involved very much in "hands-on" administration of any charitable projects but has concentrated on providing funds to others for that purpose. The main reason for this is that the trustees of the foundation are all very busily engaged in other activities with little time to become more directly involved in the way its funds are used although there are some instances in which help has been provided to needy individuals. Administration costs are kept to a minimum (in the year ending 31 March 2001 amounting to 11% of income) since at present the foundation has no office establishment of its own and has comparatively few overhead expenses other than the cost of the professional time of its solicitors (who deal with much of the administration as well as legal work), an appeals and bursaries secretary and, of course, its auditors/accountants.

'Because of the foundation's limited monitoring resources, it has tended to concentrate its funding on other registered charities who are supervised in the conduct of their affairs by the Charity Commissioners [in England and Wales], but the foundation not infrequently makes exceptions, particularly where overseas applicants and individuals are concerned.'

The trust provided details about grantmaking in 2000/01, when grants totalled £756,000, down from £1 million in the previous year. It noted long-standing connections with University of Oxford and Royal National Theatre, and discussed the winding-up of its Bui-Doi Fund – this was a channel of grants for the relief of people in developing countries. The foundation's Drama School Bursary Award Scheme was referred to, which supports students to study for an accredited drama course and had entered into its final year of running. Information on Arts 4 Everyone and other major donations was also provided, as follows, and no further grant beneficiaries were listed in the report.

Arts 4 Everyone

On 21 November 1998 the foundation pledged £500,000 over the next five years in conjunction with Arts Council of England and the regional Arts Councils' new 'Arts 4 Everyone' scheme (the main scheme and not the 'Express' scheme for grants of £5,000 or less). Under this arrangement the foundation provides an agreed sum each year to be distributed in pre-determined proportions, for approved beneficiaries. During 2000/01 the foundation paid £100,000 under this arrangement, leaving £150,000 still to be paid.

Other donations

During the year these were: £30,000 to The National Student Drama Festival Limited; £20,000 to Mallaig & Morar Community Centre Association; £16,000 to Christ's Hospital; and £15,000 to Regional Theatre Young Directors' Scheme.

Only two other grants on the grants list, for £5,000 each, were obviously made to Scottish charities – University of the Highlands and Islands Project and ILM (Highland) Limited. Grants of under £5,000 were not listed however, and the trust confirmed that a number of organisations in Scotland were supported.

The foundation classifies its grants as follows with the percentage of grant total in 2000/01 (1999/2000 in brackets):

Theatre and the performing arts	50%	(48%)
• Theatre companies and buildings	19%	(20%)
• Promotion of new theatrical works and classical music repertoire	7%	(7%)
• Theatrical training and education	23%	(19%)
• Theatre related pastoral care	1%	(1%)
The homeless	11%	(15%)
Children and education	11%	(12%)
Medical	18%	(9%)
Community projects	8%	(6%)
The environment	2%	(1%)
Unclassified (including overseas)	1%	(3%)

Grants were distributed by size as follows:

	2000/ 2001	1999/ 2000
£100,000 – £149,999	1	1
£50,000 – £99,999	–	2
£20,000 – £49,999	2	4
£10,000 – £19,999	15	19
£5,000 – £9,999	42	42
£1,000 – £4,999	49	139
Less than £1,000	148	99
Total	257	306

Exclusions Religious or political activities are not supported. Apart from the foundation's drama award and some exceptions, applications from individuals are discouraged.

Applications In writing to the correspondent. The trustees meet in May and November in plenary session, but a grants committee meets weekly to consider grants of up to £10,000.

The Maclay Murray & Spens Charitable Trust

Health and social welfare

About £10,000 (2000)

Beneficial area Scotland

c/o Maclay Murray & Spen, 151 St Vincent Street, Glasgow G2 5NJ

Tel. 0141 248 5011 **Fax** 0141 248 5819

e-mail dmw@maclaymurrayspens.co.uk

Website www.maclaymurrayspens.co.uk

Correspondent The Trustees

Trustees *Ms J D Johnson; D M White.*

Inland Revenue no. SC012364

Information available Information was provided by the trust.

General The trust receives its annual income through deeds of covenant. In 2000 it had an income of about £10,000, all of which was given in grants.

The trust supports the following causes: childen/young people, older people, people who are disabled and social welfare causes generally and also health and medical causes, including hospices, hospitals and medical research. Grants usually range from £200 to £500. Most grants are recurrent and the following organisations receive regular support: ChildLine Scotland, Macmillan Cancer Relief, Prince and Princess of Wales Hospice and St Columba's Hospice.

Applications In writing to the correspondent. The trustees meet irregularly to consider grants.

The MacLennan Trust

Homelessness, children, young people, education

£6,700 (1997/98)

Beneficial area UK, with some preference for Scotland

Royal Bank of Scotland plc, Private Trust & Taxation Office, 2 Festival Square, Edinburgh EH3 9SU

Tel. 0131 523 2658 **Fax** 0131 228 9889

Correspondent The Trust Manager

Inland Revenue no. SC010562

Information available Information was provided by the trust.

General The trust supports homelessness projects, children and young people. Education and religious appeals are also considered. The trust's total assets for 1997/98 amounted to £289,000 and the income was £11,000. Grants totalled £6,700. They usually range between £500 and £1,500. Examples of grants include £650 to Carberry Tower for the Religious Instruction of Youth, £500 each to Boys' Brigade, The Big Issue, Children 1st, Girl Guides Scotland, Moffat After School Care, St Columba's Hospice and Scottish Council for Spastics and £200 to Scotland Yard Adventure Centre.

Exclusions No grants to individuals.

Applications In writing to the correspondent. Trustees meet in February to consider grants.

The MacRobert Trust

General

£748,000 (2000/01)

Beneficial area UK, mainly Scotland

Cromar, Tarland, Aboyne, Aberdeenshire AB34 4UD

Tel. 01339 881444 **Fax** 01339 881676

Website www.themacroberttrust.org.uk

Correspondent Maj. Gen. J A J P Barr, Administrator

Trustees *Mrs C J Cuthbert; D M Heughan; J Mackie; W G Morrison; Group Capt. D A Needham; R M Sherriff; A M Summers; Cromar Nominees Ltd; J Swan; H Woodd.*

Inland Revenue no. SC031346

Information available Accounts for the no longer operating MacRoberts Trusts were provided by the trust, at the cost of £25 (see below).

General Established on 6 April 2001 by the assets of the no longer operating MacRobert Trusts, a collection of four charitable trusts and two holding companies, which merged into the new, single The MacRobert Trust. The trust expects the amalgamation will lead to greater simplicity and transparency and reduce the administration and management costs by £25,000 each year.

The following information is taken from the financial year 2000/01 and relates to the former MacRobert Trusts. The grant-making policy will remain and the income and assets will stay at much the same levels, although hopefully the administration and management costs will be reduced to lead to a larger grant total.

Grants are given to recognised charities UK-wide, but with a preference for Scotland. The categories under which the trustees consider support are:

- science and technology
- youth (especially uniformed and similar groups)
- services and sea
- ex-service hospitals and homes
- disablity
- education
- community welfare
- agriculture and horticulture
- arts and music
- medical care
- Tarland and Deeside.

The trust is prepared to make core/revenue grants where appropriate, but favours projects. The trustees recognise that, at present, experiment and innovation are much more difficult to fund and the trust's role in funding them the more significant.

It also runs Douneside House as a subsidiary charitable activity, which serves as a holiday county house for serving and retired officers of the armed forces and their families. To help cover the costs for this, Douneside House runs at commercial rates in the winter months as a conference centre.

In 2000/01 the now amalgamated trusts had combined assets totalling £49 million, comprised of Douneside House and an estate of 1,800 acres of woodland and 5,000 acres of farmland and associated residential properties let by the trust. The surplus income generated from these assets, following management and administration costs, was donated in grants. Grants to organisations totalled £748,000. The accounts also showed £149,000 in non-montery donations, comprised of the difference between the rental value of assets and the peppercorn rents of three organisations.

Grants were broken down as follows:

Ex-servicemen's hospitals – 5 grants totalling £180,000
The largest grant was £110,000 to Princess Louise Scottish Hospital (Erskine Hospital). Other beneficiaries included Scottish Veterans Residencies (£25,000) and King Edward VII's Hospital for Officers (£10,000).

Education – 7 grants totalling £69,000
Beneficiaries included Gordon Foundation (£15,000), Royal Scottish Geographical Society (£10,000) and Scottish Field Studies Association for the Kindrogan Field Centre (£6,100).

Armed services and merchant marine – 10 grants totalling £40,000
Recipients included Lord Roberts Workshops (£5,000), Royal Air Forces Association – Aberdeen branch (£1,000), Scottish Society for the Employment of Ex-regular Sailors, Soldiers and Airmen (£500) and Soldiers, Sailors and Airmen Families Association – Aberdeen (£400).

Disability – 14 grants totalling £114,000
The largest grants went to Scottish Centre for Children with Motor Impairments (£25,000), Hansel Foundation and Treloar Trust – Hampshire (£20,000 each) and AbilityNet and Leonard Cheshire Foundation – Edinburgh (£10,000 each). Other recipients included Aberdeen Day Centre (£3,000), Clyde Cruising Club Seamanship and Pilotage Trust (£2,000) and Thistle Foundation – Edinburgh (£1,800).

Community welfare – 15 grants totalling £107,000
The largest grants were £25,000 to Abbeyfield (Ballachulish) Society – Glencoe, £11,000 to Salvation Army and £10,000 each to Compass Christian Centre, Shelter Scotland – Edinburgh and WRVS. Other beneficiaries included Aberdeen Cyrenians and Jura Residential Care Ltd (£5,000 each), Aberdeen Samaritans (£1,500), Voluntary Service Aberdeen (£1,200) and Montrose Day Care Centre (£500).

Music and the arts – 12 grants totalling £48,000
The largest grants were £15,000 to Piping Centre and £10,000 to Scottish Opera. Other beneficiaries included Lochaber Music Charitable Trust (£5,000), Walk the Plank – Scotland (£4,500), Kaleidoscope Aberdeen International Childrens' Festival (£2,000) and Edinburgh Youth Orchestra (£400).

Medical care – 6 grants totalling £36,000
Beneficiaries included Queen Margaret University College (£12,000), Debra (£10,000), CHAS for the Muirfield golf day (£250) and Marie Curie Cancer Care for a childrens' Christmas party in Ardoe (£50).

Youth – 19 grants totalling £96,000
The largest grants were £20,000 to Sail Training Association and £10,000 each to Merseyside Youth Association and Prince's Trust – Scotland.

Other recipients of larger grants included Govan Ecumenical Association (£7,500), Aberdeen International Youth Festival and Girl's Brigade – Scotland (£5,000), YMCA and YWCA (£4,600 each for their respective Scottish National Councils), Wick Youth Club (£3,000), Scout Association for its Scottish headquarters (£1,800), RSSPC for the Touch of Tartan Ball (£500) and ATC Aberdeen & NES Wing Lady MacRobert Memorial Trophy (£310).

Science and technology – 4 grants totalling £39,000
These went to Glasgow Science Centre Charitable Trust (£25,000), Royal Academy of Engineering for leadership awards (£7,500), The Royal Institute (£4,600) and Locaber and District Fisheries Trust (£2,000).

Tarland and Deeside – 12 grants totalling £3,300
Beneficiaries included Cromar Parish Church
– Tarland for the fabric fund (£800), St Thomas'
Church – Aboyne (£630), Strathdee Music Club
– Aboyne (£500), Tarland Show (£400), Aboyne
& Upper Deeside Rotary Club (£100) and Logie
Coldstone Welfare Trust (£60).

*Agriculture and horticulture – 7 grants totalling
£16,000*
These went to Younger (Benmore) Trust
(£6,500), Worshipful Company of Farmers
(£2,300), Royal Highland Education Trust for the
Royal Northern Countryside Initiative (£2,000),
Scottish Association of Young Farmers Clubs
(£1,900), Royal Scottish Agricultural Benevolent
Institution (£1,800), Scottish Gardens Scheme
(£1,100) and Cromar & District Horticultural
& Industrial Society (£60).

Exclusions Grants are not normally provided
for:

- religious organisations (but not including
  youth/community services provided by them,
  or projects of general benefit to the whole
  community, or local churches)

- organisations based outside the UK

- individuals

- endowment or memorial funds

- general appeals or mail shots

- political organisations

- student bodies (as opposed to universities)

- fee-paying schools (apart from an educational
  grants scheme for children who are at, or need
  to attend, a Scottish independent secondary
  school and for which a grant application is
  made through the headteacher)

- expeditions

- retrospective grants

- departments within a university (unless the
  appeal gains the support of, and is channelled
  through, the principal).

Applications The application form and full
guidelines can be downloaded from the website.

Ian Mactaggart Fund

Education & training, culture, welfare and disability

£60,000 (1999)

Beneficial area UK, with a possible
preference for Scotland

63a South Audley Street, London W1K 2QS

Correspondent Ms H Warren

Trustees *Sir John Mactaggart; P A Mactaggart;
R Rogerson Easton Pender; Jane L Mactaggart;
Fiona M Mactaggart; Lady Caroline Mactaggart.*

Inland Revenue no. SC012502

Information available Limited information was
available on this trust.

General The trust supports education and
training, culture, the relief of people who are
poor, sick, in need or disabled. In 1999 the trust
had an income of £410,000 and gave 34 grants
totalling £60,000.

Applications In writing to the correspondent.

W M Mann Foundation

The arts, education, medical research, music

£24,000 (2000/01)

Beneficial area Scotland

201 Bath Street, Glasgow G2 4HY

Tel. 0141 248 4936 **Fax** 0141 221 2976

Correspondent Bruce M Mann, Trustee

Trustees *W M Mann; B M Mann; A W Mann;
S P Hutcheon.*

Inland Revenue no. SC010111

Information available Full accounts were
provided by the trust.

General Grants are generally given to
organisations based in Scotland or serving the
Scottish community, in the fields of music, arts,
education, medical research and care and so on.

In 2000/01 the trust had assets of £1.7 million and an income of £381,000. This included covenanted income of £306,000. Grants totalled £24,000. The surplus funds were reinvested.

The largest grant was £4,000 to Trades House of Glasgow. Other larger grants of £1,000 to £2,300 included those to City of Glasgow Chorus, East Park Home, Macmillan Cancer Relief and St Margaret's Hospice. There were 21 smaller grants of £50 to £1,000 including those to Ayrshire Hospice Appeal, Children 1st, Garelochhead Primary School and Scottish Down's Syndrome Association.

Applications In writing to the trustees at the address above.

The Marquess of Lothian's Charitable Trust

Christian, welfare

£14,000 (1999/2000)

Beneficial area UK, with some preference for Scotland

Brodies WS, 15 Atholl Crescent, Edinburgh EH3 8HA

Tel. 0131 228 3777

Trustees *Dr Margaret White; Dr V E Hartley Booth; Lady M von Westenholz.*

Inland Revenue no. SC013362

Information available Full accounts were available from the trust.

General The trust's primary aim is to 'assist with the study of Jesus Christ and the putting into practice of his teaching according to the commandments'. It supports the Order of Christian Unity as the main way in which it can fulfil this aim. It also supports other Christian and welfare organisations.

In 1999/2000 it had assets of £544,000 and an income of £16,000. Grants totalling £14,000 were given to 12 organisations and ranged from £500 to £3,000. The largest grant of £3,000 went to the Scottish Order of Christian Unity, with two other

branches also receiving donations. Other large grants went to Elizabeth Fitzroy Homes and St Elizabeth's Centre (both £2,000) with £1,000 each to Barnabas Fund, SPUC Educational Research Trust – The Anna Fund, and Care.

Grants of £500 were also given to five different organisations.

Exclusions Only registered charities are supported.

Applications In writing to the correspondent. However, the trust is fully committed at present and is unable to consider new applications.

The Martin Charitable Trust

General

£75,000 (2000)

Beneficial area Scotland, particularly Glasgow and the West of Scotland

c/o Miller Beckett & Jackson, 190 St Vincent Street, Glasgow G2 5SP

Tel. 0141 204 2833 **Fax** 0141 248 7185

Correspondent Norman A Fyfe, Trustee

Trustees *A C Fyfe; N A Fyfe; G H W Waddell.*

Inland Revenue no. SC028487

Information available Brief information was provided by the trust.

General The trust supports general charitable purposes in Scotland, particularly Glasgow and the West of Scotland. In 2000 it had an income of £69,000 and gave £75,000 in grants.

Exclusions No grants to individuals.

Applications In writing to the correspondent, including up-to-date accounts.

The Nancie Massey Charitable Trust

Education, medical research, the arts, young and older people

£164,000 (1999/2000)

Beneficial area Scotland, particularly Edinburgh and Leith

61 Dublin Street, Edinburgh EH3 6NL

Tel. 0131 558 5800 **Fax** 0131 558 5899

Correspondent J G Morton, Trustee

Trustees *J G Morton; M F Sinclair; Ann Trotman.*

Inland Revenue no. SC008977

Information available Information was provided by the trust.

General The trust was established in 1989 to help organisations supporting older people, young people, medical research, education and the arts. Assistance is primarily given to projects established in the Edinburgh and Leith areas. The trustees state they have considered accumulating part of the income to make a large donation to one project but, to date, have not identified a suitable project.

'Donations generally range from £500 to £2,000, larger donations may be made on the basis that the trustees may wish to verify how the donation has been spent.'

In 1999/2000 the trust had assets of £5 million and gave grants totalling £164,000 from an income of £180,000. The grants list only noted those beneficiaries which received donations exceeding 2% of the gross income of the trust (i.e. £3,600). Nine beneficiaries were listed, of which four had also received support the previous year. The largest grants went to The Donaldson's Development Project (£25,000) and Royal Zoological Society of Scotland (£20,000). Seven grants of £5,000 were given, to Age Concern – Edinburgh and Lothian, Edinburgh Macmillan Cancer Relief, The Drama Practice, Queen's Hall, RSPCC, St Mary's Cathedral Workshop Ltd and Sue Ryder Foundation.

Exclusions Grants are not given to individuals.

Applications Write to the correspondent requesting an application form. Trustees meet three times a year in February, June and October. Applications need to be received by January, May or September.

The Mathew Trust

General

£229,000 to organisations (1999/2000)

Beneficial area Dundee and district

Henderson Logie, Royal Exchange, Panmure Street, Dundee DD1 1DZ

Tel. 01382 201234

Correspondent Fiona Bullions

Trustees *D B Grant, Chair; Lord Provost of Dundee; G S Lowden; A F McDonald.*

Inland Revenue no. SC016284

Information available Full accounts were provided by the trust.

General The trust makes grants and loans for:

- the advancement of the education of adults in the following local government areas: City of Dundee, Angus, Perth and Kinross, and Fife

- the advancement of the vocational and professional training of such people

- the relief of poverty by providing assistance in the recruitment of such people who are unemployed, or who are likely to become unemployed in the near future.

In 1999/2000 grants totalled £243,000, much higher than in 1998/1999 when the total was £122,000. Grants to organisations totalled £229,000. Assets stood at £7 million at the end of the period, and the income for the year was £197,000. The trust lists those grants of £5,000 or more in its accounts. In 1999/2000 there were 14 such grants. The major beneficiary was Dundee Repertory Theatre which received a £50,000 capital grant and a £25,000 revenue grant. Other beneficiaries included NineWells Cancer Campaign (£25,000), Dundee College 'The Space' Theatre Project (£20,000), Dundee Heritage Trust (£15,000) and Dundee Science

Centre (£13,000). Grants to 28 individuals totalled £14,000 and ranged from £300 to £1,700.

The trust had grant commitments amounting to £356,000 at April 2000, of which £185,000 was marked as conditional.

Applications Contact the correspondent at the above address.

Gwen Mayor Memorial Trust

Primary schools

About £6,000

Beneficial area Scotland

46 Moray Place, Edinburgh EH3 6BH

Tel. 0131 225 6244 **Fax** 0131 220 3151

Correspondent The Secretary

Trustees *President, vice-president and past president of the Educational Institute of Scotland; Mrs Claire McLeod; Mrs Esther Proctor.*

Inland Revenue no. SC025852

Information available Brief information was supplied by the trust.

General The trust gives donations to primary schools and 'departments' in Scotland for projects in the area of the arts, culture, music and sport. It gives a maximum of £750 to a single project.

Exclusions Projects which cost in excess of £2,000 will not be supported.

Applications Applications to be made by 30 September via schools. Each primary school in Scotland is sent information on the trust.

The Meyer Oppenheim Trust

Jewish organisations, arts, education, social welfare

£4,500 (2001)

Beneficial area UK, but mainly Scotland

c/o KPMG, 24 Blythswood Square, Glasgow G2 4QS

Tel. 0141 226 5511

Trustees *P Oppenheim; Mrs E Quornburg; Management Trust Company.*

Inland Revenue no. SC004976

Information available Information was supplied by the trust.

General The trust supports the arts, Jewish organisations, education and social welfare. In 2001 the trust made grants totalling £4,500. Beneficiaries included Barnardos, Salvation Army, Nightingales, Jewish Care Scotland, Jewish Child Day and Applied Arts Scotland. In 1999 it had an income of £10,000, no grants were made during that year.

Applications In writing to the correspondent.

The Mickel Fund

General

£50,000 (1998)

Beneficial area UK, with a preference for Scotland

126 West Regent Street, Glasgow G2 2BH

Tel. 0141 332 0001 **Fax** 0141 248 4921

Correspondent A Smith

Trustees *J C Craig; D A Mickel; B G A Mickel; A Smith; A L Bassi*

Inland Revenue no. SC003266

Information available Information was provided by the trust.

General In 2001 the trust had an income of £75,000 to be allocated in grants. Unfortunately we were unable to obtain further recent information. The fund awards grants for general charitable purposes and grants typically range between £100 and £500, although larger amounts to a maximum of £10,000 are considered. Grants totalled £50,000 in 1998, but no information on recipients of support was available since that for 1993/94. In that year grants totalled £33,000, including support to British Red Cross, East Park Home, Edinburgh and Leith Old People's Welfare Committee, Edinburgh Youth Orchestra, Ewan Marwick Memorial Trust, and The Reservce Forces Ulysses Trust.

Exclusions Unsolicited applications from individuals will not be acknowledged.

Applications In writing to the correspondent.

The Miller Foundation

General, animal welfare

£161,000 (1999)

Beneficial area UK, with a preference for Scotland, especially the West of Scotland

c/o Maclay Murray & Spens,
151 St Vincent Street, Glasgow G2 5NJ

Tel. 0141 248 5011 **Fax** 0141 248 5819

Correspondent A Biggart, Secretary to the Foundation

Trustees *C Fleming-Brown; C C Wright; G R G Graham; J Simpson; G F R Fleming-Brown.*

Inland Revenue no. SC008798

Information available Information was provided by the trust.

General The trust supports the following:

- charities in Scotland, especially in the West of Scotland
- UK, animal welfare charities.

It will support a wide range of charities in Scotland. In 1999 grants totalled £161,000 and ranged from £1,000 to £2,000. Several grants were recurrent. Examples of beneficiaries were not available.

Exclusions No grants to individuals.

Applications On a form available from the secretary. Trustees meet twice a year to consider grants in April and November. Applications should be received by the end of March and October respectively.

The Hugh and Mary Miller Bequest Trust

Disability

£85,000 (1999/2000)

Beneficial area Mainly Scotland

Maclay Murray & Spens, 151 St Vincent Street, Glasgow G2 5NJ

Tel. 0141 248 5011 **Fax** 0141 248 5819

e-mail asb@maclaymurray&spens.co.uk

Website www.maclaymurray&spens.co.uk

Correspondent Andrew S Biggart

Trustees *G R G Graham; H C Davidson*

Inland Revenue no. SC014950

Information available Information was provided by the trust.

General The trust supports disability causes with most grants going to organisations rather than individuals. The majority of grants are for £6,000 and given to regular beneficiaries. In 1999/2000 it had an income of £87,000 and gave grants totalling £85,000.

Exclusions Only registered charities are supported.

Applications In writing to the correspondent. Trustees meet in spring and autumn to consider grants; applications should be received by March and October respectively.

The Mitchell Trust
(*also known as* Mrs M A Lascelles' Charitable Trust)

General

£53,000 (1999/2000)

Beneficial area Scotland and the developing world

c/o Pagan Osborne, 12 St Catherine Street, Cupar KY15 4HN

Tel. 01334 653777 **Fax** 01334 655063

Correspondent Mrs M A Lascelles, Trustee

Trustees *Mrs M A Lascelles; C W Pagan.*

Inland Revenue no. SC003495

Information available Accounts were provided by the trust at a cost of £10.

General The accounts of this trust are in the name of Mrs M A Lascelles' Charitable Trust, but publicly it is known as The Mitchell Trust. The trust gives for general charitable purposes to recognised Scottish charities.

In 1999/2000 it had assets totalling £1.7 million and an income of £86,000. Grants totalled £53,000, including £4,900 to Scottish Youth Dance Festival. 99 other grants were made of which 14 were for £1,000 or more. The largest went to SITA (£4,000), Seer Centre (three grants totalling £4,000), Intermediate Technology (£1,300) and Oxfam (£1,200). Recipients of £1,000 were British Red Cross, Byre Theatre, Kirkmichael, Straloch & Glenshee Church, Marie Stopes International and Children 1st. Smaller grants were given to a range of charities in Scotland and to organisations working in developing countries.

Exclusions Only recognised Scottish charities are supported.

Applications In writing to the correspondent. Applications should be received by 30 April and 31 October .

Monamy Trust

See below

nil but see below (2000/01)

Beneficial area Principally, but not exclusively, Scotland

The Courtyard, 130 Constitution Street, Leith, Edinburgh EH6 6AJ

Tel. 0131 553 6848 **Fax** 0131 553 4813

e-mail ndk.ltd@ukgateway.net

Correspondent J Norman, Trustee

Trustees *John Norman; Jack Kerr; Richard Burrell; David Tippett.*

Inland Revenue no. SC024267

Information available Accounts were provided by the trust.

General The objects of the trust are:

- alleviation of poverty generally, and among homeless and unemployed people

- research into the causes of poverty

- conservation and protection of the environment

- promotion of good race relations

- alleviation and care for those with disability or infirmity

- rehabilitation of former prisoners and relief of stress among prisoners' families.

Grants are only given to constituted groups and organisations and are to a maximum of £500 each. In 2000/01 it had assets of £160,000, which generated an income of £7,600. No grants were given during the year. The trust informed us that grants would be 'getting underway on a regular basis' in 2001/02, and the accounts for 2000/01 did not show a typical year for grantmaking, but were relevant for the income.

Exclusions No grants to individuals.

Applications On a form available from the administrator at the trust's address. The trustees meet in March and September to award grants; applications must arrive by the end of February and August.

The J P Morgan Fleming Educational Trust

(*formerly* Save & Prosper Educational Trust)

Education

£957,000 (1999/2000)

Beneficial area UK, with a special interest in Islington, outer parts of east London/Essex, and a specific budget for work in Scotland

Finsbury Dials, 20 Finsbury Street, London EC2Y 9AY

Tel. 020 7742 6332

Correspondent Duncan Grant, Director

Trustees *J P Morgan Fleming Ltd, who have appointed the following Managing Committee: C J Rye, Chair; M L Bassett; S Dyer; D Grant.*

Inland Revenue no. 325103

Information available Excellent annual report and accounts. A good guidance leaflet for applicants.

General Formerly Save and Prosper Educational Trust, this trust is now part of the J P Morgan Fleming Asset Management. Originally founded in 1974. It was established as part of a tax-avoiding school fees planning service. Further recruitment of parents into the scheme has been stopped by the Inland Revenue and the corresponding income for this trust will diminish to zero by the year 2014.

However, another charity, the J P Morgan Fleming Foundation (formerly Save & Prosper Foundation), is being built up as the old one declines.

In 1999/2000 the Educational Trust had assets of £274,000 and an income of £918,000. Grants totalled £759,000, including £200,000 to the Foundation. The Foundation had assets of almost £4 million and an income of £349,000. This included the £200,000 from the Educational Trust. Grants totalled £198,000. Support is for UK-based educational projects, with an emphasis on special needs, which generally fit into one of the following categories:

- special needs education including youngsters disadvantaged by disability, background or lack of opportunity
- giving something back to the community by way of children's projects that offer education and training that widen the opportunities for youngsters, particularly those children who are in trouble or 'at risk'
- primary and secondary schools, universities and museums
- supporting school age children and students in all art forms, helping them to gain access to the arts and to better appreciate them
- generally, it does not give support direct to individuals but some scholarships and bursaries are made to organisations supporting educational fees and maintenance
- new and innovative ways of advancing education in the UK.

J P Morgan Fleming Foundation has a modest unrestricted portion of its budget that is generally used for donations to children's charities.

Within these guidelines consideration will focus on projects dealing with:

- drugs and education
- homelessness and education
- literacy and numeracy.

Applications are welcome from throughout the UK but the main focal areas are areas of Scotland, and also Islington and Romford. Some consideration will be given to 'core cost' funding.

About £50,000 was distributed in grants in Scotland during 1999/2000, possibly more, as grants may have been awarded to local branches of UK charities in Scotland.

'In recent years, we have provided educational grants which have ranged in size from £100 to £10,000. Usually, we fund a project for no more than two years. This means we can support a variety of different projects and that we do not face long term commitments. In a few cases, however, we agree to review funding annually.

'We find it useful to have regular reviews of projects that we support. For example, we sometimes ask for written reports or for a questionnaire to be completed, and for larger levels of funding we arrange review visits.'

The following list of beneficiaries are taken from the annual reports of Save and Prosper Educational Trust (SPET) and the Save and Prosper Foundation (SPF). The source of the grant is indicated in brackets.

Beneficiaries in Scotland include: University of Dundee to fund the chair of Scottish Art, and YouthLink Scotland to fund training and equipment costs for youth projects in Glasgow, Dundee and Edinburgh (£10,000 each SPET); Royal College of Surgeons – Edinburgh (£10,000 SPF); Skill in Scotland (£5,000 SPF) to fund training for a development officer working with disabled students; Royal Scottish National Orchestra (£3,000 SPET) for education outreach work; Scottish Society for Autistic Children for computer equipment and Abbey View Women's Centre – Dunfermline for literacy and numeracy resources (£2,500 each SPET); Edinburgh Puppet Company (£1,000 SPET) to fund schools workshops; University of Paisley and Dumfries and Galloway College (£750 each SPF); Edinburgh Greenbelt Trust (£600 SPET) to fund braille and tactile visitors guides; Glasgow City Council and Scottish European Educational Trust for the annual euroquiz for schools (£500 each SPET); and Edinburgh University Children's Holiday Venture (£250 SPET) to fund educational outings.

Exclusions Projects not usually supported include:

- open appeals from national charities
- building appeals
- charity gala nights and similar events
- anniversary appeals
- appeals by individuals for study grants, travel scholarships or charity sponsorships.

Applications To apply for funding please write a brief letter (not more than two sides of A4) to Duncan Grant, the director. Please set out your reasons for applying and enclose any relevant publicity material and accounts.

Applications are always acknowledged. 'If your application is unsuccessful, we suggest you wait at least a year before re-applying.' Trustees meet in March, May, July, September and December. Applications need to arrive at least a month before the relevant meeting.

The Stanley Morrison Charitable Trust

Education, general, sports for young people

£43,000 (2000)

Beneficial area The west coast of Scotland, with a preference for Glasgow and Ayrshire

O'Connell Consulting, McGregor House, Southbank Business Park, Kirkintilloch, Glasgow G66 1XF

Tel. 0141 578 2252 **Fax** 0141 578 2248

e-mail tom@oconnell-consulting.com

Correspondent Tom O'Connell

Trustees *S W Morrison; J H McKean; Mrs M E Morrison; T F O'Connell; G L Taylor; A S Dudgeon.*

Inland Revenue no. SC006610

Information available Information was provided by the trust.

General The trust states that grants are awarded to:

- sporting activites in Scotland, with particular emphasis on the encouragement of youth involvement
- charities which have as their principal base of operation and benefit the west coast of Scotland, and in particular the Glasgow and Ayrshire areas.
- those charities whose funds arise from or whose assistance is provided to people having connection with the licensed trades and in particular the whisky industry.
- scottish educational establishments.

There is also a preference for organisations known to the trustees.

In 2000 it had assets of £2 million and an income of £81,000. Grants totalled £43,000 and ranged from £100 to £8,000. Beneficiaries included Princess Royal Trust for Carers, Scottish Cricket Union, Save the Children and Scottish School Badminton Union.

Applications In writing to the correspondent. Applicants should include details on the purpose of the grant, what funding has already been secured and the actual sum that they are looking for.

The Morton Charitable Trust

General
About £70,000

Beneficial area Scotland

Turcan Connell, Princes Exchange, 1 Earl Grey Street, Edinburgh EH3 9EE

Tel. 0131 228 8111 **Fax** 0131 228 8118

Inland Revenue no. SC004507

Information available This trust is one of 10, probably all small, trusts administered by Turcan Connell. The company would not provide us with any information on these trusts, only agreeing to send each trust's accounts for the cost of £20 each. We did not think this was reasonable for such small trusts.

General This trust gives about £70,000 each year to charitable organisations at the trustees' discretion. Unfortunately, no further information was available on the size or number of grants made, or beneficiaries.

Applications In writing to the correspondent.

The Mugdock Children's Trust

Children up to the age of about 14 who are ill or disabled

£40,000 (1999/2000)

Beneficial area Scotland

135 Wellington Street, Glasgow G2 2XE

Tel. 0141 248 3904 **Fax** 0141 226 5047

Correspondent L J McIntyre

Trustees *Rosamund Blair; Joyce Duguid; Anne Leask; Avril Meighan; G M Philips; A J Struthers; Moira Bruce.*

Inland Revenue no. SC006001

Information available Full accounts and further information was supplied by the trust.

General The trust makes grants for the welfare of children up to the age of about 14 within the following categories:

- poor children from Glasgow or other districts of Scotland who are in need of convalescent treatment for sickness or any other disability

- organisations of a charitable nature whose objects either consist of or include the provision in Scotland of rehabilitation, recreation or education for children convalescing or still suffering from the effects of illness, injury or disability

- organisations of a charitable nature whose objects either consist of or include the provision in Scotland of accommodation or facilities for children who are in need of care or assistance.

It tends to support organisations rather than individuals. In 1999/2000, the trust had assets of £540,000 and an income of £47,000. Grants totalled £40,000 and were divided as follows:

Charities regularly supported without specific application
Nine grants, ranging from £1,000 to £8,000 were given, totalling £25,000. Examples include Camphill Centres, Riding for the Disabled, St Mungo Group and Salvation Army.

Charities sent application forms without request
Five grants were given ranging from £300 to
£2,000. Beneficiaries were Boys' Brigade, Sighthill
Youth Centre, Boys and Girls Club of Scotland
and the Epilepsy Association, all for general
purposes, and Stepping Stones in Scotland for
physical play equipment.

Other applications
12 grants of £500 to £3,000 were given totalling
£10,000. These included £3,000 to Sargent Cancer
Care for Children towards Link House extension
project, £1,000 each to Edinburgh Family Service
Unit for work with children in Pilton and
Muirhouse, Ochil Tower School towards a
replacement minibus and Visual Impairment
Services towards equipment for a music
workshop, £750 to Sense for playdays for
children.

Applications On a form available from the
correspondent. Trustees meet in March and
November.

Murdoch Trust
(*formerly* Euroscot Trust)

Christian religion
See below

Beneficial area Scotland

c/o Cook and Co., Suite 536, Baltic Chambers,
50 Wellington Street, Glasgow G2 6HJ

Tel. 0141 226 4100

Correspondent Mr Cunningham

Inland Revenue no. SC007591

Information available Limited information was
available on this trust.

General This trust gives funds to Christian
organisations and serves to promote the Christian
religion. It contributes to existing Christian
charities, responds to disaster appeals, supports
ministers and missionaries, supports the
production of literature and the teaching of
Christianity. Unfortunately, no further
information was available on the amount given
each year or beneficiaries.

Applications The trust states that unsolicited
applications are not welcome as all funds are
committed.

The James & Elizabeth Murray Charitable Trust

General
About £1,500 a year

Beneficial area Scotland, but mostly
Aberdeenshire

c/o Adam Cochran & Co.,
6 Bonn-Accord Square, Aberdeen AB11 6XU

Correspondent The Trustees

Trustees *Mrs G Murray; D G Morgan.*

Inland Revenue no. SC012263

Information available Information was provided
by the trust.

General This is a relatively small trust.
It receives about 50 applications a year, although
it only gives three grants each year totalling
£1,500. Previous beneficiaries have included
Aberdeen Hospitals Relay Association, Grampian
Tape Services for the Blind, Salvation Army and
Voluntary Services Aberdeen Fuel Fund.

Applications The trust is receiving far too
many appeals for the small number of grants
available and can no longer consider unsolicited
applications.

Mrs Jean Murray's Charitable Trust

General
About £15,000 a year

Beneficial area Scotland

Messrs Mitchells Roberton, George House,
36 North Hanover Street, Glasgow G1 2AD

Tel. 0141 552 3422 **Fax** 0141 552 2935

e-mail jamc@mitchells-robertson.co.uk

Correspondent J A M Cuthbert, Trustee

Trustees *J A M Cuthbert; D A R Ballantyne; Revd P D Thomson; Mrs A D S Bell.*

Inland Revenue no. SC020144

Information available Information was provided by the trust.

General This trust gives about £15,000 each year for general charitable purposes.

Applications In writing to the correspondent.

The Bill and Margaret Nicol Charitable Trust

General

£6,000 (1997)

Beneficial area Scotland

Messrs MacRoberts, 152 Bath Street, Glasgow G2 4TB

Tel. 0141 332 9988 **Fax** 0141 332 8886

Correspondent David MacRobert

Information available Limited information was available from the trust.

General In 1997 the trust had an income of £7,000 and gave grants totalling £6,000. It supports a wide variety of organisations in Scotland.

Applications Unsolicited applications are unlikely to be successful.

Noble Resolve Gospel and Temperance Mission Auxiliary

Temperance movement, religion, welfare

£18,000 (2000/01)

Beneficial area Scotland, some preference for Kilmarnock and Ayrshire

c/o 1 Howard Street, Kilmarnock KA1 2BW

Tel. 01563 572727 **Fax** 01563 527901

e-mail ccsandco@aol.com

Correspondent A A Stewart

Inland Revenue no. SC010270

Information available Information was provided by the trust.

General The trust supports the temperance movement, religion and welfare causes. In 2000/01 the trust gave 22 grants totalling £18,000. Grants ranged from £250 to £3,000 with most grants around £500. The same organisations are supported each year. The largest grants went to Ayrshire Council for Alcohol (£3,000), three local schools (£1,500 each) and Church of Scotland Board of Social Responsibility (£1,300). Other grants included those to Ayrshire Echo Association, Ayrshire Society for the Deaf, Barnardos, Buchanan Centre, Kilmarnock Tape Services for the Blind, Quarriers Home, Scottish Spina Bifida, Samaritans and UNICEF. A one-off grant was given to Scottish Council of Alcohol.

Applications Applications are not invited.

The North British Hotel Trust

Welfare, health

£974,000 (2000/01)

Beneficial area UK, but mainly Scotland

1 Queen Charlotte Lane, Edinburgh EH6 6BL

Tel. 0131 554 7173

Correspondent C Leivesley, Secretary to the Council

Trustees *W G Crerar, Chair; I C Fraser.*

Charity Commission no. 221335

Information available Perfunctory annual report, accounts, uncategorised grants list.

General The trust makes over 50 grants a year. Giving is concentrated in areas where the North British Trust Hotels company operates (a holding of shares in that company constitutes the charity's endowment). It is possible that the trust operates as the recipient of applications addressed to the company's hotels. There are over 20 such hotels in Scotland, covering much of the country. There are also four hotels in England, with grants being made close to those in Scarborough, Harrogate and Barnby Moor in Yorkshire, and Eastbourne in East Sussex.

Most identifiable grants are for welfare purposes, especially those benefiting older or disabled people, or for health.

In 2000/01 its assets totalled £6 million and its income was £559,000. Grants totalled £974,000.

Beneficiaries of larger grants were Samaritans, Inverness (£23,000), Old People's Associations (£18,000), Scottish Chamber Orchestra (£15,000), Couple Counselling – Scotland, Duke of Edinburgh Award Scheme, Friends of Warrender Baths – Edinburgh and The New School, Butterstone (£10,000 each), Lomond Mountain Rescue (£7,600), Council for Music in Hospitals (£6,900) and Grantown Youth Project and Guide Dogs for the Blind (£6,000 each). The smallest grant was for £500.

The trust has funded 'homes from home' in both Edinburgh and Glasgow for CLIC (Cancer and Leukaemia in Childhood) for major programmes. In 2000/01 the programmes were nearing completion and grants were £20,000 and £405,000 respectively. Another major award, of £320,000, was made to Argyll and Clyde Acute Hospitals NHS Trust.

Applications In writing to the correspondent.

The Northern Rock Foundation

Disadvantaged people

£11 million (2001)

Beneficial area North east of England, also Scotland, Cumbria, Yorkshire and north west England under certain programmes

21 Lansdowne Terrace, Gosforth, Newcastle upon Tyne NE3 1HP

Tel. 0191 284 8412 **Fax** 0191 284 8413

Minicom 0191 284 5411

e-mail generaloffice@nr-foundation.org.uk

Website www.nr-foundation.org.uk

Correspondent The Grants Manager

Trustees *P R M Harbottle, Chair; D F Baker; David Faulkner; L P Finn; Lord Howick of Glendale; Frank Nicholson; Lady Russell; Julie Shipley; J P Wainwright; John Ward.*

Charity Commission no. 1063906

Information available Excellent report, accounts, guidelines and application forms were provided by the trust.

General The aim of the foundation is to help those who are disadvantaged in society, mainly, but not exclusively, in the north east of England. No grants are made for work south of Yorkshire or the Manchester area, or in Wales or Northern Ireland, but work in Scotland is supported.

The foundation gets its income under a covenant from Northern Rock plc, which transfers five per cent of its pre-tax profits to the foundation each year.

Grants may be made for limited capital, core or project funding and for varying periods of time. Support from other funders 'helps establish confidence in your project'. In 2001 grants totalled £11 million. It operated 15 grant-making programmes, some of which only give in the core region of Durham, Northumberland and Tyne and Wear. (For information on these see *A Guide to the Major Trusts Volume One.*) The grant programmes including Scotland are:

Helping the very young (£768,000 in 35 grants) The foundation welcomes imaginative proposals which enable young people aged 0 to 7 to have the best and fairest start in life. Particular areas of interest include:

- projects helping mothers-to-be and new parents to understand how to care for themselves and their children

- the effects on children of parental problems, including separation, refuge from domestic violence, refugees, substance abuse and bereavement

- initiatives which promote health and safety of the very young, combat physical and sexual abuse and help children who have been abused

- projects which give children access to a full creative and cultural life including physical development through sport and active play as well as encouraging children to make their own decisions and make their voices heard.

Grants average £20,000. No support is given to projects that can achieve their objectives using local or central governmental resources. This programme is intended to meet the needs of all children. Projects addressing the needs of children who are disabled, for example, should apply through the disability programme outlined above.

In 2001 Scottish beneficiaries included Family Mediation Scotland for a coordinator (£50,000 over three years), Grandparent Support Group for respite and training courses for people in Glasgow who are caring for their grandchildren as a result of drug misuse within the family (£19,000 over two years), Scottish Committee for the 100 Languages of Children Exhibition for an outreach programme (£10,000).

Grants to small organisations
(£177,000 in 30 grants)
This programme offers grants of up to £10,000 to smaller organisations with an income of under £25,000 a year who work in the area of disadvantage. Support is given for core costs, projects and capital purposes, making it wide-ranging and flexible. The idea is to offer grants to smaller organisations which do not have the time or expertise for major fundraising, and to introduce their staff to applying to trusts in as friendly and accessible way as possible. The trust has an application form for these grants which is intended to simplify the procedure and attract more applicants. Organisations do not need to be registered but most have a legal framework and

a charitable purpose if unregistered (for these organisations the grant will be paid through a registered charity such as a CVS).

Beneficiaries included Cruse Bereavement Care for volunteer training (£10,000), Elswick Community Minibus for office equipment and running costs (£5,700) and Argyll Couple Counselling Service towards the development, training and supervision of relationship councillors (£3,000).

Community training awards
(£21,000 in 6 grants)
This programme is more proactive than reactive, giving grants towards staff training and development where the trust's grant assessors believe some introspection will benefit the organisation. Recipients included Need a Listening Ear for a consultant to produce a development plan (£1,000).

Creative communities: the arts in social
regeneration (£467,000 in 41 grants)
The trustees launched this programme in 2000. It was created to encourage the use of the arts and skills of artists in helping communities to grow and develop. The foundation believes that 'involvement in the arts can impact upon a community in real and positive ways'. Through this arts-based programme it supports projects working to: help people to deal with change and loss; instil confidence and self-worth; promote understanding between different people and groups; support communities; and improve health. Likely causes to be supported include:

- projects combating crime and social exclusion

- projects giving confidence and skills to unemployed people

- creative work with prisoners

- work by artists with youth groups, in factories or other workplaces

- projects involving the arts in health

- creative approaches to literacy teaching

- helping people on low incomes to enjoy the arts as a cultural right.

Arts-related beneficiaries included Northern Recording for a community music project in County Durham (£70,000), Ashton Group Contemporary Theatre for a programme leading to the production of 25 community plays in Barrow-in-Furness (£40,000) and Triangle

Residents Association for artists to work with residents on a deprived housing estate (£7,000).

Outside-in (£127,000 in 10 grants)

This programme aims to tackle overt and concealed discrimination of gay men and lesbians, from open violence to more subtle harassment, by helping organisations which try to educate the public and deal with the consequences of discrimination. Projects most likely to succeed are those which deal with:

- supporting vulnerable gays and lesbians in, for example, housing and homelessness
- combating violence and bullying at home, school, work etc.
- prevention or treatment of alcohol and drug misuse
- promotion of safe sexual behaviour
- mental health advice
- supporting families of gay people.

Beneficiaries included Borders Gay Lesbian and Transgender Youth Group for a development worker (£43,000).

Staff-matched funding (£165,000)

The trust matches all funds given by employees of Northern Rock plc to organisations.

In 2000 the trust had an income of £25 million. This was unusually high due to the trust being able to sell back to Northern Rock plc £4 million of their shares of no market value, generating £12 million. Total expenditure was £10 million (including just £340,000 in management and administration fees), after which £15 million was transferred to assets. It gave grants totalling £9.5 million, broken down as follows:

	No.	Success rate	Amount	% of total
Cleveland/Teesside	21	57%	£454,000	5%
Durham	39	53%	£676,000	7%
national	1	50%	£5,000	–
north east region	24	73%	£1,051,000	11%
north west	35	54%	£610,000	6%
northern region	13	65%	£1,532,000	16%
Northumberland	15	47%	£511,000	5%
Scotland	20	47%	£307,000	3%
Tyne & Wear	99	59%	£3,804,000	41%
Yorkshire	34	60%	£560,000	6%
total	301	51%	£9,511,000	100%

Exclusions Applications for local projects outside the north east of England, Cumbria, Yorkshire and the north west of England and Scotland will not be considered, nor:

- organisations which are not registered charities or which do not have purposes recognised as charitable in UK law
- charities which trade, have substantial reserves (normally over 50% of annual running costs in unrestricted reserves) or are in serious deficit
- national charities which do not have a regional office or other representation in the north east of England
- grant-making bodies seeking to distribute grants on the foundation's behalf
- open-ended funding agreements
- general appeals, sponsorship and marketing appeals
- corporate applications for founder membership of a charity
- loan or business finance
- retrospective grants
- endowment funds
- replacement of statutory funding
- activities primarily the responsibility of central or local government or health authorities
- individuals and organisations that distribute funds to individuals
- animal welfare
- mainstream educational activity
- medical research, hospitals and medical centres
- environmental projects which do not accord with the main objectives of the foundation
- fabric appeals for places of worship
- promotion of religion
- expeditions or overseas travel
- minibuses and other vehicles
- holidays and outings.

The foundation is unlikely to make

- An unbroken series of grants to the same organisation. You should leave a gap of at least six months from the date on which you submitted your final report.

- Numerous grants which incorporate an element of core costs to the same organisation.

- If your application is turned down you cannot reapply for the same purpose unless your rejection letter explicitly tells you that you can and under what circumstances.

- You should not normally have more than one grant from the foundation at a time. Once your grant has expired i.e. it has been used for the term and purpose for which it was given, and you have reported as requested, you may apply again six months later.

- It may occasionally be possible to extend core or project funding for an organisation that has received a grant over several years. You should discuss this with your grants officer before your grant expires. Such extensions will be rare: you should start looking for new sources as soon as you receive a grant from the foundation.

Applications Applications must be made on the foundation's two page application form. This comes with full instructions and guidance. In brief, the form will have to be accompanied by:

- brief supporting statement (not more than two pages)

- current budget and recent management accounts

- most recent annual report and accounts (or equivalent for very small organisations)

- the 'objects' and 'dissolution' parts of your constitution

- your budget for the project, how much you are asking for and how you hope to get the rest.

The brief supporting statement needs to cover:

- your organisation and its qualifications for taking on this project

- the need for the project, its importance, scale and urgency

- what you plan to do and how

- the level of user involvement at all stages

- how you will measure its success and learn from your experience, if appropriate

- the timetable for the project

- how, if appropriate, you would continue when a grant expires.

Information should be accurate and comprehensive. If something essential is missing the foundation will ask you to supply it and therefore the processing of your application will be delayed. Your application will be acknowledged and the foundation will let you know straight away if it is ineligible. If it is eligible, you will be told which staff member will assess it. There should normally be a response within four months (for the small organisations scheme, two months).

'Please remember that all foundations receive many more requests than they can help. Undoubtedly we will have to turn down many good applications.'

The Northwood Charitable Trust

Health, general

£924,000 (1999)

Beneficial area Scotland, especially Dundee and Tayside

22 Meadowside, Dundee DD1 1LN

Tel. 01382 201534

Correspondent The Secretary

Trustees *B H Thomson; D B Thomson; A F Thomson; Prof. A J McDonald; A McDougall.*

Inland Revenue no. SC014487

Information available There was no response to a request for a copy of the charity's annual report and accounts (despite the statutory requirement to the contrary).

General This trust is connected to the D C Thomson Charitable Trust, DC Thomson & Company and the Thomson family. It was established by Eric V Thomson in 1972 and has received additional funding from other members of the Thomson family. It has general charitable purposes, with preferences for universities and medical and educational projects.

In 1999 it had assets of £15 million and an income of £1.3 million. Grants totalled £94,000.

University of Dundee received three large grants, £94,000 for the department of Psychiatry and

£50,000 each for mollecular and cellular pathology and its biomedical research centre. Other large grants were £60,000 to Macmillan Cancer Relief for its Roxburghe House project and £54,000 to Tayside Institute of Child Health.

Applications The trust's funds are fully committed and it states that no applications will be considered or acknowledged. The trust did not wish to appear in this guide and did not confirm the address.

Novum Trust

Church of Scotland

About £17,000 (2000/01)

Beneficial area UK and overseas, with a preference for Scotland

Department of National Mission, Church of Scotland Offices, 121 George Street, Edinburgh EH2 4YN

Tel. 0131 225 5722 **Fax** 0131 226 6121

e-mail amillar@cofscotland.org.uk

Correspondent Revd Alex M Millar, Secretary Depute

Inland Revenue no. SC021277

Information available Information and guidelines for applicants were provided by the trust.

General 'The Novum trust provides small short-term grants to initiate projects in Christian research and action which cannot be readily financed from other sources. Special consideration is given to proposals aimed at the welfare of young people, the training of lay people, and new ways of communicating the faith.'

Examples of areas the trust are likely to support include:

- research into and application of ideas for the maintenance and improvement of the spiritual and moral welfare of young people in the United Kingdom

- research into and application of new methods and improvements in existing methods of communicating the Christian message

- work in association with overseas churches or on behalf of immigrants in Scotland

- Christian education and training for ministers and laymen of the Scottish churches.

At the May 2001 trustee's meeting seven grants were approved totalling £8,600.

Beneficiaries have included Hillington Park Parish Church – Glasgow for the employment of a new youth worker (£1,000), Kepplewray Project towards a mini-bus and sports equipment (£750), RAF Chaplaincy for multi-media equipment (£700) and The Well – Asian Information and Advice Centre – Glasgow for a bible correspondence course in Urdu (£300).

Exclusions 'It is not intended that the trust should simply supplement funds already available from church or state resources. Primarily it is intended that the trust should provide funds for projects that cannot readily be financed from other sources. If such projects after a year or two still need money, this would normally be obtained elsewhere; the Novum Trust would by then have "primed the pump" and allow a new enterprise the chance to prove itself.'

Applications On a form available from the applications secretary, or by e-mail from the trust. The trustees meet twice a year, applications should arrive by 1 April for the May meeting and 1 October for the November meeting.

Ochil Trust

School pupils, general

About £100,000 a year

Beneficial area UK

Strathallan School, Forgandenny, Perth PH2 9EG

Tel. 01738 812504 **Fax** 01738 813269

Correspondent Maj. Keith George Legge, Secretary

Inland Revenue no. SC026991

Information available Information was provided by the trust.

General The trust makes grants primarily in the form of bursaries or scholarships to pupils and prospective pupils of Strathallan School. Grants are also made to charitable organisations, for a wide range of purposes. Grants total about £100,000 a year.

Applications On a form available from the correspondent.

The Harold Oppenheim Charitable Trust

General

£16,000 (1999/2000)

Beneficial area Unrestricted

16 Rutland Square, Edinburgh EH1 2BB

Tel. 0131 229 8751

Correspondent Miss Linda Millar, Secretary to the Trustees

Trustees *Mrs E M Oppenheim Sandelson; Mrs J P Prevezer; Mrs R S Bello; Mrs F L Arghebant.*

Inland Revenue no. SC008028

Information available Accounts were available from the trust.

General It has been a policy of the trust to support charities known personally to the trustees and whose charitable activities the trustees admire and consider worthy of support. In 1999/2000 the trust had assets of £222,000 and an income of £11,000. It gave grants totalling £16,000 to University of Edinburgh (£6,000), West London Synagogue (£5,000), St Columba's Hospice (£2,000), Macmillan Cancer Relief (£2000), and the Children's Hospice Association Scotland (£1,000).

Exclusions None.

Applications In writing to the correspondent but note the above.

Orrin Charitable Trust

General

£47,000 (1999/2000)

Beneficial area Mainly Scotland

c/o Hedley Foundation Limited, 9 Dowgate Hill, London EC4R 2SU

Tel. 020 7489 8076

Correspondent The Secretary

Trustees *Mrs E V MacDonald-Buchanan; J MacDonald-Buchanan; H MacDonald-Buchanan.*

Charity Commission no. 274599

Information available Full accounts were on file at the Charity Commission.

General The trust makes grants mainly to Scottish organisations, although certain charities elsewhere in the UK may be supported. Beneficaries include conservation charities, galleries, hospitals and community projects. The trust tends to mainly support organisations known to the trustees rather than supporting unsolicited applications.

In 1999/2000 it had assets of £582,000 and an income of £45,000. Grants ranged from £250 to £13,000 each and totalled £47,000.

Beneficiaries included Wester Ross Fishing Trust (£13,000), National Galleries of Scotland (£8,000), Highland Hospice (£4,000), and Macmillan Cancer Relief Scotland and National Trust for Scotland (£2,000 each).

Exclusions Grants are not given overseas or to individuals.

Applications In writing to the correspondent for consideration at meetings twice a year, but note the comments above.

Mrs M E S Paterson's Charitable Trust

Church of Scotland, young people, general

£35,000 (2001)

Beneficial area Scotland

Lindsays Solicitors, 11 Atholl Crescent,
Edinburgh EH3 8HE

Tel. 0131 477 8721

Correspondent Callam S Kennedy

Inland Revenue no. SC004835

Information available Information was provided
by the trust.

General The trust divides its grant total as
follows:

* one-third towards the restoration of churches
* one-third to Church of Scotland
* one-third for general charitable purposes, with
  a preference for young people's organisations.

The largest grants available are for £3,000, but
they usually range from £1,000 to £2,000 each.
In 2001 grants totalled £35,000.

Exclusions No grants to individuals.

Applications In writing to the correspondent.
Trustees meet once a year in July to consider
grants.

Andrew Paton's Charitable Trust

General

£61,000 (1999/2000)

Beneficial area Unrestricted but with
a preference for the West of Scotland

190 St Vincent Street, Glasgow G2 5SP

Tel. 0141 204 2833

Correspondent G A Maguire, Trustee

Trustees *G A Maguire; N A Fyfe; R G Dingwall.*

Inland Revenue no. SC017502

Information available Information was provided
by the trust.

General This trust has general charitable
purposes with a preference for Scotland,
particularly the Glasgow and West of Scotland
area. Among over-represented sectors of the
varied grant list were medical, welfare and
nautical charities.

In 1999/2000 this trust had assets of £1 million
and an income of £44,000. Grants to 81
organisations totalled £61,000.

The largest grants included £5,000 to St Andrew's
Hospice, £4,000 to David Cargill House, £3,000 to
Church of Scotland Mission Aid Fund, £2,000 to
Scottish Motor Neurone Disease Association and
£1,500 to Salvation Army.

There were 15 recipients of £1,000 each. These
included Abbeyfield (Glasgow) Society Ltd,
Children 1st, Glasgow Old People's Welfare
Association, King George's Fund for Sailors,
Sense Scotland and West of Scotland Deaf
Children Society.

Other grants included £750 to MS Society –
Scotland; £500 each to Boys' Brigade Glasgow
Battalion, Ocean Youth Trust Scotland, Paintings
in Hospitals – Scotland, Royal National Mission
to Deep Sea Fishermen, Scottish Adoption
Association, Scottish Committee for the Hundred
Languages of Children, Adam Smith Foundation;
Visual Impairment Services – Scotland; £400 to
West of Scotland Lung Foundation, £250 each to
Glasgow City Mission, Glasgow Semen's Friend
Society, Royal Society for the Relief of Indigent
Gentlewomen of Scotland, Scottish Crusaders,
TOCH Scotland; and £200 to Gartnavel General
Hospital Rheumatology Research.

Applications In writing to the correspondent.

Paw Print Charitable Trust

General

Nil (1999)

Beneficial area Scotland

Turcan Connell, Princes Exchange,
1 Earl Grey Street, Edinburgh EH3 9EE

Tel. 0131 228 8111 **Fax** 0131 228 8118

Correspondent The Trustees

Inland Revenue no. SC025671

Information available This trust is one of 10,
probably all small, trusts administered by Turcan
Connell. The company would not provide us with
any information on these trusts, only agreeing to
send each trust's accounts for the cost of £20

each. We did not think this was reasonable for such small trusts.

General The trust supports a wide variety of charitable causes. In 1999 the trust had both an income and an expenditure of £10,000. No grants were distributed during the year. No further information was available.

Applications In writing to the correspondent.

Penpont Charitable Trust

Medical research, music, visual arts

£1,700 (2000/01)

Beneficial area Scotland

25 Lauder Road, Edinburgh EH9 2JG

Tel. 0131 668 3378 **Fax** 0131 662 4111

e-mail jimcook@nestor15.freeserve.co.uk

Correspondent James Cook, Chair

Trustees *James Cook, Chair; Patricia Cook; Douglas Connell.*

Inland Revenue no. SC023685

Information available Information was provided by the trust.

General Grants are given to organisations working in the areas of music, the visual arts and medical research. The maximum single grant is usually £500. In 2000/01 it gave £1,700 in four grants. These were £500 each, to St Giles Cathedral for an organ recital, Scottish Chamber Orchestra and The Tunnell Trust for young musicians; and £200 to British Federation of Young Choirs.

Exclusions Grants are given to recognised charities only.

Applications In writing to the correspondent.

The Earl of Perth's Charitable Trust

Not known

£5,400 (1998/99)

Beneficial area UK, with a preference for Scotland

Stobhall, Perth PH2 6DR

Tel. 01821 640332

Correspondent Lord Perth

Trustees *Rt Hon. Earl of Perth; Rt Hon. Viscount Strathallan.*

Charity Commission no. 231130

Information available Accounts were on file at the Charity Commission, without a grants list.

General This trust has so far failed to file a grants list with its accounts at the Charity Commission, so we do not know what types of causes it supports.

In 1998/99 the income of the trust was £1,100 from assets of £23,500. Grants totalled £5,400. In the previous year, grants also exceeded income with grants totalling £18,000 and the income only £2,000. Transfers from the capital fund have covered the years' deficits, with corresponding decreases in the remaining assets.

Exclusions No grants to individuals.

Applications In writing to the correspondent. Unsuccessful applications are not acknowledged.

The P F Charitable Trust

General

£130,000 in Scotland (1998/99)

Beneficial area UK, with apparent special interests in Oxfordshire and Scotland

Ely House, 37 Dover Street, London W1S 4NJ

Tel. 020 7409 5600

Correspondent Mrs Val Richards, Secretary, or Geoffrey Fincham

Trustees *Robert Fleming; Valentine P Fleming; Philip Fleming; R D Fleming.*

Charity Commission no. 220124

Information available Inadequate annual report. Accounts listing the 50 largest grants; basic grant information sheet.

General The trust was set up in 1951 by the banker Philip Fleming, and is still run by family members. Its grant-making ability was enhanced considerably in 1983 when the settlor's son, Robert Fleming, made substantial donations to the trust. In 1998/99 the trust had high investment management costs (£41,000) in relation to the low investment income (£1.5 million), and further capital losses of £1.1 million on investment assets of nearly £52 million. Administration costs were also high, at £120,000, partly as a result of a 52% rise in staff salary costs, to £35,000 from £23,000 in the previous year.

It has previously been reported that the trust will provide both core and revenue funding, although it is not keen to support salaries of staff members of organisations. The trust may renew its commitments after the first three years are completed and occasionally makes commitments for up to five years for medical research projects.

The trust has in the past expressed its belief that charities should do more to improve the efficiency of their administration. This is particularly important when the trust makes, for example, a three-year commitment to provide a certain amount each year, because frequently it makes such commitments and after the first year receives letters asking for a repeat donation, when it has already been promised. It also frequently receives more than one letter from the same organisation requesting the same thing, but from different people, and this is something that the trust wishes to avoid.

In 1998/99 the 50 largest grants were listed in the accounts and totalled £711,000. Almost 20% of this went to Scottish organisations totalling £130,000. The proportion to Scotland may in fact have been higher, but it was not possible to determine from the grants list where some of the beneficiaries were located.

The largest grant in Scotland was £51,000 to the Caledonian Foundation (now the Scottish Community Foundation). Others were to University of Dundee (£36,000), Scottish

Churches Architecture Heritage Trust (£15,000), Scottish Division of British Federation of Young Choirs and University of Abertay Dundee Foundation (£10,000 each), Aberdeen City Council (£5,500) and Cornerstone Community Care (£5,000). A wide range of organisations are supported.

Exclusions No grants to individuals or non-registered charities. The trust no longer gives to:

- individual hospices (but instead supports Help the Hospices)
- individual churches (but instead gives grants to the Historic Churches Preservation Trust, Scottish Churches Architectural Heritage Trust and to the Baptist Union Home Missions and Methodist Church Home Missions).

Applications To the correspondent at any time, in writing with full information. Replies will be sent to unsuccessful applications if an sae is enclosed. Trustees meet monthly.

A M Pilkington's Charitable Trust

General

£130,000 (1999/2000)

Beneficial area UK, with a preference for Scotland

Carters, Chartered Accountants, Pentland House, Saltire Centre, Glenrothes, Fife KY6 2AH

Tel. 01592 630555

e-mail cartersca@sol.co.uk

Correspondent G J Carter

Inland Revenue no. SC000282

Information available Information was provided by the trust.

General The trust supports a wide variety of causes in the UK. In practice there is a preference for Scotland and probably half the grants are given in Scotland. In 1999/2000 the trust had assets of £3.1 million and an income of £172,000. It gave grants to 146 charities totalling £130,000. There is a preference for giving recurring grants.

Grants normally range from £500 to £1,500. Details of the beneficiaries were not available.

Exclusions Grants are not given to overseas projects or political appeals.

Applications The trustees state that, regrettably, they are unable to make grants to new applicants since they already have more than enough causes to support.

The Portrack Charitable Trust

General

£23,000 (1999/2000)

Beneficial area Some preference for Scotland

Bank of Butterfield (UK) Ltd, St Helen's, 1 Undershaft, London EC3A 8JX

Tel. 020 7816 8100 **Fax** 020 7816 8206

Correspondent K H Galloway, Trustee

Trustees *Charles Alexander Jencks; Keith Harold Galloway; John Keswick Jencks.*

Charity Commission no. 266120

Information available Full accounts are on file at the Charity Commission.

General In 1999/2000 the trust had assets of £182,000 and an income of £24,000. The trust gave 36 grants totalling £23,000. The largest two grants of £6,000 went to Maggie Jencks Cancer Care Centre. The remaining grants ranged from £200 to £500.

Examples of beneficiaries in Scotland include New School Edinburgh, Roman Catholic Diocese of Galloway – Retired Priests Fund and St Teresa's Church, Dumfries, which received two separate payments. Other beneficiaries included Alzheimer's Disease Society, Breast Cancer Campaign, Holywood Church, Mental Health Foundation and Scope.

Exclusions Grants are not given to individuals.

Applications In writing to the correspondent.

The Priory of Scotland of the Order of St John of Jerusalem

Health, welfare, disability

£314,000 (1999/2000)

Beneficial area Scotland

21 St John Street, Edinburgh EH8 8DG

Tel. 0131 556 8711 **Fax** 0131 558 3250

e-mail scotstj@aol.com

Correspondent Mrs Joan Blair

Inland Revenue no. SC000262

Information available The yearbook was provided by the trust.

General The 2000/01 yearbook stated: 'In its early years, the order provided training in first aid and related subjects in Scotland, as in other parts of the United Kingdom. However, the Scottish-based St Andrew's Ambulance Association existed to undertake identical activities, both in Scotland and England. In 1908 it was agreed that St Andrew's would cease first aid training south of the border and St John north of it.

'In the 1940's, some of its members felt there was scope for the order to undertake a variety of public services in Scotland. In 1947, the Scottish Priory of the Order was formed and since then, from a standing start, it has achieved remarkable success in meeting a wide diversity of need. Over the years the priory has responded to changes of some of these needs brought about by development such as the creation and evolution of the National Health Service. More recently it has extended its support to mountain rescue teams in Scotland through the provision of vehicles and bases and has funded minibuses for other needy organisations. A brief history of the priory of Scotland was published to make its 50th anniversary.

'Today in Scotland the priory provides, amongst other things, a palliative care clinic and unit, sheltered and nursing residential accommodation, and holiday/respite homes for disabled people and their carers. A branch of

St John Cadets provides an outlet for the enthusiasm of its younger members. Also, the priory supports many local initiatives which provide services and supplies for people of all ages who are ill, disabled, infirm or in danger. The Scottish priory has always supported the order's hospital in Jerusalem and currently sponsors its chief executive officer.'

Its objectives were listed as including:

- the encouragement of all that makes for the spiritual and moral strengthening of mankind

- the encouragement and promotion of all work of humanity and charity for the relief of people in sickness, distress, suffering or danger

- the provision of assistance to the St John Eye Hospital in Jerusalem and its clinic and research projects

- the provision and maintenance of nursing homes, sheltered housing, hospices and rest and residential homes in Scotland

- the provision of a library and museum.

In 1999/2000 it had assets of £14 million and an income of £1.1 million, half of which was received from fees and rents for its homes. Direct charitable expenditure totalled £1 million, broken down as follows:

cost of running homes	£720,000
St John Eye Hospital	£15,000
mountain rescue vehicles	£183,000
minibuses	£71,000
Loch Lomond Boat House	£15,000
palliative care in Stranraer	£5,600
other donations	£24,000

Applications In writing to the correspondent. Trustees meet in November and December; applications should be received the preceding two months.

The Pyke Charity Trust

Disability, welfare, community, general

£114,000 (2000)

Beneficial area Mostly local to the trust

11 Fountain Close, 22 High Street, Edinburgh EH1 1TF

Tel. 0131 557 2995

Correspondent Tom Harvie Clark, Trustee

Trustees R van Zwanenberg; J Macpherson; T Harvie Clark.

Charity Commission no. 296418

Information available Accounts were provided by the trust, but without a list of grants.

General The 2000 accounts state: 'The general areas of the trustees' interest remain the disabled, social welfare and community needs. However, due to the volume of applications that were being received the trustees have decided not to accept speculative applications. Instead only local charities well known to the trustees will be considered.'

In 2000 it had assets of £3.7 million and an income of £87,000. Grants totalled £114,000 and were broken down as follows:

	2000		1999	
	total	%	total	%
Disabled	£5,800	5	£10,000	8
Education	–	–	£2,500	2
General	£25,000	22	£23,000	19
Medical	£4,000	4	£3,500	3
Old people	£500	–	£2,600	2
Youth	£5,300	5	£8,600	7
School fees	£73,000	64	£69,000	58

A grants list was not included in the accounts, with the trust stating: 'We have found over many years that the disclosure of individual grants has been misleading and does not convey a proper understanding of the charity's activities.'

Applications The trust told us in July 2001 that 'it no longer accepts speculative applications and instead its trustees approach charities that they honour and respect'.

Quaker Tax Witness Fund

Welfare, health, employment, general

£6,000 (2001)

Beneficial area South east Scotland (i.e. Edinburgh and the Lothians, the Borders and Fife)

Quaker Meeting House, 7 Victoria Terrace, Edinburgh EH12 2J1

Tel. 0131 225 4825

Correspondent David Turner

Information available Information was provided by the trust.

General The fund is interested in assisting local groups working within their community supporting, amongst other projects, healthy eating schemes, health projects, community care, employment initiatives and housing repair schemes. Priority is given to organisations which 'help people to help themselves' tackle poverty. There is also a preference to support new projects which could not be established without funding from the trust. It operates in Edinburgh, the Lothians and parts of the Borders and Fife. Grants range from £25 to £500 each. In 2001 they were given to 20 organisations and averaged £300 each.

Exclusions No grants to individuals or towards day-to-day running costs or political groups.

Applications In writing to the correspondent for an application form. Applicants do not need charitable status, but they do need a constitution and a bank account operated by at least two signatures.

Radio Forth Help a Child Appeal

Children with special needs

£126,000 (1999)

Beneficial area East central Scotland

Forth House, Forth Street, Edinburgh EH1 3LF

Tel. 0131 556 9255 **Fax** 0131 475 1221

e-mail lesley.fraser@srh.co.uk

Website www.forthonline.co.uk

Correspondent Lesley Fraser, Charity Coordinator

Trustees *B Malcolm; T Gallagher; D Mackinlay; A Wilkie; M Scott; Lady Dunpak; J Kennedy.*

Inland Revenue no. SC005626

Information available Information was provided by the trust.

General The trust raises money for children with special needs in east central Scotland. It organises appeals and events through the radio station and encourages listeners to hold their own fundraising events. The following are examples of the types of projects supported:

- holiday home for young people with disabilities
- minibuses for several local children's charities
- emergency equipment for special baby units
- wheelchairs and specially adapted seating
- play area for children who are blind
- modern equipment to improve the lives of children with disabilities
- help with therapies and treatment
- outdoor play, e.g. toys and climbing frames
- specially adapted sensory rooms and equipment
- toys and computers
- music room for terminally ill children
- music therapy for autistic children
- riding for children with disabilities.

Unfortunately we were unable to obtain financial information for 1999, other than the grant total of £126,000.

Applications Contact the correspondent for further information.

The Carol Richmond Charitable Trust

General

£3,700 (1998/99)

Beneficial area Mainly Scotland

Lomynd, Knockbuckle Road, Kilmalcom, Renfrewshire PA13 4JT

Tel. 01505 872716

Correspondent P D Bowman, Secretary/Treasurer

Inland Revenue no. SC008728

Information available Information was provided by the trust.

General The trust will support a wide variety of causes, including: social welfare; education/training; medical and health organisations; environment, conservation and heritage; and religious appeals. It mainly supports organisations in Scotland but will occasionally support international emergency appeals. It will give one-off or recurrent grants, ranging from £50 to £2,200.

In 1998/99 it had assets of £80,000 and an income of £3,500. It gave grants totalling £3,700. Beneficiaries included Cash for Kids, Giffnock South Parish Church of Scotland, Glenalmond Appeal, Hurricane Appeal Nicaragua, RNID and Trades Hall of Glasgow Restoration Appeal.

Exclusions Grants are not given for animal welfare, the arts, overseas projects (except emergency appeals), political appeals, sports or recreation.

Applications In writing to the correspondent at any time.

RNVR Club (Scotland) Memorial Trust

Maritime, naval

About £7,000

Beneficial area Scotland, mainly the west coast

The Little House, Pier Road, Rhu G84 8LH

Tel. 01436 820382

Correspondent I J Scott, Treasurer

Inland Revenue no. SC018009

Information available Information was provided by the trust.

General This trust was set up in memory of the Scottish Officers of the Royal Navy Volunteer Reserve. The trust has a number of aims including: to educate the public in maritime and naval matters; to assist in the preservation of ships and articles of naval significance; to provide facilities for education, character training and development both on and off shore for deserving men and women; and to assist voluntary organisations with similar aims such as Sail Training Association and Outward Bound Scheme. Grants total about £7,000 a year.

Applications In writing to the correspondent, requesting an application form.

The Robertson Trust

Care, education, medical, drugs prevention and treatment, general

£4.8 million (2000/01)

Beneficial area Scotland

PO Box 15330, Glasgow GI 2YL

Tel. 0141 304 4533 **Fax** 0141 304 4569

e-mail admin@therobertsontrust.org.uk

Website www.therobertsontrust.org.uk

Correspondent Sir Lachlan Maclean, Secretary

Inland Revenue no. SC002970

Information available A detailed annual review was provided by the trust.

General The Robertson Trust was established in 1961 by the Robertson sisters, who inherited a controlling interest in a couple of whiskey companies for their father and wished to ensure the dividend income from the shares would be given to charitable purposes. A wide range of organisations are supported each year, although the trust tends to focus on care, education, medical charities and drug prevention and treatment. During 2000/01 a small grants programme was created to allow smaller charities to apply for one-off donations of up to £3,000 for a particular project or activity. Outside of this programme, there is no set minimum or maximum grant size.

In 1992 the trust established a sister charity, The Robertson Scholarship Trust, to provide bursaries for young students with outstanding ability, which it continues to support (£230,000 in 2000/01).

In 2000/01 The Robertson Trust had assets of £215 million which generated an income of £5.2 million. Out of over 1,000 applicants, 380 grants were awarded totalling £4.8 million.

Grants were broken down as follows (figures in brackets are the 1999/2000 totals):

Care	£800,000	(£780,000)
Drugs	£400,000	(£200,000)
Educational	£1,150,000	(£950,000)
Medical	£600,000	(£1,200,000)
Alcoholic research	£175,000	(£175,000)
Animal welfare	£75,000	(£75,000)
Arts	£200,000	(£175,000)
Community service	£425,000	(£375,000)
Disability	£500,000	(£250,000)
Environmental issues	£100,000	(£25,000)
Heritage/conservation	£100,000	(£200,000)
Sport	£400,000	(£50,000)

Number of grants were also given, broken down by size, as follows:

up to £1,000	40	(40)
£1,001 – £5,000	190	(135)
£5,001 – £10,000	90	(85)
£10,001 – £20,000	45	(40)
over £20,000	35	(35)

The following information was taken from the annual review: 'The geographical distribution of donations is monitored each year. The trust seeks to support charitable organisations throughout Scotland at both a national and local level. There is some preference towards funding activities which take place in close proximity to the sites operated by The Edrington Group which include amongst other Drumchapel, Perth and Speyside. It is clear from the statistics that much still has to be done to raise the profile of the trust in some areas of Scotland, particularly away from the central belt and amongst smaller community-based organisations. It is pleasing however to see that most communities in Scotland have benefited in some way from The Robertson Trust …. The majority of awards, both by number and amount, were made to national organisations and those based in the city of Glasgow. The central area (Stirling, Perth and Falkirk) did not receive a large number of donations but the largest donation made by the trust last year was a payment of £750,000 to the University of Stirling for a new swimming pool and fitness centre. Edinburgh City and the Highland and Islands received a significant number of smaller donations.'

Other grants included: £100,000 to East Park towards the opening of four community houses for residential care for young people who are disabled in Glasgow; £20,000 to The Coach House Trust towards refurbishments; £15,000 to Breast Cancer Care Scotland to develop an information resource; £10,000 each to Alness Community Association Ltd towards a building purchase and ChildLine Scotland towards running costs; £5,000 to CAFE (Community Alcohol Free Environment) Project for a part-time youth worker; and £4,500 to Artlink, Edinburgh and the Lothians, to expand their services.

Beneficiaries of smaller grants included: Multi Ethnic Aberdeen Ltd to publish an ethnic directory of groups and services in the area (£3,000); The Sea Watch Foundation to work with communities around the Moray Firth coastline to encourage good environmental stewardship and Shopmobility Ayr for the running costs of a minibus (£2,000 each); and Rutherglen/Cambuslang Drugs Forum for a one-day event for 170 primary schoolchildren involving sports activities and drug education to promote healthy lifestyles (£1,000).

Exclusions The trust does not support:

- individuals or organisations which are not recognised as charities by the Inland Revenue or the Charity Commission
- general appeals or circulars, including contributions to endowment funds
- local charities whose work takes place outside of Scotland
- projects which are exclusively or primarily intended to promote political beliefs
- organisations which have applied within the last 12 months
- students or organisations for personal study, travel or for expeditions, whether in Scotland or not.

The trust is unlikely to support:

- projects which are properly the subject of statutory funding
- projects which collect funds to distribute to others.

Applications In writing to the correspondent, including the most recent annual report and accounts. The trustees meet every two months and it is unusual for organisations to wait more than three months for a decision.

Full guidelines are available from the correspondent or on the website.

Royal Scots Benevolent Society

Services and ex-services

£46,000 to individuals and organisations (2001)

Beneficial area UK

RHQ, The Royal Scots (Royal Regiment), The Castle, Edinburgh EH1 2YT

Tel. 0131 310 5016 **Fax** 0131 310 5019

e-mail rhqroyalscots@edinburghcastle.fsnet.co.uk

Website www.royalscots.co.uk

Trustees D J C Meehan, Chair; H K Young; G E Lowder; KPMG.

Information available Information was provided by the trust.

General The trust supports soldiers and former soldiers, and their dependants, of the Royal Scots (The Royal Regiment) who are in need. The trust will also give to organisations which help the same people. In 2001 £46,000 was given in total.

Applications Applications should be made via SSAFA Forces Help or British Legion.

The Hector Gordon Russell Trust

Air force charities, young people, general

Possibly about £5,000

Beneficial area Greenock, Inverness and Campbeltown

Henderson & Co., Chartered Accountants, 73 Union Street, Greenock PA16 8BG

Tel. 01475 720202

Correspondent R T Henderson, Trustee

Trustees D Caldwell; D R Fairbairn; R T Henderson.

Inland Revenue no. SC000679

Information available Information was provided by the trust.

General The late Hector Gordon Russell was a local Greenock businessman who had interests in a number of organisations, mainly located in Inverness, Greenock and Campbeltown.

In 2000 the trust's income was £6,800. A grant total figure and list of grant beneficiaries was not available for this year.

Past beneficiaries have included Erskine Hospital, Greenock Medical Aid Society, Campbeltown Sea Cadets and Polish Air Force Association in Great Britain.

Applications The trust states that: 'No applications whatsoever should be made for any financial assistance, as none will be forthcoming in response to any such application'.

The Russell Trust

General

£244,000 (1998/99)

Beneficial area UK, especially Scotland

Rothes, Markinch, Glenrothes, Fife KY7 6PW

Tel. 01592 753311

Correspondent Mrs Cecilia Croal, Secretary

Inland Revenue no. SC004424

Information available Information was provided by the trust.

General In 1998/99 the trust had assets of £375,000 and an income of £300,000. Grants totalled £244,000. Grants are one-off and usually range from £250 to £10,000. The average grant is £1,000. It usually supports specific services or projects and prefers to give start-up grants for new initiatives. Grants range from £250 to £10,000. Recipients of £10,000 were Edinburgh Green Belt Trust for an educational initiative, National Galleries of Scotland to set up a 'friends' scheme, National Trust for Scotland for Hew Lorimer project at Kellie Castle, Royal Society of Edinburgh, and St Andrews University for PhD awards. Other grants included £6,000 to Liberating Scots Trust for a military museum to commemorate Scots in the Second World War and £5,000 went to Clovenstone Primary School for a new playground and Craighead Institute.

Exclusions Only registered charities are supported.

Applications On a form available from the correspondent.

St Andrew Animal Fund Ltd

Animal welfare

£17,000 (2000)

Beneficial area UK and overseas, with a preference for Scotland

10 Queensferry Street, Edinburgh EH2 4PG

Tel. 0131 225 2116 **Fax** 0131 220 6377

e-mail advocates.animals@virgin.net

Website www.advocatesforanimals.org.uk

Correspondent Les Ward

Trustees *Prof. Timothy Sprigge; Murray McGrath; Christopher Mylne; Eileen Aitken; David Martin; Dr Jane Goodall; Heather Petrie; Rebecca Ford; Shona McManus; Stephen Blakeway; Ginny Hay; Emma Law.*

Inland Revenue no. SC005337

Information available Full accounts and policy information were provided by the trust.

General The fund was formed in 1969 to carry out charitable activities for the protection of animals from cruelty and suffering. Grants are awarded only to fund or to part-fund a specific project, e.g. building work, renovation, repairs and so on; an animal project – spaying/neutering, re-homing and so on; animal rescue/animal sanctuary – providing care for unwanted, ill or injured animals.

The activities during 2000 included making grants and awards to further animal welfare projects in Scotland and elsewhere, including overseas. The fund continued its involvement in a project dealing with the force feeding of ducks and geese in the production of foie gras, and with Focus on Alternatives, a group promoting the development, acceptance and use of humane alternatives to animals in research.

The trustees consider that the priorities for the charity in the next few years are support for the development of non-animal research techniques, funding farm animal and companion animal and wildlife projects to improve welfare and enhance the welfare of animals.

In 2000 the income to the fund was £113,000, with charitable grants totalling £17,000. Other charitable expenditure amounted to £56,000. Grants of £1,000 went to Crosskennan Lane Animal Sanctuary, Norwegian School of Veterinary Science, Hessilhead Wildlife Rescue Trust, World Animal Net and Orkney Seal Rescue, with three grants of £1,000 to £2,000 being given to Tinto Kennels, Foie Gras, and for quarantine for a dog called Bruno rescued from Croatia. Several grants were to Scottish charities, but others were given elsewhere in the UK and also overseas.

Exclusions No support for routine day-to-day expenses.

Applications In writing to the correspondent. The trustees meet in April and applications must reach the fund by 31 December for consideration at the next meeting. Applications should include a copy of the latest accounts, the name and address of a referee (e.g. veterinary surgeon, bank manager, pet food supplier and so on), the purpose for which any grant will be used and, where relevant, two estimates. Receipts for work carried out may be requested and the fund states that visits by representatives of the fund to those organisations receiving grants will be made at random.

The Saltire Society

Culture

£30,000 (1999)

Beneficial area Scotland

9 Fountain Close, 22 High Street, Edinburgh EH1 1TF

Tel. 0131 556 1836 **Fax** 0131 557 1675

e-mail saltire@saltire.org.uk

Website www.saltire-society.demon.co.uk

Trustees *Revd A Black, Chair; S Aitken; Marillyn Gray; I M Hume; Madame May MacKerrell of Hillhouse; C Rankin; Moria Stratton; Dr D Wilkie; Anne Warren; Dr D Purves; J Gibson.*

Inland Revenue no. SC004962

Information available Information was available on the website.

General The trust describes itself as 'looking to the future as well as the past encouraging creativity in Scotland as well as cultural heritage'. Its aims and objectives are to:

- 'increase public awareness of Scotland's distinct natural and cultural heritage in all its richness and diversity and foster the cherishing and enrichment of all aspects of this heritage, including the Scots and Gaelic languages
- 'enhance the quality of Scotland's contribution to all of the arts and sciences by encouraging creativity, inventiveness and the achievement of the highest standards of excellence in these fields
- 'build on the achievements of the past to advance Scotland's standing as a vibrant, creative force in European civilisation
- 'improve all aspects of Scottish life and letters at home and abroad and strengthen Scotland's cultural links with other countries and people.'

In 1999 the trust had an income of £130,000 and gave grants totalling £30,000.

Applications In writing to the correspondent.

The Andrew Salvesen Charitable Trust

General

£30,000 (1994)

Beneficial area UK, with a preference for Scotland

c/o Meston Reid & Co., 12 Carden Place, Aberdeen AB10 1UR

Tel. 01224 625554

Correspondent Mark Brown

Trustees *A C Salvesen; Ms K Turner; V Lall.*

Inland Revenue no. SC008000

Information available Limited information was available from the trust.

General The trust gives grants for general charitable purposes, in particular it will support the arts, education/training, medical sciences, and welfare of people who are older, young or ill.

In 1998 it had an income of £60,000 but the grant total was not available. Unfortunately we were unable to obtain further up-to-date information.

In 1994 a total of £30,000 was awarded. Beneficiaries included Royal Zoological Society of Scotland (£7,500), Sick Kids Appeal (£5,000), Bield Housing Trust and Scottish Down's Syndrome Association (£3,500 each), Sail Training Association (£3,000), Multiple Sclerosis Society in Scotland (£2,400) and William Higgins Marathon Account (£1,500). A number of miscellaneous distributions were also made, totalling £4,000.

Applications The trustees only support organisations known to them through personal contact. The address holders told us that all applications sent to them are thrown in the bin.

Mr & Mrs John Salvesen's Charitable Trust

General

£8,500 (1994/95)

Beneficial area Unrestricted, but with a preference for Scotland

Turcan Connell, Princes Exchange, 1 Earl Grey Street, Edinburgh EH3 9EE

Tel. 0131 228 8111 **Fax** 0131 228 8118

Trustees *J I McC Salvesen; Mrs A M Salvesen; D A Connell.*

Information available This trust is one of 10, probably all small, trusts administered by Turcan Connell. The company would not provide us with any information on these trusts, only agreeing to send each trust's accounts for the cost of £20 each. We did not think this was reasonable for such small trusts.

General The trust's funds totalled £102,000 in 1994/95. Grants totalled £8,500 and ranged from £500 and £5,000.

Beneficiaries were Edinburgh Festival Theatre Trust (£5,000), Scottish Children's Hospice (£2,000), Anthony Nolan Bone Marrow Trust (£1,000) and Royal Scottish Agricultural Benevolent Institution (£500).

Applications In writing to the correspondent.

The Scotbelge Charitable Trust

Housing, arts, culture, recreation, health, conservation, community facilities

£26,000 (1999/2000)

Beneficial area UK, with a preference for Scotland

Bank of Butterfield (UK) Ltd, St Helens, 1 Undershaft, London EC3A 8JX

Tel. 020 7816 8100 **Fax** 020 7816 8206

Correspondent K H Galloway, Trustee

Trustees *Mrs A Wetherall; S L Keswick; K H Galloway; A J J Stanford.*

Charity Commission no. 802962

Information available Full accounts were provided by the trust.

General The trust will support organisations concerned with housing, arts and culture, recreation, health, conservation and community facilities. It will give one-off or recurrent grants for core costs and building costs and funding for up to three years will be considered.

In 1999/2000 the trust had assets of £309,000, an income of £27,000 and gave grants totalling £26,000. The largest grants were £2,500 to both The Piping Centre and Friends of Sciennes Primary School. Ida Wynefred Keswick Trust received £2,000, with £1,500 to Dynamic Earth Charitable Trust and £1,000 each going to eight charities including Deafblind UK, Orkney Sea Cadets and Scottish International Children's Festival. There were 20 grants of £500, and one for £100. Organisations receiving £500 included Big Issue Foundation – Scotland; Manic Depression Fellowship – Scotland; and Scottish Council for Alchohol.

Exclusions No grants to individuals, expeditions or travel bursaries.

Applications In writing to the correspondent. Telephone calls are not welcome.

The John Scott Trust

General

£91,000 (1999/2000)

Beneficial area Scotland

63 Loudoun Road, Newmilns, Ayrshire KA16 9HG

Tel. 01560 320092

Correspondent John D Scott, Trustee

Trustees *J D Scott.*

Inland Revenue no. SC003297

Information available Accounts were provided by the trust.

General The trust supports general charitable purposes. In 1999/2000 the trust had assets of £1 million and an income of £69,000. It gave grants totalling £91,000. A list of beneficiaries was not available. In the past the following organisations have received support: Ayrshire Fiddle Orchestra, Summerhill Youth Club, Nith Inshore Rescue, WRCS, Tom Allan Centre, Dumfries Area Scout Council, Salvation Army, Barnardos and National Trust for Scotland.

Applications Applications are not invited.

Mark Scott Foundation

Young people

£30,000 (1999)

Beneficial area Scotland

McGrigor Donald, Pacific House, 70 Wellington Street, Glasgow G2 6SB

Tel. 0141 221 5178 **Fax** 0141 248 6677

Correspondent Cathie Higgins, Foundation Administrator

Trustees *J N Scott; J Scott; G Brown; Father G Tartaglia; R Woods; N J Scott.*

Inland Revenue no. SC025254

Information available Information was provided by the trust.

General 'The purpose of this foundation is to bridge a funding gap between the financial resources a person has and what he or she needs to begin, continue or complete a course, project, idea or dream. The foundation is here to help meet that gap. Eligible applicants should generally be aged between 16 and 25 and resident in Scotland.'

Most grants are given to individuals, although some groups have been supported such as netball teams etc. In 1999 the trust had an income of £40,000 and gave £30,000 in grants.

Applications In writing to the correspondent.

The Scottish Chartered Accountants' Trust for Education

Education and research into accountancy

£20,000 (1998)

Beneficial area UK, with a preference for Scotland

CA House, 21 Haymarket Yards, Edinburgh EH12 5BH

Tel. 0131 347 0100

Correspondent Angela Ellis

Trustees *Mrs V A Dickson; A M Halthorn; H M M Johnston; I M Stubbs.*

Inland Revenue no. SC008368

Information available Information was provided by the trust.

General The trust awards grants for:

* research conferences organised by Scottish Institute and for related publications

- research into teaching methods for the accountancy profession
- research on accounting and related subjects as well as other research projects relevant to the profession
- visits by academics to give addresses to members of the institute and students
- visits by practitioners from overseas to participate in the institute's educational programme.

It recently used a large part of its capital funds to support a building project for the educational department of Scottish Institute. As a result the trust's expenditure is now about £20,000.

Previous beneficiaries have included research projects on environmental issues in accountancy and on financial reporting and user needs; an advanced management programme; National Auditing Conference; and Scottish accountancy academics to attend overseas conferences.

Applications In writing to the correspondent.

The Scottish Churches Architectural Heritage Trust

Scottish church buildings

£191,000 (1999)

Beneficial area Scotland

15 North Bank Street, The Mound, Edinburgh EH1 2LP

Tel. 0131 225 8644

Correspondent Mrs Florence MacKenzie, Director

Trustees *Lord Penrose, Chair; Donald S Erskine; Magnus Magnusson; Lady Marion Fraser; John Gerrard; Revd Malcolm Grant; Ivor Guild; Revd Kenneth Nugent; Prof. Frank Willett; Revd Douglas Galbraith.*

Inland Revenue no. SC000819

Information available A detailed report was provided by the trust.

General This trust was established 'to assist congregations of any denomination in Scotland in the preservation and upkeep of church buildings which are in regular use for public worship, principally by raising funds for their repair and restoration and by acting as a source of technical advice and assistance on maintenance and repair'.

In 1999 it had assets of £677,000 and an income of £147,000, including £101,000 in donations received. Grants totalled £191,000.

The largest grants were £20,000 to Edinburgh Reid Memorial Church for replacement of the roof, £10,000 each to Monymusk Aberdeen for stonework repairs and Westray Orkney for re-harling, £9,000 to Glasgow St Georges Tron for general repairs and £8,000 each to Kilmarnock St Kentigern's for window and roof repairs and Thurso St Peter's for repairs to the roof and vaulted ceiling.

Applications On a form available from the correspondent. The grants committee meets four times a year in February, May, October and November.

Scottish Churches Community Trust

Community projects, including church-run projects

About £200,000

Beneficial area Scotland

200 Balmore Road, Possilpark, Glasgow G22 6LJ

Tel. & Fax 0141 336 3766

Website www.scct.org.uk

e-mail admin@scct.org.uk

Correspondent John Dornan, Development Coordinator

Trustees *Gordon Armour; Sandra Carter; Christina Davis; Alan Grist; Christopher Lyon; Elizabeth McQuade; Frank Maxwell; Ian Moir; Robert Owens; Richard Toller.*

Information available Information was provided by the trust.

General Grants are given in support of causes in Scotland, with priority to areas of greatest deprivation. The trust funds work developed by churches and community groups meeting real and identified needs in either a local community or among groups of disadvantaged people.

Grants can be one off or for up to four years, normally in the range £3,000 to £5,000. The maximum normally available is £20,000 over four years; or up to one third of the total costs.

This is a newly established trust, hence no financial information. The projected grant total for 2001 was £200,000.

Exclusions No funding for: work developed by organisations working in isolation from others; building work being done solely in compliance with legislation or not in direct support of a project for community benefit; one-off short-term activities such as trips or excursions, holiday clubs, mission events and festivals; work developed by organisations whose primary purpose is the promotion of abortion, euthanasia or artificial contraception; or work not carried out by recognised charities or properly constituted groups.

Applications Guidelines are available from the correspondent.

Scottish Coal Industry Special Welfare Fund

Miners' welfare

£90,000 (2000)

Beneficial area Scotland

50 Hopetoun Street, Bathgate, West Lothian EH48 4EU

Tel. 01506 635550

Correspondent The Trustees

Inland Revenue no. SC001200

Information available Information was provided by the trust.

General The fund was set up to improve the conditions of people employed in the mining industry and their families. It supports individuals in need and also through the provision of recreational facilities, youth clubs and courses. In 2000 the trust had an income of £200,000 and gave grants totalling £90,000.

Applications In writing to the correspondent.

The Scottish Community Foundation

Community

£2.8 million (2001/02)

Beneficial area Scotland

126 Canongate, Edinburgh EH8 8DD

Tel. 0131 524 0300 **Fax** 0131 524 0329

e-mail mail@scottishcommunityfoundation.com

Website www.scottishcommunityfoundation.com

Correspondent Louise Massara and Lorraine Corbett, Grants Officers

Trustees *Alastair Dempster, Chair; Alastair Balfour; Anne Boyd; John Frame; Michael Gray; Iain Johnston; Sir Hamish Macleod; George Menzies; Graeme Millar; Martin Sime; Graeme Simmers.*

Inland Revenue no. SC022910

Information available Information was provided by the trust and was taken from the trust's website.

General The broad aim of this foundation is to assist charities working to improve the quality of life and life chances in Scotland, especially in circumstances where funding is particularly hard to find and where a grant can achieve a significant impact in enabling charities to fulfil their own objectives. Grants are made to groups across a wide spectrum of social welfare and community development activities. While larger organisations are not excluded from applying, the majority of funding is directed at locally-based work involving, and often initiated by, members of that local community.

In 2001/02 the foundation made grants totalling £2.8 million, broken down as follows:

Scottish Executive Foot and Mouth Disease Matched Funding Programme	£1,800,000
main, small and specialist grant programmes	£525,000
rapid response grants programme for rural communities	£325,000
Chase Millennium Awards Programme	£150,000

The largest grant given was as part of the foundation's work in administering the Scottish Executive Foot and Mouth Disease Matched Funding Programme, giving over £1 million to Royal Scottish Agricultural Benevolent Institution.

The foundation's main grant programme provides awards of up to £5,000 to local charities and community groups. The small grants programme is a fast track grants programme providing grant awards of up to £1,000 to local charities and community groups.

Other initiatives include:

• Millennium awards for Youth (Scotland) – £1.3 million was received by the foundation to donate in grants to young individuals

• New Millennium Fund for Scotland – the foundation aims to engage 1% of limited companies in Scotland in pledging money to an endowment fund in excess of £10 million (£380,000 pledged 2000/01)

• personal endowment – by March 2002, seven individuals and families had established endowment funds within the foundation ranging from £10,000 to £100,000.

Exclusions Grants are not made towards:

• individuals

• advancement of religion or a political party

• major fundraising appeals

• secondhand vehicles

• payment of debts or other retrospective funding

• payments towards areas generally understood to be the responsibility of statutory authorities.

Applications On an application form available from the correspondent. There is no closing date for applications. Grant decisions in 2001 for the main grants programme (requests from £1,000 to £5,000) were in January, April, July and October. Decisions for the small grants programme (up to £1,000) are made within four weeks of receipt of the application. Up-to-date information was not available.

The trust stated: 'Please indicate on the application form which programme you are applying to [small or main grants programme]. You may only apply to one programme at a time. However, groups may apply to both programmes during the course of the year and, if successful, may hold one grant under each programme in any one year.

'Guidelines are available to help you complete the application form.

'If you require any further information please contact the office and we will give you any further help we can.

'We cannot assess groups for a grant without sight of their constitution (or other founding deed) [which has been adopted and/or signed by the management committee/board] and up-to-date accounts [that have been audited/signed as accepted by the management committee/board]. Please ensure you include those when returning your application form to avoid any delay in processing your application.

'If you would like us to acknowledge safe receipt of your application, please address, stamp and return the postcard [enclosed with your application pack].

'Applications to the main grants programme are allocated to assessors. An assessor will contact you to arrange a suitable time to conduct a short telephone assessment. A report will then be considered by a funders committee.

'If you have applied to the small grants programme, then the grants officer will contact you to arrange a suitable time to conduct a short telephone assessment. A report will then be sent to the board for their consideration.

'If you are successful you will receive a letter informing you of the grant awarded and from which fund. You will also be sent a grant acceptance form outlining the terms of the grant. Grants will be paid by cheque. [Applicant groups must have a bank or building society account in the name of the group.]'

Scottish Disabled Sports Trust

Sports events for people who are disabled

£5,000 (2000/01)

Beneficial area Scotland

7 Westerton of Mugdock, Milngavie, Glasgow G62 8LQ

Tel. 0141 956 6415

Trustees *A G Mills, Chair; Miss C M Baldwin; R C Brickley; J B Mason; A R Mitchell.*

Inland Revenue no. SC005435

Information available Information was provided by the trust.

General This trust was originally established to further the aims of Scottish Disabled Sports, although it can aid other organisations and individuals concerned with the promotion of sports for people who are disabled. The 2000/01 accounts stated:

'Donations come from many sources but donors generally indicate the area of sport they would wish to assist and are therefore retained in named funds. Money is placed on long or short term investments appropriate to the time when grants are expected to be sought. The net investment income of the trust is allocated fairly between and added to named funds.'

In 2000/01 it had assets of £68,000 which generated an income of £4,000. New donations received totalled only £4,000. The only grant made was £5,000 to Sports Disabled Scotland for the Scottish team taking part in the Nordic Games in Sweden. There was also a commitment of £5,000 to Scottish Anglers National Association for disability facilities at a proposed National Game Angling Centre at Loch Leven.

Applications As the trust effectively operates as a banking house, no unsolicited applications can be considered.

The Scottish Hospital Endowments Research Trust

Medical research

£1.2 million (1999/2000)

Beneficial area Scotland

Turcan Connell, 1 Earl Grey Street, Edinburgh EH3 9EE

Tel. 0131 228 8111 **Fax** 0131 228 8118

e-mail sshert4578@aol.com

Website www.shert.com

Correspondent The Secretaries to the Trust

Trustees *Lord Kilpatrick of Kincraig, Chair; Prof. Margaret Alexander; Prof. William Bowman; Alastair Dempster; Prof. Kevin Docherty; Dr Alexander Proudfoot; Mrs Brenda Rennie.*

Inland Revenue no. SC014959

Information available Full accounts were provided by the trust.

General The 1999/2000 accounts stated:'

The objectives of the trust are to:

- receive and hold endowments, donations and bequests

- make grants from these to promote medical research in Scotland

- engage in fundraising activities for the purposes of the trust

- develop and exploit ideas and exploit intellectual property.

'The trust aims to improve health standards by funding research of the highest quality into the cause, diagnosis, treatment and prevention of all forms of illness and genetic disorders, and into the advancement of medical technology.

'The trust fulfils its objects by supporting research-minded members of the scientific, medical and allied professions by giving them the opportunity to pursue high-calibre research either independently or in collaboration with colleagues in their own or other universities, major hospitals and research units in Scotland.

'The trust intends to:

* increase its provision of research scholarships and fellowships in further encouragement of young doctors and scientists

* expand its funding of specialist equipment

* augment the funds available to it to help sustain the outstanding contributions of Scottish medical research to healthcare throughout the world.'

In 1999/2000 it had assets of £29 million and an income of £1.8 million, comprised of £1.2 million in investment income, £568,000 in legacies and donations and £42,000 in royalties. Grants totalled £1.2 million and were given for research projects, fellowships and scholarships, research workshops and travel grants.

Exclusions Grants are only for projects carried out in Scotland.

Applications Contact the correspondent for further information.

The Scottish International Education Trust

Education, the arts, economic and social welfare

£109,000 (1998/99)

Beneficial area Scotland

22 Manor Place, Edinburgh EH3 7DS

Tel. & Fax 0131 225 1113

Correspondent E C Davison, Director

Trustees *J D Houston, Chair; W Menzies Campbell; Sir Sean Connery; Tom Fleming; Lady Gibson; Alexander Goudie; Sir Norman Graham; Andy Irvine; Prof. Alistair Macfarlane; Kenneth McKellar; Jackie Stewart.*

Inland Revenue no. SC009207

Information available A brochure is available from the trust.

General The Scottish International Educational Trust is a charitable organisation set up in 1971

on the initiative of Scottish born actor Sean Connery.

The trustees regard their two primary purposes to be as follows:

* To assist young Scots who have demonstrated excellence in their initial course of higher education and wish to take their studies or professional training further.

* To support projects which seem to the trustees especially valuable in contributing to the cultural, economic or social development of Scotland or the improvement of the Scottish environment.

The trust gives grants to organisations and individuals contributing to the cultural, economic and social development of Scotland. One-off grants are given ranging from £400 to £2,000.

In 1998/99 it had assets totalling £2.2 million, generating an income of £360,000. Grants totalled £109,000.

Exclusions No grants to commercial organisations, for capital work, general maintenance, courses (e.g. undergraduate study) for which there is support from statutory bodies/public funds.

Applications In writing to the director.

Scottish Silver Jubliee & Children's Bursary Fund

Young people under 25, local community

£5,300 (1999/2000)

Beneficial area Scotland

1 Woodside Road, Tullibody, Alloa FK10 2QQ

Tel. 01259 723935

e-mail iscambus@aol.com

Correspondent Ian Sutherland, Hon. Secretary

Trustees *George S Geary; Ian Sutherland; Ronald Beasley; Richard J Marks; Hon. E David*

Bruce; Ian F H Grant; Mrs. Sheila Robertson; Mrs Fiona Waite.

Inland Revenue no. SC005154

Information available Information was provided by the trust, including guidelines for applicants.

General The trust supports projects in Scotland which are planned and undertaken by young people and which benefit the community in general. It also helps to provide play equipment to playgroups. Projects can be from an established organisation which helps communities abroad. Individuals are only supported in exceptional circumstances. Funds are sometimes available to young people undertaking voluntary work to benefit those in need overseas. Young people must be under 25 and can apply either as part of a group or on their own.

Types of projects supported include:

- help to older people and people who are disabled, e.g. letter writing, gardening, redecoration, entertainment, company

- creating or repairing nature walks, gardens, walls, fencing

- provision of equipment to playgroups and parent and toddler groups

- youth information and resource projects

- activities for underprivileged children.

The annual review for the trust states that 46 applications were made during the year; 22 grants were awarded. The maximum award has been increased to £1,000 and awards to those giving service overseas has been increased, commensurate with the time being spent abroad. During the year eight grants were given, ranging from £100 to £400. Grants are usually one-off. In 1999/2000 the trust had assets of £74,000 and an income of £6,000. Grants totalled £5,300. Beneficiaries included Kaimes Special School Association (£400), St Peters under 5s', Galashiels (£400), Gifford Play Group (£300) and the Scottish Adoption Association, Edinburgh (£250).

Applications On a form available from the correspondent. Applications should be countersigned by a supporter, e.g. youth leader, minister of religion, community policeman, teacher and so on. Constructive monitoring and reporting on the progress of a project is desirable but not essential. Cheques are made payable to a group bank account, local or national agency or organisation or suppliers. Trustees meet in March and October. Guidelines for applicants are available from the trust.

The Scottish Slimmers Charitable Trust

Poverty, education, health

See below

Beneficial area UK, with a preference for Scotland

11 Bon Accord Square, Aberdeen AB11 6DJ

Tel. 01224 256103

Correspondent Ms E Rennie

Trustees *J L Reid; Ms C Tolson; Ms A Lewis.*

Inland Revenue no. SC021002

Information available Limited information was available from this trust.

General This trust's income is raised purely from fundraising events. It raises about £30,000 each year to be donated in grants. In recent years the trust's support has focused on large national healthcare charities such as Cancer Relief Macmillan Fund, Breakthrough Breast Cancer and British Heart Foundation. However, Scottish hospices such as Strathcarron Hospice in Glenny, Ayrshire Hospices and Inverness Highland Hospice were also supported. Amounts given vary, but are usually to a maximum of £500 each.

Exclusions Grants are not awarded to animal charities or to overseas organisations.

Applications In writing to the correspondent.

Scottish Sunday School Union For Christian Education

Christian education

Not known

Beneficial area Scotland

2 Fraser Avenue, Newton Mearns, Glasgow G77 6HW

Tel. 0141 571 7359

Correspondent Mrs Lynne Collingham, Secretary/Treasurer

Inland Revenue no. SC011263

Information available Limited information was available on this trust.

General The trust funds Scottish children's Christian education. It gives grants to Sunday schools and other Christian youth organisations, and will fund training and research.

Applications In writing to the correspondent.

Scottish Trust for the Physically Disabled

Disability

£54,000 (2000)

Beneficial area Scotland

Craigievar House, 77 Craigmount Brae, Edinburgh EH12 8YL

Tel. 0131 317 7227 **Fax** 0131 317 7294

Correspondent Peter Mountfield-Smith

Trustees *Allan J McFarlane, Chair; Richard Gregory; Philip Harris; Miss Mary R Hope; David W McDonald; William S Miller; John M Sheridan; Grant Carson; Miss Eileen A Mackay; Wladyslaw Mejka; Robin Burley.*

Inland Revenue no. SC049682

Information available Full accounts were provided by the trust.

General The trust informed us in January 2002 that it was undergoing a review and by the summer of 2002 may have a different policy.

This trust promotes the welfare of people with physical disabilities in Scotland, as well as supporting the residents of the Margaret Blackwood Housing Association through the Margaret Blackwood Foundation.

In 2000 it had assets of £142,000 and an income of £44,000, including £36,000 in a donation received from The Robertson Trust. Donations made totalled £54,000 and were broken down as follows: Margaret Blackwood Foundation (£35,000), Margaret Blackwood Housing Association (£12,000),Glasgow Disabled Persons Housing Service (£6,800).

The accounts also listed the following commitments made in 2000: Margaret Blackwood Technical Consultants Ltd as an interest-free loan (£60,000); Centre for Independent Living – Glasgow for administrative support services (£15,000 over two years); and Belses Gardens for administration costs for a volunteer project (£10,000 over three years), and towards identifying needs regarding individual house purchases (£6,000).

Applications In writing to the correspondent for consideration in March, June or September.

The Patricia and Donald Shepherd Trust

General

£77,000 to organisations (1999/2000)

Beneficial area Worldwide, particularly in the north of England and Scotland

PO Box 10, York YO1 1XU

Correspondent Mrs Patricia Shepherd, Trustee

Trustees *Mrs P Shepherd; Mrs J L Robertson; Patrick M Shepherd; D R Reaston; I O Robertson; Mrs C M Shepherd.*

Charity Commission no. 272948

Information available Full accounts were on file at the Charity Commission.

General The trust makes grants to benefit people in need and society in general. There is a preference for supporting charities in the north of England and Scotland, or those connected with the trustees, particularly those involving young people.

In 1999/2000 it had assets of £489,000, generating an income of £93,000. After management and administration charges of £450, grants totalled £80,000, of which £3,000 was given to individuals.

Beneficiaries included WellBeing (£6,500), St Leonard's Hospice (£5,000), Wilberforce Home for the Blind (£4,000), Timewarp 2000 Schools Project (£2,500) and The Children's Society (£1,000).

Applications In writing to the correspondent.

This entry was not confirmed by the trust but was correct according to information on file at the Charity Commission.

The A Sinclair Henderson Trust

General, religion, medical, education, historic building maintenance

£17,000 (1998/99)

Beneficial area UK, with a preference for Scotland

Messrs Thorntons, 50 Castle Street, Dundee DD1 3RV

Tel. 01382 229111 **Fax** 01382 228208

Correspondent A F McDonald, Trustee

Trustees *J S Fair; Mrs A Thoms; Mrs V Oyama; A F McDonald; Mrs M S Grundberg.*

Inland Revenue no. SC016110

Information available Information was supplied by the trust.

General In 1998/99 the trust had assets of £659,000 and an income of £21,500. Grants totalled £17,000 and ranged between £250 and £2,500. They are made throughout the year to a range of organisations, including medical

charities, youth organisations and historic buildings preservation societies.

Exclusions Grants are not available for individuals.

Applications In writing to the correspondent. Trustees meet in May and applications should be received by the previous month.

The Society in Scotland for Propagating Christian Knowledge

Church of Scotland, missionary work

See below

Beneficial area UK, with a preference for Scotland

Tods Murray, 66 Queen Street, Edinburgh EH2 4NE

Tel. 0131 226 4771

Correspondent The Trustees

Inland Revenue no. SC000270

Information available Information was provided by the trust.

General This trust supports missions in the Highlands and Islands and the work of the Church of Scotland. We were informed in January 2002 that there are no surviving trustees and as such nobody has the authority to donate funds from the trust. A few existing commitments are continuing to be paid, with the remaining funds being accumulated for such time as the trust is able to resume its grantmaking. The trust was in the process of obtaining a court order to instate trustees whilst this research was being conducted so the 'available' funds of around £7,000 a year can be distributed.

Applications The trust will be unable to accept any applications until its trust deed is altered.

The Souter Charitable Trust
(*formerly* The Souter Foundation)

Social welfare, Christianity

£1.4 million (2000)

Beneficial area UK, but with a strong preference for Scotland; overseas

PO Box 7412, Perth PH1 1WH

Tel. 01738 634745 **Fax** 01738 440275

Correspondent Linda Scott, Secretary

Trustees *Brian Souter; Elizabeth Souter; Mrs Ann Allen.*

Inland Revenue no. SC029998

Information available Accounts and an information sheet were provided by the trust.

General The foundation was established in 1991 with an endowment from Brian Souter, a creator of the Stagecoach Company, who continues to make substantial donations.

From January 2001 the grant-making activities of The Souter Foundation were taken over by The Souter Charitable Trust, a related charity which was formed in 2000. This entry provides financial information and examples of past beneficiaries of the older trust using the 2000 accounts. The trust's annual report in 2000 stated that The Souter Foundation charity would continue to operate until all grants under its existing commitments had been paid out.

The Information Sheet for The Souter Charitable Trust says: 'Our stated policy is to assist "projects engaged in the relief of human suffering in the UK or overseas, particularly those with a Christian emphasis". We tend not to get involved with research or capital funding, but would be more likely to provide a contribution towards the revenue costs of a project. Applications for building projects, personal educational requirements or personal expeditions will not generally be considered.'

In 2000 The Souter Foundation received donations of £411,000 (£1.2 million in 1999), and the total income was £624,000 (£1.7 million).

Grants totalling £1.4 million (£1.6 million in 1999) were made to 386 beneficiaries, of which 323 received grants for £1,000 or less, including 56 individuals who received grants totalling £16,000. Assets totalled £3.5 million at the year end (£8.1 million in 1999). The annual report stated that most grants were one-off and only a small number of projects were supported for up to three years.

From the 28 recipients listed, it appears that more than half of the money went to Scottish causes, a substantial proportion of them with Christian connections.

Main beneficiaries in 2000 (1999 in brackets) included:

Goudie Paintings	£150,000	(–)
The Christian Institute	£102,000	(£50,000)
Scotland Against Drugs	£100,000	(–)
Church of the Nazarene	£90,000	(£133,000)
Children's Hospice Association Scotland	£50,000	(£50,000)
Friends of Carberry	£50,000	(–)
Bethany Christian Trust	£40,000	(£40,000)
Save the Children	£38,000	(£50,000)
Scripture Union	£30,000	(£30,000)
Church of Scotland	£25,000	(–)
Mercy Ships	£25,000	(£6,300)
Fanfare for a New Generation	£25,000	(£50,000)
Oasis Trust (Faithworks)	£25,000	(–)
UNICEF (Mozambique)	£25,000	(–)
Scottish Offenders Project	£21,000	(£11,000)
Parentalk	£21,000	(£20,000)

Other grants of over £10,000 that went to organisations in Scotland were £20,000 to Glasgow City Mission, £15,000 to Scottish Crusaders, £12,000 to Prison Fellowship Scotland and £10,000 each to CancerBacup Scotland and Scottish Bible Society.

Exclusions Building projects, personal education grants and expeditions are not supported

Applications In writing to the correspondent. Please keep applications brief and no more than two sides of A4 paper: you may send audited accounts, but please do not send brochures, business plans, videos and so on. The trust states that it will request more information if necessary. The trustees meet every two months or so, and all applications will be acknowledged in due course, whether successful or not. An sae would be appreciated. Subsequent applications should not be made within a year of the initial submission.

Special Nursery Trust

Neonatal care and research

£28,000 (1997)

Beneficial area Grampian region, Orkney and Shetland

68 Station Road, Banchory, Kincardinshire AB31 5JY

Correspondent Mrs F Burnett, Trustee

Trustees *Mrs F Burnett; Ms C Barron; M U L Hutton; Dr D J Lloyd.*

Inland Revenue no. SC014910

Information available Limited information was available on this trust.

General The trust aims to help babies in special care and support research into neonatal care in the beneficial area. Grants can be one-off, or for research projects for up to two years. Capital projects will also be supported. In 1997 the trust had an income of £25,000 and gave grants totalling £28,000. Beneficiaries have included Woman and Child Health Endowment Fund which received £14,000 for research funding of the Neonatal Data Bank. The maximum grant given is £25,000.

Applications In writing to the correspondent. Applications should be sent by January each year.

The Sportsman's Charity

Sport; people who are disadvantaged or disabled; children and young people

About £80,000 (1999/2000)

Beneficial area Scotland

30 Murrayfield Road, Edinburgh EH12 6ER

Tel. 0131 346 0077 **Fax** 0131 313 1023

Correspondent Alan Hobbett, Chief Executive

Trustees *D McLean; A Cubie.*

Inland Revenue no. SC015424

Information available Information was provided by the trust.

General The charity was established in 1983 to raise money for distribution to charitable organisations throughout the UK. In practice support is given to Scottish organisations which promote sport or work for people who are disadvantaged and disabled, and children and young people.

In 1999/2000 grants totalled around £80,000 and were made to a range of charities. A list of grant beneficiaries was not provided by the trust.

Past beneficiaries have included Drum Riding Centre for the Disabled, Clyde Cruising Club, Salvation Army for the Christmas Cheer programme, Myelin Project, Craigroyston Community High School for a field trip programme and Endeavour Scotland. Other organisations supported in the past include Scottish Adoption Association, Scottish Association for the Deaf, Scottish Council for Spastics, Scottish Disabled Sailors Association, Scottish Society for Autistic Children, Scottish Dyslexia Trust Appeal, Scottish Spina Bifida Fund, Lothian Federation of Boys' Clubs, Edinburgh Walk in Numeracy Centre and Highland Hospice.

Applications Applications should be made in writing to The Scottish Community Foundation, 27 Palmerston Place, Edinburgh EH12 5AP. Direct applications to The Sportsman's Charity are not invited.

The Spurgin Charitable Trust

Social welfare

About £3,500

Beneficial area Scotland

Applehouse, Finlaystone, Langbank, Renfrewshire PA14 6TJ

Tel. 01475 540285

Correspondent G G MacMillan, Trustee

Trustees *G G MacMillan; Mrs L C Richardson.*

Inland Revenue no. SC019799

Information available Limited information was available on this trust.

General The trust had assets amounting to £73,000 in 1991, generating an income of £7,600. Grants, which totalled £3,500, were awarded to social welfare organisations in Scotland. Both recurrent and one-off grants are awarded. Up-to-date information was not available.

Applications In writing to the correspondent at the above address.

The address for this trust was confirmed, but we were unable to receive confirmation on the rest of the entry.

The Hugh Stenhouse Foundation

General

£25,000 (1998/99)

Beneficial area Mainly Scotland, with an emphasis on the west coast

Lomynd, Knockbuckle Road, Kilmacolm, Renfrewshire PA13 4JT

Tel. 01505 872716

Correspondent P D Bowman, Secretary and Treasurer

Trustees *Mrs P R H Irvine Robertson; M R L Stenhouse; P H A Stenhouse; R G T Stenhouse; Mrs R C L Stewart.*

Inland Revenue no. SC015074

Information available Information was provided by the trust.

General The trust will support social welfare causes, children and young people, medical and health organisations and the environment/ conservation and heritage. It supports organisations in Scotland, especially on the west coast. In 1998/99 it had assets of £805,000 and an income of £26,000. It gave grants totalling £25,000. Grants usually range from £100 to £3,000. Beneficiaries included Boys Brigade

(Glasgow battalion), Community Millennium Project Group, Maxwelton House Trust and Tarbolton Mothers and Toddlers Group.

Exclusions Grants are not given for political appeals.

Applications In writing to the correspondent. Trustees meet in January and June. Applications should be received by December and May respectively.

The Rennie Stenhouse Foundation

General

£1,800 (1998/99)

Beneficial area Mainly Scotland, with an emphasis on the west coast

Lomynd, Knockbuckle Road, Kilmacolm, Renfrewshire PA13 4JT

Tel. 01505 872716

Correspondent P D Bowman, Secretary

Inland Revenue no. SC010974

Information available Information was provided by the trust.

General The trust supports a wide variety of causes. It will consider animal welfare, children/ young people, disability, education/training, environment, conservation and heritage, medical and health organisations, overseas projects and religious appeals.

Grants can be one-off or recurrent and usually range from £60 to £250. In 1998/99 the trust had assets of £73,000 and an income of £3,100. It gave grants totalling £1,800. Beneficiaries included Anwoth & Girthon Church of Scotland, Loch Arthur Community, Prince's Scottish Youth Business Trust, RNMDSF, RSPB, Society of Deacon's & Preseses of Glasgow and Trades Hall of Glasgow Restoration Appeal.

Exclusions Grants are not given for: the arts, political appeals, social welfare and sports recreation.

Applications In writing to the correspondent. Trustees meet in March and September, applications should be received by the beginning of the month.

Alexander Stone Foundation

General

£10,000 (1998)

Beneficial area Not known

c/o Burness, 242 West George Street, Glasgow G2 4QY

Tel. 0141 248 4933 **Fax** 0141 204 1601

Correspondent Steven Phillips

Inland Revenue no. SC008261

Information available Limited information was available from the trust.

General The trust supports a range of charities, with a possible preference for Scotland. In 1998 it had an income of £30,000 and gave grants totalling £10,000.

Applications In writing to the correspondent.

The address for this trust was confirmed, but unfortunately we were unable to confirm the rest of the entry.

Talteg Ltd

Jewish, welfare

£110,000 (2000)

Beneficial area UK, with a preference for Scotland

90 Mitchell Street, Glasgow G1 3NA

Tel. 0141 221 3353

Correspondent F S Berkeley, Trustee

Trustees *F S Berkeley; M Berkeley; A Berkeley; A N Berkeley; M Berkeley; Miss D L Berkeley.*

Charity Commission no. 283253

Information available Accounts were on file at the Charity Commission, but without a grants list or a narrative report.

General In 2000 the trust had assets of £2.6 million, an income of £284,000 and an expenditure of £115,000. Grants totalled £110,000. Unfortunately, no grants list was included with the accounts.

No grants list has been available since 1993 when the trust had an income of £175,000 (£134,000 from donations) and gave £92,000 in grants. Of the 48 grants made in the year, 34, including the larger grants, were to Jewish organisations. British Friends of Laniado Hospital received £30,000 and £20,000 each was given to Centre for Jewish Studies and Society of Friends of the Torah. Other larger grants were to JPAIME (£6,000), Glasgow Jewish Community Trust (£5,000), National Trust for Scotland (£2,300) and Friends of Hebrew University of Jerusalem (£1,000).

The remaining grants were all for less than £1,000 with several to Scottish charities, including Ayrshire Hospice (£530), Earl Haig Fund – Scotland (£200) and RSSPCC (£150). Other small grants went to welfare organisations, with an unusual grant of £780 to Golf Fanatics International.

Applications In writing to the correspondent.

The Tay Charitable Trust

General

£200,000 (2000/01)

Beneficial area UK, with a preference for Scotland

6 Douglas Terrace, Broughty Ferry, Dundee DD5 1EA

Tel. 01382 779923

Correspondent Mrs Elizabeth A Mussen, Trustee

Trustees *Mrs E A Mussen; Mrs Z C Martin; G C Bonar.*

Inland Revenue no. SC001004

Information available Financial information was provided by the trust.

General This trust has general charitable purposes, supporting both local and national charities. In 2000/01 it had assets of £4.7 million and an income of £165,000. Grants totalled £200,000. They included £30,000 to RNLI, £10,000 to Ninewells Cancer Campaign and £5,000 each to Amnesty International, Imperial Cancer Research Campaign, Link, Maggie Centre, Maritime Volunteers, Ninewells Hospital and Medical School, and Prince's Scottish Youth Business Trust.

Exclusions Grants are only given to charities recognised by the Inland Revenue. No grants to individuals.

Applications No standard form; applications in writing to the correspondent, including a financial statement. An sae is appreciated.

The T C Charitable Trust

General, education

£8,500 (2000)

Beneficial area Mainly Scotland

KPMG, 24 Blythswood Square, Glasgow G2 4QS

Tel. 0141 226 5511

Correspondent The Secretary

Trustees *D G Coughtrie; R J Thomson; W J M Kinnear.*

Inland Revenue no. SC017335

Information available Information was provided by the trust.

General The trust supports general charitable purposes and education. Grants are usually to organisations. It tends to give fewer, larger grants. In 2000 five grants were given totalling £8,500. The largest grants were £3,000 each to Adam Smith Foundation and Harmeny Education Trust Ltd, although grants are not usually this high. The other beneficiaries were a school and an individual for teaching abroad.

Applications In writing to the correspondent. Applications should be received by the end of January for consideration in February. Grants are distributed in March.

The Len Thomson Charitable Trust

Young people, local projects, medical research

£30,000 (1993/94)

Beneficial area Scotland

Turcan Connell, Princes Exchange, 1 Earl Grey Street, Edinburgh EH3 9EE

Tel. 0131 228 8111 **Fax** 0131 228 8118

Correspondent Linda Bruce, Secretary

Trustees *D A Connell; Mrs E Thomson; S Leslie.*

Inland Revenue no. SC000981

General The trust supports young people, local community organisations and medical research. In 1993/94 the trust's total funds amounted to £493,000 and grants to voluntary organisations totalled £30,000. Grants which ranged between £1,000 and £15,000 were awarded to Youth Clubs – Scotland (£15,000), Save the Children (£7,000), Radiation Oncology Endowment Fund at Lothian Health Board (£5,000), Girls' Brigade (£2,000) and Newtongrange Parish Church (£1,000).

Applications In writing to the correspondent.

Scott Thomson Charitable Trust

Relief of poverty, education, Christian

£16,000 (1993/94)

Beneficial area Scotland

36 Norwood Drive, Glasgow G46 7LS

Correspondent R Scott Thomson, Trustee

Trustees *R H Craig; R Scott Thomson, Ms M B Thomson.*

Inland Revenue no. SC004071

Information available Limited information was available on this trust.

General In 1993/94 grants totalled £16,000 and were awarded to organisations concerned with the relief of poverty, the advancement of education and the Christian religion.

Up-to-date information was unavailable from this trust, which did not wish to have an entry in this guide.

Applications Contact the correspondent in writing for further details.

Trinity Park Foundation

Health, medical research

£10,000 (1998)

Beneficial area Scotland

Trinity Park House, South Trinity Road, Edinburgh EH5 3SE

Tel. 0131 552 6255

Correspondent Alan Harper

Trustees *A S Hamilton; J D Thomson; J G Adamson.*

Inland Revenue no. SC004807

Information available Limited information was available on this trust.

General The trust supports the improvement of the phyisical and mental health of people in Scotland. This includes medical research, healthcare and the prevention, diagnosis and treatment of illness. In 1998 the trust had an income of £20,000 and gave £10,000 in grants.

Applications In writing to the correspondent.

Tulip Charitable Trust
(*formerly* K C Charitable Trust)

Medical research, drug abuse, children, young people and older people

Not known

Beneficial area Mainly Scotland, especially Edinburgh

Kleinwort Benson Trustees Limited, P O Box 191, 10 Fenchurch Street, London EC3M 3LB

Tel. 020 7956 6600

Correspondent John Degan

Information available Limited information was available from the trust.

General The trust makes donations to small, local charities or to other charitable organisations. It supports groups working in fields such as medical research, drug abuse, children and young people and older people. It has an interest in supporting unemployed young people through training schemes and workshops.

Exclusions No grants are made to individuals.

Applications In writing to the correspondent. Applications are considered half-yearly.

The John Tunnell Trust

Chamber music

£44,000 (2000/01)

Beneficial area UK, with some preference for Scotland

4 Royal Terrace, Edinburgh EH7 5AB

Tel. & Fax 020 8241 9330

e-mail tunnelltrust@aol.com

Correspondent The Secretary

Inland Revenue no. SC018408

Information available Information was provided by the trust.

General The trust was set up in 1988 as a tribute to John Tunnell, who was leader of the Scottish Chamber Orchestra from its foundation in 1974 until his death in 1988.

The trust aims to promote chamber music, advance the education of young musicians and provide performance opportunities for talented chamber musicians. Grants are given to British groups and societies of two to eight chamber music players aged 27 or under.

Its main programme is to support Scottish chamber music clubs and societies for tours of Scotland. Other grants are usually given for residential chamber music courses and concerts elsewhere in the UK.

Applications Application forms are available from the correspondent at the above address. The deadline is 30 June, with auditions for potential recipients held in November.

The Unemployed Voluntary Action Fund

Voluntary projects engaging unemployed people as volunteers

£795,000 (1999/2000)

Beneficial area Scotland

Comely Park House, 80 New Row, Dunfermline, Fife KY12 7EJ

Tel. 01383 620780 **Fax** 01383 626129

e-mail uvaf@uvaf.sagehost.co.uk

Website www.uvaf.org.uk

Correspondent Mrs Sandra Carter, Administrator

Inland Revenue no. SC005229

Information available Full accounts, report and review were provided by the trust.

General The fund has the following aims:

- 'overcoming social exclusion through providing opportunities for unemployed people to volunteer

- introducing 'purpose' through volunteering for people with higher support needs

- promoting job readiness through volunteering

- promoting racial equality and reducing racial disadvantage through funding and benefiting ethnic minority groups

- providing opportunities for volunteering, for its intrinsic value, which are inclusive

- assisting projects in the fields of health, social and community development which tackle social exclusion across Scotland.'

'Projects must aim to meet needs in one or more of the fields of social and community development or health. The voluntary activity must develop a service which will positively assist those involved as volunteers and its beneficiaries. Projects should show how they will:

- combat exclusion by reducing isolation, improving communication and increasing self-worth and independence

- provide ongoing, regular, structured voluntary work

- enhance and improve skills which promote job readiness, educational opportunities and personal development.

'This application should show evidence of the need for the service and assess realistically what measurable change can be achieved.'

In 1999/2000 the fund had assets of £23,000 and an income of £1.2 million, of which £868,000 was received in 'grant-as-aid' from The Scottish Executive to distribute to local projects which create opportunities for volunteering primarily for people not in work, £275,000 was received from the Ethnic Minority Grant Scheme (EMGS) to promote racial equality and reduce racial disadvantage, and £25,000 came from National Lottery Charities Board (now Community Fund). Grants totalled £795,000, given across the following programmes:

Major grants programme – 37 grants totalling £757,000

These were broken down geographically as follows:

	no. grants	grant total
Borders/Dumfries & Galloway	5	£111,000
Central Scotland	2	£30,000
Fife	4	£61,000
Angus/Dundee	3	£74,000
Aberdeen/Aberdeenshire/Moray	4	£97,000
Highland/Western Isles	2	£38,000
West of Scotland (excluding Glasgow)	6	£125,000
Glasgow	3	£55,000
Lothians	2	£46,000
Edinburgh	6	£121,000

Grants are given for three years. Organisations receiving their first payment included Home-Start Deveron – Aberdeenshire 'to involve volunteers in providing practical help through regular home-visiting and in giving encouragement and support to access local services to young families experiencing difficulties' (£27,000); Edinburgh Voluntary Organisations Council 50+ Project to develop voluntary opportunities for people aged over 50 who are unemployed through redundancy or early retirement and to explore new approaches to recruitment and support (£22,000); Contact Point in East Dunbartonshire 'to involve volunteers in providing information on disability matters through outreach clinics in local village access points and to develop information services to meet the needs of the black and ethnic communities for information on disability matters' (£17,000); and Fife Society for the Blind 'to recruit and train visually impaired volunteers to assist with the activities of the organisation' (£3,900).

Organisations receiving continued funding included Dumfries and Galloway Council on Alcohol 'to set up a volunteer befriending project to offer practical help, advice and support to people with alcohol related problems, their families and friends' (£29,000); Penumbra Youth Project – Borders 'to establish out-of-hours activities with buddy volunteers, and recruit supportive flatmates for young people with

mental health problems living in the Scottish Borders' (£27,000); Knowetop Community Farm's Friends of the Farm Project – Dumbarton 'to establish and develop volunteer involvement, including volunteers with learning difficulties in the day-to-day running of the community farm and with visitors' (£19,000); and New Horizons Drop-in Project – Borders 'to involve key volunteers in assisting users of mental health services to operate local self-help drop-in centres in Galashiels, Hawick, Kelso and Pebbles' (£18,000).

Small grants scheme – 6 grants totalling £17,000

'For some organisations a small grant in the range of £1,500 to £4,000 provides a timely injection of funds to pilot a new project and to assess the elements to develop it further. These include improving management skills as well as the services volunteers will be involved in.

'Six grants totalling £17,000 were approved.

'The Small Grants Scheme is a rolling programme in which funding is taken up throughout the year.

'Nine projects from 1999/2000 and the previous year reported back.

'During the year 170 volunteers were recruited. In an average week in the Small Grants Scheme 89 volunteers were active, of which 79% were unemployed.

'The average time commitment was 8.2 hours.'

Beneficiaries included Young Ideas – Islay 'to develop the project and organisational and management skills through training for committee members and volunteers' (£4,000); Inverness Volunteer Centre – Handyperson's Scheme 'to help older members of the community, including those with disabilities, by providing a small repair and assistance service' (£3,300); and WRVS – Forres 'to pilot a Good Neighbour Scheme in the Forres area with a view to extending it to cover all of Moray' (£2,100).

Supplementary grants – 8 grants totalling £11,000

Beneficiaries included New Horizon – Borders (£2,200); LEAP at The LIFE Project – Cambuslang (£1,900); and Dumfries and Galloway Rape Crisis Centre (now known as South West Rape Crisis and Sexual Abuse Centre) (£500).

Training bursary scheme – 14 grants totalling £9,800

Recipients included Contact Point in East Dunbartonshire (£1,100); Creich, Croick and Kincardine District Day Care Association (£910); CARD Carers' Centre – Renfrewshire (£650); and DOSTI – The Muslim Community Groups, Edinburgh (£190).

Ethnic minority grants scheme – 13 grants totalling £275,000

These grants are administered by the fund on behalf of The Scottish Executive and are given to voluntary organisations in Scotland for projects designed to reduce discrimination and promote racial equality in the fields of employment, education, health, social welfare and law.

Exclusions Schemes which cannot be considered include exhibitions, arts clubs and performances; business co-operatives; credit unions; food co-operatives; out-of-school care; housing and hostel welfare; formal educational or vocational courses and skills and training; clean-ups and one-off projects; holidays and camps; conservation schemes; building projects, including playgrounds; social clubs; sports centres and sports activities; campaigning and political activities.

Applications Apply in writing, or telephone for a detailed guidelines pack from the correspondent. The deadline for applications for the main grants programme is 30 June; decisions are made in December. Applications to the small grants scheme are considered throughout the year.

The Anthony Walker Charitable Trust

General, environment

£7,000 (1998/99)

Beneficial area Some preference for the Barnsley area and for Scotland

Messrs Bury & Walkers, Britannic House, Regent Street, Barnsley S70 2EQ

Tel. 01226 733533

Correspondent Ben Nicholson, Clerk

Trustees *M J M Walker; Mrs H E Porteous; Mrs J R Lees.*

Charity Commission no. 326187

Information available Accounts were on file at the Charity Commission.

General The trust supports general charitable purposes and in particular environmental causes. The settlor was from Barnsley and is now living in Scotland; this is reflected to some extent in the grants list which shows a preference for Scotland. There may also be some preference for Barnsley but this is unclear. It had an income of £2,500 in 1997/98 and no grants were given in this year. In January 1999 the trust distributed an accumulated income of £7,000.

Beneficiaries included ActionAid; Friends of the Earth – Scotland; Friends of Homeopathy; John Muir Association; National Medicine Society; Oxfam; Save the Children; Search and Rescue Dog Association; The Soil Association; and Tree Aid. It is not known whether grants to UK charities were to local branches.

Exclusions Grants are not normally given to individuals.

Applications In writing to the correspondent.

The Waterside Trust

Christian, welfare

£3.9 million (2000)

Beneficial area UK and overseas

56 Palmerston Place, Edinburgh EH12 5AY

Tel. 0131 225 6366 **Fax** 0131 220 1041

Correspondent Robert Clark

Trustees *Irvine Bay Trustee Company.*

Inland Revenue no. SC003232

Information available Annual report and accounts were provided by the trust.

General The trust supports Christian causes in the UK and overseas. Grants are made to organisations which 'provide adult Christian formation and pastoral care of the young, offer educational and recreational activities for disadvantaged young people, and provide care and support for the elderly, the unemployed and deprived families, especially those with young children. The trust supports projects in the areas of community development, the homeless, the mentally ill, ex-offenders, refugees and those with a history of substance abuse'. Support for this latter category is now minimal.

In 2000 the income was £3.2 million, of which £3 million was from donations. It received 290 applications and 25 grants were made totalling £3.9 million. The assets decreased to £2.9 million. The major beneficiary in 2000 and 1999, to the extent of £2.8 million and £1 million respectively, was Rathbone Jersey Ltd. The other grants made are categorised as general, religious and charitable grants (totalling £27,000) and overseas donations (which totalled £939,000). Overseas donations ranged from £18,000 to £209,000, and most being around £50,000 to £70,000.

The largest grants were as follows: Children's National Medical Centre – USA (£208,500); Stitching Porticus – The Netherlands (£75,000); St Augustine College of South Africa (£70,600); and the Association of Sisterhoods of Kenya (£69,000).

During the year the trust received 290 applications and 25 grants were made.

Exclusions No grants to individuals, environmental projects, arts organisations, conservation groups, endowment appeals or major research projects.

Applications In writing to the correspondent for consideration on an ongoing basis.

The James Weir Foundation

Health, social welfare, heritage, research

£151,000 (1999)

Beneficial area UK, with a preference for Scotland

84 Cicada Road, London SW18 2NZ

Tel. & Fax 020 8870 6233

Correspondent Louisa Lawson, Secretary

Trustees *Simon Bonham; William J Ducas.*

Charity Commission no. 251764

Information available Full accounts were provided by the trust.

General The trust's 1999 accounts stated: 'The trustees are directed to apply the trust funds in the payment of donations or subscriptions to such charitable bodies or institutions for all or any of the charitable objects or purposes as the trustees in their absolute discretion think fit and the following charities are specifically named as potential beneficiaries in the trust deed:

• The Royal Society

• The British Association for Advancement of Science

• The RAF Benevolent Fund

• The Royal College of Surgeons

• The Royal College of Physicians

• The University of Strathclyde.

'As a matter of practice the trustees give priority to charities which meet the following criteria:

• local charities in Ayrshire and Glasgow

• charities with which Mr James Weir or his family were particularly associated

• schools and educational institutions with which Mr James Weir or his family were particularly associated

• charities with which the trustees are personally associated and where they are able to judge the value of the work

• other Scottish or national charities

• other local charities.'

In 1999 it had assets of £6.4 million and an income of £222,000. After administration charges of £50,000 (including £39,000 in investment managers' charges), grants to 125 organisations totalled £151,000. There were 25 grants of £2,000 each, 97 of £1,000 each and 3 of between £100 and £500.

Beneficiaries of £2,000 included Army Benevolent Fund – Scotland; Child Psychotherapy Trust; Crossroads Care for Carers – Scotland; Hansel Foundation; Penumbra; Royal Society of Edinburgh; Scottish Council on Alcohol; and University of Strathclyde Foundation. Recipients of £1,000 included Association for the Protection of Rural Scotland; Big Issue Foundation – Scotland; Capability Scotland; Church of Scotland; Family Mediation Scotland; Glasgow and South West Scotland Federation of Boys' and Girls' Clubs; Head Injuries Trust for Scotland; Karten CTEC Centre; National Trust for Scotland; Nancy Oldfield Trust; Reality of Work in Scotland; Royal Caledonian Schools; Scottish Adoption Service; Scottish Spina Bifida Association; and Youth Clubs Scotland. Beneficiaries of smaller grants were Gap (£500), St John Ambulance (£250) and Prospect House Appeal (£100).

Exclusions Grants are given to recognised charities only. No grants to individuals.

Applications In writing to the correspondent. Distributions are made twice yearly in June and November when the trustees meet. Applications should be received by May or October.

The Whitaker Charitable Trust

Education, environment, music, personal development

£300,000 (1999/2000)

Beneficial area UK, but mostly Nottinghamshire, Northern Ireland and Scotland

c/o Currey & Co., 21 Buckingham Gate, London SW1E 6LB

Tel. 020 7828 4091

Correspondent Edward Perks, Trustee

Trustees *D W J Price; Mrs E J R Whitaker; E R H Perks.*

Charity Commission no. 234491

Information available Accounts were on file at the Charity Commission.

General The trust has general charitable objects, with preferences for:

* local charities in Nottinghamshire and East Midlands

* music education

* agricultural and silvicultural education

* countryside conservation

* Scottish and Northern Irish charities

* spiritual matters

* prison-related charities.

In 1999/2000 the assets stood at £6 million and the income was £211,000. Grants totalling £300,000 were given to 87 organisations. The largest grants by far went to Atlantic College which received £100,000 and Opera North which received £54,000. Other beneficiaries included Marlborough College (£15,000), Babworth PCC (£7,000) and Game Conservancy – Scotland (£3,500). There were 43 other grants of £1,000 or more, recipients included Leith School of Art (£3,000), Bassetlaw Hospice (£2,000), Mencap Lincolnshire (£2,000) and Sail Training Association (£1,000). Smaller grants included £500 each to Aberdeen International Youth Festival, Dyslexia Institute, East Kilbride Befriending Project, Scottish Wildlife Trust, Scottish Opera and YMCA Scotland.

Exclusions Support is given to registered charities only. No grants are given to individuals or for the repair or maintenance of individual churches.

Applications In writing to the correspondent.

J and J R Wilson Trust

Older people, animal welfare

£105,000 (1999/2000)

Beneficial area Mainly Scotland, particularly Glasgow and the west coast of Scotland

Tho and J W Barty, 61 High Street, Dunblane, Perthshire FK15 0EH

Correspondent The Clerk

Trustees *Hugh M K Hopkins; John G L Robinson.*

Inland Revenue no. SC007411

Information available Information was provided by the trust.

General The trust supports older people and also wild or domestic animals and birds. In 1999/2000 it gave £105,000 in grants. Of this, £84,000

went to charities in support of older people, and £21,000 went to charities in support of animals and birds. The total given was less than the previous year, when £123,000 was given in grants and donations.

Examples of grants given to charities related to older people are: Crossroads (Scotland) Care Attendance Scheme (£6,000); Age Concern Scotland and Alzheimers Scotland (£5,000 each); Marie Curie Cancer Care for their home nursing service and Prince and Princess of Wales Hospice (£3,000 each). There were 12 grants of £2,000 each, and 18 of £1,000. Other grants not exceeding £1,000 came to £13,000.

Of the grants given to animal and bird related organisations, Central Scotland Countryside Trust (West Quarter Glen) received £8,000, and 10 charities received £1,000 each including PDSA, Scottish Projects Conversation Trust, Scottish Wildlife Trust (Peregrine Protection Appeal) and Zoological Society of Glasgow and the West of Scotland. Other grants not exceeding £1,000 came to about £3,000.

Exclusions No grants to individuals.

Applications In writing to the correspondent. The trustees meet once a year, usually in January, to consider grants.

The Edith & Isaac Wolfson (Scotland) Trust

Higher education, general

£88,000 (1999)

Beneficial area Scotland

8 Queen Anne Street, London W1G 9LD

Tel. 020 7323 5730 **Fax** 020 7323 3241

Correspondent Dr Victoria Harrison, Secretary

Trustees *Lord Wolfson of Marylebone; Lord Quirk; Lord Quinton.*

Inland Revenue no. SC006281

Information available Accounts were provided by the trust.

General In 1999 the trust's assets totalled £919,000, and there was an income of £75,000.

Grants are given to educational organisations, for special needs equipment. Grants committed during the year totalled £70,000. However, none of these were paid during the year, although £88,000 was given in grants committed in previous years.

Commitments were £20,000 each to Balnacraig School, Perth (for an extension to school for teenagers with special needs), Royal Blind Asylum and School, Edinburgh (for furniture for 20 bedrooms), and Beaconhurst School, Bridge of Allan (for IT equipment), and £10,000 to Edinvar, Edinburgh (for technology for people with special needs).

Exclusions No grants to individuals.

Applications Contact the correspondent at the above address for further information. The trustees meet annually in December. This charity works jointly with the Wolfson Foundation, to whom applicants should refer.

The James Wood Bequest Fund

General

£67,000 (2000)

Beneficial area Glasgow and the 'central belt of Scotland'

Messrs Mitchells Roberton, George House, 36 North Hanover Street, Glasgow G1 2AD

Tel. 0141 552 3422

Correspondent The Trustees

Inland Revenue no. SC000459

Information available Accounts are available from the trust.

General The trust gives to home and foreign missions of the Church of Scotland and other charitable organisations in the beneficial area. Grants totalled £67,000 in 2000. They are one-off and usually range from £500 to £2,000.

Exclusions Registered charities only. Grants cannot be made to individuals.

Applications In writing to the correspondent, including if possible a copy of the latest accounts, a budget for the project, sources of funding received and other relevant financial information. Trustees meet in January, April, July and October. Applications should be received by the preceding month.

The Konrad Zweig Trust

Ecology, environment and conservation

About £10,000

Beneficial area UK, with a preference for Scotland

House with Arches, Ormiston Hall, Tranent, East Lothian EH35 5NJ

Tel. 01875 340541

Correspondent Mrs Francesca Loening, Trustee

Trustees U Loening; Mrs F Loening; Prof. A Manning; Ms A Marland; Ms M Ashmole; Ms A Rookwood.

Inland Revenue no. SC004375

Information available Information was supplied by the trust.

General The trust funds charities and individuals undertaking academic and/or practical projects based on environmental concerns or on economic or social concerns which have an environmental dimension. It is interested in 'an ecologically sustainable and equitable balance between people and the environment'. Priority is given to the following types of projects:

- ecological education: aiming for a better understanding of ecological sustainability at all levels of society

- ecological economics: research projects concerned with the academic and practical development of the subject

- practical projects which provide the means towards sustainability.

It may consider arts, education or animal welfare projects if they are closely related to environment and conservation issues. The trustees are themselves engaged in ecological teaching and practical work and welcome discussion about potential projects. They like to be kept in touch with the developments of projects they have supported.

One-off or recurrent grants can be given and they usually range from £200 to £1,500. In 1998/99 the trust had assets of £136,000 and an income of £3,100. It gave £35,000 in grants, which is higher than usual; the grant total is usually about £10,000 a year. Grants included £2,000 to SUSTRANS for safe routes to school; £1,500 each to Habitat Scotland for developing an information service and Friends of the Earth for sustainable Scotland community development; £1,000 to Trees for Life for reafforestation of Glen Affric; and £500 to Venture Scotland for an organic vegetable garden.

Exclusions Beneficiaries must be registered charities. The trust does not support students for higher degrees although it may consider a specific research project which forms part of a higher degree.

Applications The trust has recently made the decision to change its funding policy. It no longer invites applications but uses its funds for specific projects identified by the trustees. The trust is also considering joining with other trusts to form a consortium of trusts with broadly similar objectives. If this is successful the policy may be changed once again.

It would therefore not appear to be appropriate for unsolicited applications to be made to this trust.

Aberdeen & Perthshire

The Aberdeenshire Educational Trust Scheme

Education

£64,000 (2000/01)

Beneficial area The former county of Aberdeen

Aberdeenshire Council, Woodhill House Annexe, Westburn Road, Aberdeen AB16 5GB

Tel. 01224 664678 **Fax** 01224 664214

Correspondent The Director of Education & Recreation

Information available Information was provided by the trust. Guidelines for applicants are available from the trust.

General The trust makes educational grants to people who live in the former county of Aberdeen, including pupils or students whose parents are resident in the former county of Aberdeen. Educational grants include, for example, apprentices, postgraduate scholarships, bursaries, travel grants and grants for further education. (For more information about grants to individuals see *The Educational Grants Directory*.)

Grants are also made to Aberdeen County schools and further education centres, as well as to clubs and organisations benefiting people in the county.

In 2000/01 it had an income of £64,000, all of which was given in grants. The maximum grant is £200. Details of beneficiaries were not provided.

Grants can be given to:

- assist in providing and maintaining playing fields and other sports facilities including equipment as the Education Authority sees fit

- schools and further education centres to assist in providing special equipment

- clubs, societies and organisations which include amongst their activities work of an educational nature

- schools and organisations to assist education in art, music and drama

- individuals and bodies to undertake educational experiments and research which will be for the benefit of people belonging to Aberdeen County. Help may also be given towards 'regional and national enterprises of an educational nature'.

All grants are seen as a minimal contribution towards the total cost of a project. Grants to individuals normally range between £10 and £200 depending upon need.

Applications On the relevant application form available from Angie Smith at the above address.

The Joseph Alexander Trust

Arts, general

About £6,000

Beneficial area Kirriemuir

53 East High Street, Forfar, Angus DD8 2EL

Correspondent J M G Blair, Solicitor

Inland Revenue no. SC014277

Information available Information was provided by the trust.

General The trust gives grants in Kirriemuir: to musical societies; for the study of art and drama; and for prizes to school children and to voluntary groups promoting interest in literature, art and recreation. It also supports local charities in

Kirriemuir. It has about £6,000 to give away each year. The maximum grant given is £5,000. Recent beneficiaries have included the local boys' brigade, scout groups and local schools for art and drama purposes.

Exclusions Only registered charities are supported. No grants to individuals.

Applications In writing to the correspondent. Trustees meet twice a year in the spring and autumn.

Boyd Anderson Bequest

Improving amenities

£940 (2001)

Beneficial area Lossiemouth

Moray Council Headquarters, High Street, Elgin IV30 1BX

Tel. 01343 543451

Correspondent The Chief Executive

Inland Revenue no. SC019068

Information available Information was provided by the trust.

General The trust operates in Lossiemouth, primarily funding improvements to local amenities. It was established in 1952. In 2001 it gave £940 in grants. The total available is usually around this amount.

Applications In writing to the correspondent.

Angus Council Charitable Trusts

General

About £2,000

Beneficial area The Angus area

Angus Council, St James's House, St James's Road, Forfar DD8 2ZE

Tel. 01307 473466

Correspondent Eileen Whittet or Fiona Anderson

Inland Revenue no. SC025065

Information available Information was provided by the trust.

General This is a collection of over 100 trusts which are managed by the council and give about £2,000 each year in total. Each trust has different specific criteria and operates individually. Those trusts which consider unsolicited applications usually advertise locally when money is available. The other trusts tend to have councillors acting as trustees, who decide how the funds should be donated.

Applications Contact the correspondents for further information.

The Arbroath Improvement Trust

Arts, education, young people

£6,200 (2000)

Beneficial area Arbroath and district

Thorntons, Brothockbank House, Arbroath, Angus DD11 1NF

Tel. 01241 872683 **Fax** 01241 871541

Correspondent A Derek Scott, Hon. Secretary & Treasurer

Trustees *Dr A W Fraser; Revd V Allen; A Smith; G McNicol; Dr R B Speirs; A D Massie; A Lauchlan; A Carnegie; E F Gilbert; R C Matthew; T R R Wood; A King; B M C Milne; Mrs S Welsh.*

Inland Revenue no. SC005622

Information available Annual accounts are available from the trust.

General The objects of the trust as outlined in the trust's accounts are described as including 'the improvement and beautifying of the town; acquiring works of art for the art gallery; purchasing books for the benefit of local students in supplement to those provided out of the library funds; encouragement of promising pupils from the town schools in any way not provided for by the educational authorities; encouragement of youth movements; in fact, anything on these or similar lines that will make the town a better place to live in, and tend to give the inhabitants a greater pride and produce a greater interest in their native town'.

Grants usually range between £200 and £500 and in 2000 totalled £6,200 given to 28 local organisations. The trust tends to make recurrent grants. The assets of the trust stood at £154,000 and the income for the year was £9,900.

A total of £1,400 was distributed between seven Arbroath primary schools and £800 between two secondary schools. The other grants were all for £200 with the exception of £400 to Arbroath Old Abbeychurch Hall Appeal. Recipients of £200 included a male voice choir, boys' brigade, horticultural society, swimming club and instrumental band.

Exclusions Churches and organisations with liquor licences are not considered.

Applications In writing to the correspondent providing full details of the organisation, the scheme requiring funding, costings and details of other funds sought/received. Trustees meet in March and October and applications should be received by the preceding month.

The Astor of Hever Trust

Youth, medical research, education

£50,000 (2000)

Beneficial area UK and worldwide, with a preference for Kent and the Grampian region of Scotland

Frenchstreet House, Westerham, Kent TN16 1PW

Tel. 01959 562051 **Fax** 01959 561286

Correspondent Lord Astor of Hever, Trustee

Trustees *John Jacob, Third Baron Astor of Hever; Irene, Lady Astor of Hever; Hon. Philip D P Astor.*

Charity Commission no. 264134

Information available Full accounts were on file at the Charity Commission.

General The trust gives grants UK-wide and internationally. It states that there is a preference for Kent and the Grampian region of Scotland, although the preference for Kent is much stronger.When Gavin Astor, 2nd Baron Astor of Hever, founded the trust in 1955, its main areas of support were arts, medicine, religion, education, conservation, youth and sport. Reflecting the settlor's wishes, the trust continues to make grants to local youth organisations, medical research and educational programmes. Most beneficiaries are UK charities and local branches of national charities.

In 2000 it had assets of just over £1 million, an income of £41,000, and a grants total of £50,000. Over 160 grants were awarded, mainly for £500 or under. Larger grants in Scotland included £5,000 to Lonach Hall Appeal and £2,500 each to the Scottish Grouse Research Trust and Game Conservancy Trust.

Smaller grants given in previous years in Kent and Scotland included £500 each to Age Concern – Fairbridge, Hospice in the Weald and St Thomas Church (Aboyne), £150 to Cromar, Upper Dee and Donside Agricultural Association and £100 to Riding for the Disabled – Burstow Park Group.

Applications In writing to the correspondent. Unsuccessful applications are not acknowledged.

A G Bain's Trust

Older and young people, children who are disabled

£50,000 (2000/01)

Beneficial area Aberdeen

2 Bon-Accord Crescent, Aberdeen AB1 2DH

Tel. 01224 587261

e-mail info@storiecs.demon.co.uk

Correspondent J C Chisholm, Trustee

Trustees *W S Crosby; C A B Crosby; J C Chisholm.*

Inland Revenue no. SC003250

Information available Notes and audited accounts were provided by the trust.

General The trust was set up in 1990 to work in the areas of the care, maintenance, welfare and education of people who are elderly or disabled in the Grampian region. Since then, the trustees have paid the free income of the residue of the trust fund to Voluntary Service Aberdeen, with certain sums designated to particular areas of the organisation's work.

The assets of the trust in 2001 stood at £1.2 million and generated an income of £84,000. There were also £103,000 realised gains on investments, which were reinvested with accrued gains. In 2000/01 Voluntary Service Aberdeen received £50,000 for a specific project. No other grants were made.

Applications Contact the correspondent for further details.

Blair Charitable Trust

Historic buildings, general

£1,400 (2000)

Beneficial area Pitlochry in Tayside

Atholl Estates Office, Blair Atholl, Pitlochry, Perthshire PH18 5TH

Tel. 01796 481355 **Fax** 01796 481211

Correspondent The Trustees

Trustees *Mrs S H Troughton; A Stewart; Dickinson Trust Ltd.*

Inland Revenue no. SC001433

Information available Brief information was supplied by the trust.

General The trust's main concern is the maintenance of the Blair Castle, its grounds and estates. After expenditure on the castle, surplus funds can be given in grants to other charitable organisations.

In 2000 the total income was £349,000 with expenditure on the castle and relevant historic buildings totalling £287,000. £1,400 was given in grants.

In the previous year it had an income of £49,000, expenditure on the castle totalled £28,000 and £10,000 was given in grants.

Applications In writing to the correspondent.

Miss Margaret Cameron's Trust

Young people, general

Not known

Beneficial area Forres and the county of Moray

Grigor & Young, Solicitors, 1 North Street, Elgin IV30 1QU

Tel. 01343 544077

Correspondent The Trustees

Inland Revenue no. SC008910

Information available Information was provided by the trust.

General This trust operates solely in Forres and the county of Moray. It was originally established to assist young people's organisations. Whilst it now gives for a wider variety of causes, it still mainly supports organisations such as playgroups and young people's groups. It usually supports organisations rather than individuals. No financial information was available.

Applications In writing to the correspondent. Funds are distributed once a year.

The Carnegie Dunfermline Trust

Social, recreational or cultural facilities

£181,000 (2000)

Beneficial area Dunfermline and Rosyth. Applicants must be based in, or have a strong connection with, this area

Abbey Park House, Abbey Park Place, Dunfermline KY12 7PB

Tel. 01383 723638 **Fax** 01383 721862

e-mail admin@carnegietrust.com

Correspondent William C Runciman, Secretary

Trustees *George R Atkinson, Chair;*
Dr D M Fraser, Vice-Chair; plus 16 life trustees,
three trustees appointed by Fife Council and three
honorary trustees.

Inland Revenue no. SC015710

Information available The trust publishes a very
comprehensive annual report and guidance notes
for applicants.

General The trust was founded in August 1903.
In Mr Carnegie's original instructions to the
Gentlemen of the Commission, he said the
endowment was 'all to be used in attempts to
bring into the monotonous lives of the toiling
masses of Dunfermline more of sweetness and
light ... some elevating conditions of life ... that
the child of my native town, looking back in after
years, however far from home it may have
roamed, will feel simply by virtue of being such
life has been made happier and better. If this be
the fruit of your labours you will have succeeded;
if not, you will have failed ... I have said your
work is experimental … If you can prove that
good can be done you open new fields to the rich
which I am certain they are to be more and more
anxious to find for their surplus wealth … .
Remember you are pioneers, and do not be afraid
of making mistakes; those who never make
mistakes never make anything. Try many things
freely, but discard just as freely … . As conditions
of life change rapidly, you will not be restricted as
to your plans or the scope of your activities'.

The trust states: 'Grants can usually be given to
any non-profit making organisation which is
properly constituted. They can also be given as
pump-priming or start-up grants.

'Your club, organisation or school must be based
in Dunfermline or Rosyth. Outwith these areas
help is restricted to Cairneyhill, Crossford and
Limekilns Primary Schools and Inverkeithing
High School.

'Support is given, for example, to projects in arts,
music, entertainment, education, play, sport,
recreation, local history, local research, heritage,
tourism, welfare, etc.

'New or innovative projects are especially
welcome as are schemes to help young people and
those disadvantaged.'

In 2000 the trust had assets of £11 million and an
income of £384,000. Grants totalled £181,000,
costs of generating funds were £44,000 and other
charitable expenditure came to £142,000. The
grants were given under different categories
shown below.

Category	Grant total
Arts projects and restoration	£980
Band concerts/competitions	£7,700
Celebrations for Civic Week/galas/festivals and Christmas	£12,000
Clubs (other than sporting)	£2,700
Coaching – sport	£7,200
Library support	£11,000
Exhibitions	£3,500
Guides/scouts/boys' brigade	£6,800
Heritage event support/tourism	£17,000
Interdenominational service	£1,50
Millennium clock	£4,600
Music festivals/bands	£6,200
Music in homes and hospitals	£2,500
Pittencrief Park/Glen Pavillion/Louise Carnegie Gates	£7,100
Sport and playing fields	£35,000
Support for disabled/hard of hearing/elderly/ mental health	£8,000
Town twinning	£1,700
Women's aid/young families/kids' outing	£5,600
Youth: playgroups/primary schools/ secondary schools	£36,000
Youth and community support	£3,300

In addition to the above, over £48,000 was
allocated to fund projects for local clubs and
organisations. Other funds are already set aside to
fund several long-term projects. Low interest
loans were also paid out or offered throughout
the year. Grants in 2000 included:

Arts
£5,000 towards the running costs of an arts re-
enactment of a painting.

Music
£2,700 towards the running costs for a concert of
Millennium Harmony in Carnegie Hall.

Sports
£2,500 towards equipment for Dunfermline
Fencing Club.

Schools
£13,000 towards the costs of bringing Edinburgh
International Science Festival's Roadshow to the
local 25 primary and 5 high schools.

Louise Carnegie Gates
Grants totalling £33,000, towards refurbishment
of these park gates.

Community
£5,000 to buy hand-held radio equipment for Dunfermline District Scout Council.

Exclusions No grants for:

- individuals (except in very special cases)

- closed clubs (i.e. groups not open to the general public to join – this does not exclude minority groups catering for specialised interests)

- political organisations or causes, commercial enterprises, religious or sectarian bodies, or military or warlike pursuits

- organisations which simply want help with maintenance and running costs; the trustees think these should be met out of subscription income. Exceptions might be made in special cases or for new bodies

- projects which have already been started

- overseas projects

- health and medical organisations.

Applications By letter at any time. 'It is sometimes difficult for the trust to steer the correct course between helping a deserving group and sapping its initiative.' Applicants are always expected to have applied to all relevant statutory bodies 'and to show members' willingness to commit existing reserves or to embark on special fundraising activities'. Applications are considered monthly.

Mrs Edith Beattie Dundas Trust

Community

About £7,000 a year

Beneficial area Arbroath

c/o Connelly & Yeoman, 78 High Street, Arbroath DD11 1HL

Tel. 01241 434200 **Fax** 01241 434100

Correspondent D J Mackintosh

Inland Revenue no. SC015213

Information available Information was provided by the trust.

General The trust states it will give grants in Arbroath for improving amenities and the social and cultural activities of the town. Grants are available for the benefit of individuals and organisations within the town. About £7,000 is available each year to be given, although the trust may accumulate funds in one year and therefore spend more the next.

Applications In writing to the correspondent. Applications must arrive by 1 August each year.

The Ellis Campbell Charitable Foundation

Youth, education, heritage, conservation

£59,000 (2000)

Beneficial area Hampshire, Perth and Kinross/Tayside

Shalden Park Steading, Shalden, Alton, Hampshire GU34 4DS

Tel. 01256 381821 **Fax** 01256 381921

e-mail ellis.campbell@virgin.net

Correspondent Michael Campbell, Chair

Trustees *Michael Campbell, Chair; Mrs Linda Campbell; Mrs Doris Campbell; Jamie Campbell; Mrs Alexandra Andrew; Laura Campbell; Trevor Aldridge.*

Charity Commission no. 802717

Information available Full accounts were provided by the trust.

General The trust objects are:

- education/assistance of disadvantaged people under 25

- preservation/protection/improvement of items of architectural/structural/horticultural/ mechanical heritage

- encouragement of community-based projects.

Trustees normally stipulate that recipients must be based in Hampshire, Perth or Kinross/Tayside. From 2001 a grant of £20,000 a year was awarded to the Scottish Community Foundation who will vet Perthshire/Tayside applications and make grants on the trust's behalf. £10,000 a year was committed to the Jubilee Sailing Trust until April 2003, and a grant of about £10,000 to the Countryside Foundation for Education was committed for 2002.

The trust's annual report broke down its charitable giving as follows:

	Total		Hampshire		Other		Perthshire/Scotland	
	£k	No.	£k	No.	£k	No.	£k	No.
Education	10.1	(10)	8.1	(7)	2.0	(1)	0	-
Heritage	5.1	(7)	1.1	(3)	2.0	(2)	2.0	(2)
Other	24.2	(44)	7.9	(13)	8.9	(26)	7.4	(5)
Youth	19.5	(24)	11.1	(12)	0.4	(4)	8.0	(8)
Total	58.9	(85)	28.2	(35)	13.3	(35)	17.4	(15)

In 2000 the trust received 308 applications. There was a major increase in giving to Perthshire (up from £8,400 in 1999), mostly effected via the Scottish Community Foundation which was given £15,000 to distribute.

The assets of the trust in 2000 stood at £974,000 generating an income of £61,000. Grants totalled £59,000. These included: £2,000 each to Basingstoke Sports Centre to refit a community sports centre and Music at Winchester for the Winchester Festival; £1,000 each to Arkwright Scholarships for further education/training in engineering, Prince's Trust for various projects and Gilbert White House for the conservation of a garden; and £500 to Winchester Detached Youth Work Project for youth counselling in rural areas.

In response to the foot and mouth epidemic in 2001, the trustees stated they were 'seeking out organisations to help those who are engaged in educating the urban population on to the true nature of farming and the wider rural economy in helping farmers who [were] reduced to bankruptcy.'

Exclusions No grants to individuals. Other than the grants made annually over a period, no grants will be made more regularly than every other year. No funding for annual running costs.

Applications In writing to the correspondent. Trustees meet in March, July and October. Applications should be submitted before the preceding month and they will not necessarily be acknowledged.

David Gordon Memorial Trust

Arts, youth work, Christian, community centres

About £8,000

Beneficial area Former Grampian region only

89 Beaconsfield Place, Aberdeen AB15 4AD

Correspondent Ms B L MacFarlane

Inland Revenue no. SC002664

Information available Information was provided by the trust.

General The trust supports the following:

* music, drama and the arts

* Christian ecumenical church services

* community centres for social welfare

* youth work.

It has about £8,000 to give in grants.

Applications In writing to the correspondent. The trustees meet in November, which is when most of the grants are dispersed. The finance committee meets an additional two or three times a year, when emergency grants can be considered.

Grampian Police Diced Cap Charitable Fund

Disability and illness

£35,000 a year

Beneficial area The Grampian police force area

Grampian Police, Queen Street, Aberdeen AB10 1ZA

Correspondent Inspector John Duncan

Inland Revenue no. SC017901

Information available Limited information was available on this trust.

General Grants totalling £35,000 a year are made to individuals who are ill or disabled, and to groups helping such individuals.

Applications In writing to the correspondent.

The Guildry Incorporation of Perth

Education, local community

£91,000 (2000/01)

Beneficial area Perth

42 George Street, Perth PH1 5JL

Correspondent Lorna Peacock, Secretary

Trustees *Roger Ward; Colin Carrie; David Donaldson; Alastair H Anderson; Richard W Frenz; Kenneth Darling; Louis Flood; Michael Norval; Neil Dewar.*

Inland Revenue no. SC008072

Information available Information was provided by the trust.

General The main purpose of the trust is to provide educational bursaries to members of the Guildry. A specific bursary is also given to non-members; recipients are nominated by schools in Perth. In 2000/01 it had an income of £174,000 and distributed £91,000 in donations, pensions and bursaries. These were broken down as follows:

weekly pensions	£14,000
quarterly pensions	£11,000
coal allowances	£5,200
school prizes	£1,800
charitable donations	£34,000
bursaries	£19,000

The only other information was contained in the trustees' report which stated that from the Millennium Fund £3,820 was spent on the Bridge at Guildtown and £2,500 was contributed to refurbishment costs at Balcraig School.

No further breakdown of the donations was given.

Applications In writing to the correspondent. The trust meets to consider grants on the last Tuesday of every month.

The Mary Jamieson Hall and John F Hall Trust

Social welfare

£4,000 to organisations (1998/99)

Beneficial area Aberdeen and surrounding area

Messrs Ritson Smith, Chartered Accountants, 16 Carden Place, Aberdeen AB10 1FX

Tel. 01224 643311

Correspondent Neil Farquharson

Trustees *P G R Saxon; J H Gray; J Birnie; J P Grant.*

Inland Revenue no. SC007754

Information available Information was provided by the trust.

General This trust makes 30 to 35 twice yearly grants of £500 to £600 to ex-employees of Hall and Tawse Scotland Ltd in Aberdeen, or their families. It also gives two or three grants of £500 to £1,000 twice a year to Aberdeen local charities such as Salvation Army, Samaritans and Cyrenians. In 1998/99 charitable organisations received a total of £4,000 in grants.

Applications Apply in writing to the correspondent.

The Patrick Mitchell Hunter Fund

General

About £10,000 a year

Beneficial area Aberdeen only

Wilsone & Duffus, PO Box 81, 7 Golden Square, Aberdeen AB10 1EP

Tel. 01224 641065 **Fax** 01224 647329

e-mail info@wilsoneduffus.co.uk

Correspondent The Administrator

Trustees *J T C Gillan; W Howie.*

Inland Revenue no. SC017380

Information available Information was available from the trust.

General This trust supports charities in Aberdeen. Grants range from £250 to £1,000, and total about £10,000 each year.

Exclusions Grants are not given to individuals or organisations which are not based in Aberdeen.

Applications In writing to the correspondent.

The Logie Charitable Trust

General

About £10,000

Beneficial area Mainly the north of Scotland, particularly Morayshire

Turcan Connell, Princes Exchange, 1 Earl Grey Street, Edinburgh EH3 9EE

Tel. 0131 228 8111 **Fax** 0131 228 8118

Correspondent The Secretary

Trustees *Colin Baxter; Mrs Graeme Laing; Earl of Leven and Melville.*

Inland Revenue no. SC011176

Information available Information was provided by the trust.

General The trust supports local community organisations. There is a preference for organisations which are known to the trustees and local branches of UK-wide organisations. About £10,000 is given in grants each year. Grants range from £25 to £5,000. Details of the beneficiaries were not available.

Applications In writing to the correspondent. The trustees distribute grants once a year, between November and January.

Mrs Williamina McLaren's Trust Fund

People who are poor, disabled, infirm or in need

£15,000 (2000/01)

Beneficial area Angus

Thorntons WS, 53 East High Street, Forfar DD8 2EL

Tel. 01307 466886 **Fax** 01307 464643

Correspondent J M G Blair

Inland Revenue no. SC003233

Information available Limited information was provided by the trust.

General The trust gives to organisations which assist people in need in Angus. In 2000/01 a total of £15,000 was distributed in grants.

Exclusions Only recognised Scottish charities are supported.

Applications In writing to the correspondent, with Scottish charity status number.

The Mollison Fund

Social welfare

About £9,000

Beneficial area City of Aberdeen

Craigens Solicitors, 13 Bon-Accord Crescent, Aberdeen AB11 6NN

Tel. 01224 588295 **Fax** 01224 575400

Correspondent D J Crombie

Trustees *Melville Watson; Mrs Doris Meston; Laurence Reid.*

Inland Revenue no. SC002300

Information available Information was supplied by the trust.

General The trust's deed stipulates it must fund Belmedie Eventide Home and Endowment Fund for Cornhill Hospital. The remaining income is given to social welfare charities in Aberdeen. About £9,000 is given in total each year in grants.

Exclusions The trust's deed states that applicants must not receive any central or local authority funding. Applicants are required to certify this in their application.

Applications In writing to the correspondent. The trustees meet in June/July each year; applications should be submitted by the end of May.

Miss Gertrude Pattullo Advancement Award Scheme

Young people aged 16 to 25 who are physically disabled

£4,600 to individuals and organisations (1999/2000)

Beneficial area Dundee and Angus

Help Unit, Blackadders, 30 & 34 Reform Street, Dundee DD1 1RJ

Tel. 01382 229222 **Fax** 01382 342220

e-mail solicitors@blackadders.co.uk

Website www.blackadders.co.uk

Correspondent Beth Anderson

Trustees *C F S Williamson; D N Gordon; D Sneddon.*

Inland Revenue no. SC000811

Information available Information was provided by the trust.

General This trust operates in Dundee and Angus for the benefit of 16 to 25 year-olds who are physically disabled. It operates by:

- 'awarding grants for the advancement in life of physically handicapped children and young persons including the payment of fees for special training and the purchase of books and equipment

- 'providing grants to enable physically handicapped young persons to establish themselves in a trade or profession for which they appear to be particularly suited

- 'paying subsistence grants to physically handicapped children and young people during their period of training for any trade or profession

- 'contributing to any scheme, trust, organisation or other body, other than those controlled or administered by a public or local authority, whose aims are similar to the purposes of the trust.'

In 1999/2000 it had assets of £67,000 and an income of £6,600. Grants ranged from £100 to £1,000 and totalled £4,600. Beneficiaries included Attic Young Project (£1,000), Angus Council for a computer for an individual (£600), and Princess Royal Trust Dundee Careers to allow a BSL interpreter to attend meetings (£500).

Applications On a form available from the correspondent at any time.

Miss Gertrude Pattullo Trust For Handicapped Boys

Boys aged 18 or under who are physically disabled

£5,300 to individuals and organisations (1999/2000)

Beneficial area Dundee and Angus

Help Unit, Blackadders, 30 & 34 Reform Street, Dundee DD1 1RJ

Tel. 01382 229222 **Fax** 01382 342220

e-mail solicitors@blackadders.co.uk

Website www.blackadders.co.uk

Correspondent Beth Anderson

Trustees *C F S Williamson; D N Gordon D Sneddon.*

Inland Revenue no. SC015505

Information available Information was provided by the trust.

General This trust supports boys aged 18 or under in Dundee and Angus who are physically disabled by providing grants ranging from £100 to £1,000 each. It achieves this by:

• 'making financial provision for such medical service appliances and comforts as may be required by physically handicapped boys and are not obtainable under the National Health Service facilities available at the time

• 'making financial provision whereby physically handicapped boys may enjoy a holiday in suitable surroundings with such nursing or other attention as their condition may require

• 'making grants to physically handicapped boys for the purposes of obtaining clothes and other necessaries

• 'contributing to any scheme, trust, organisation or other body, other than those controlled or administered by a public or local authority, whose aims are similar to the purpose of the trust.'

In 1999/2000 it had assets of £67,000 and an income of £6,200. Grants totalled £5,300. Beneficiaries included Crossroads Care Attendance Scheme (£500) and Barnardos Dundee Family Support Team for bedroom furniture (£500 each), and Dundee City Council for an individuals childcare costs (£300).

Applications On a form available from the correspondent.

Miss Gertrude Pattullo Trust For Handicapped Girls

Girls aged under 18 who are physically disabled

£14,000 to individuals and organisations (1999/2000)

Beneficial area Dundee and Angus

Help Unit, Blackadders, 30 & 34 Reform Street, Dundee DD1 1RJ

Tel. 01382 229222 **Fax** 01382 342220

e-mail solicitors@blackadders.co.uk

Website www.blackadders.co.uk

Correspondent Beth Anderson

Trustees *C F S Williamson; D N Gordon; D Sneddon.*

Inland Revenue no. SC011829

Information available Information was provided by the trust.

General This trust operates in Dundee and Angus benefitting girls aged 18 or under who are physically disabled by giving grants generally ranging from £100 to £1,000 each. It achieves it aims by:

• 'making financial provision for such medical services, appliances and comforts as may be required by physically handicapped girls and are not obtainable under the National Health Service facilities available at the time

• 'making financial provision whereby physically handicapped girls may enjoy a holiday in suitable surroundings with such nursing or other attention as their condition may require

• 'making grants to physically handicapped girls for the purpose of obtaining clothing and other necessaries

• 'contributing to any scheme, trust, organisation or other body, other than those controlled or administered by a public or local authority, whose aims are similar to the purposes of this trust.'

In 1999/2000 it had assets of £85,000 and an income of £8,300. Grants ranged from £100 to £1,000 and totalled £14,000. Beneficiaries included Brittle Bone Society – Dundee (£2,000) and Central Baptist Church for a building project and Enable – Dundee branch (£500 each).

Applications On a form available from the correspondent, at any time.

Perth & Kinross District Council Charitable Trusts

General

£30,000 (1996)

Beneficial area Perth & Kinross district

Council Building, 2 High Street, Perth PH1 5PH

Tel. 01738 475000

Inland Revenue no. SC019658

Information available Limited information was available on this trust.

General The trusts support general charitable purposes in the Perth and Kinross district, with a possible preference for social welfare. In 1996 the trusts had an income of £110,000 and gave £30,000 in grants. More recent information was not available.

Applications In writing to the correspondent.

The Thomas Primrose Trust

General

About £7,500 (1999/2000)

Beneficial area The City of Aberdeen

100 Union Street, Aberdeen AB10 1QR

Tel. 01224 428000 **Fax** 01224 644479

Correspondent Alan J Innes, Trustee

Trustees *A J Innes; Miss B L McFarlane.*

Inland Revenue no. SC004048

Information available Information was supplied by the trust.

General The trust awards grants to organisations of a 'philanthropic, benevolent, charitable or educational character and objects connected with the City of Aberdeen'. Organisations must be non-sectarian and non-political in their constitution and management.

In 1999/2000 the trust gave grants totalling £7,500. Grants ranged from £100 to £1,500. Beneficiaries included Aberdeen Care and Repair Group, Alzheimer Scotland – Action on Dementia, North East of Scotland Music School, Voluntary Service Aberdeen to the crisis fund and the fuel fund. A few grants were recurrent.

Exclusions Organisations must not be supported by rates, taxes or from public funds or sources. Grants are not given to individuals.

Applications In writing to the correspondent. Trustees meet once a year, in November.

Sight And Hearing New Experiences Fund

Education and welfare of sensory impaired children and young people

Not known

Beneficial area Dundee and surrounding areas

42 Castleloch Castle, Abernethy PH2 9LP

Correspondent The Chair

Inland Revenue no. SC026326

Information available Limited information was provided by the trust.

General The fund works with children and young people who have sensory impairment. It assists with improving education and general welfare, and will make grants to other organisations working in the same field.

Applications In writing to the correspondent.

This entry was not confirmed by the trust, but the address was correct according to the Scottish Charities Index.

Miss Margaret J Stephen's Charitable Trust

General

About £6,000

Beneficial area Mainly Dundee

Maclay Murray & Spens, 151 St Vincent Street, Glasgow G2 5NJ

Tel. 0141 248 5011 **Fax** 0141 248 5019

Correspondent The Trustees

Trustees *P J R Miller; G R G Graham.*

Inland Revenue no. SC017487

Information available Information was provided by the trust.

General The trust will support a wide range of organisations with a strong preference for Dundee. There also appears to be a preference for health and welfare causes. It gives about £6,000 in grants each year, ranging from £500 to £1,000. Recent beneficiaries have included Chest, Heart & Stroke Association, Crossroads Care Attendants Scheme and Girl Guides Association, all in Dundee. Past beneficiaries have included Dundee School Exchange for Muscular Dystrophy, The Good Shepherd Sisters, Scottish Council on Alcohol and Tayside Mountain Rescue Association. Individuals can also be supported but it is not the policy of the current trustees.

Applications In writing to the correspondent. Trustees meet once a year in March to consider grants.

The Verden Sykes Trust

See below

£16,000 (1998/99)

Beneficial area Aberdeen

20 Forvie Circle, Bridge of Don, Aberdeen AB22 8TA

Tel. 01224 704907

e-mail merrilees.forvie@dial.pipex.com

Correspondent Mrs Irene Merrilees, Administrator

Trustees *R Ellis; Dr James Merrilees; Revd J R McLaren; Mrs I Merrilees; Mrs A McCallum; Miss Anne Watt; A McRobb.*

Inland Revenue no. SC007281

Information available Guidelines and full accounts were available from the trust.

General The trust has a wide brief, but primarily supports:

- churches and Christian missions, especially St Nicholas United Reformed Church in Aberdeen
- religious education and music
- pensions to retired ministers

It can also support:

- education for children and adults
- work with young people
- the welfare of elderly and infirm people
- scientific research into disease and physical and mental disability
- the relief of poverty and the effects of natural disaster in any part of the world.

The trust supports projects mainly in Scotland, especially in Aberdeen. It can also give in the UK and supports UK-based organisations which work overseas. However, please note that applications are only invited from Aberdeen. The trust gives one-off grants for specific projects and not for capital costs. A few individuals are supported.

In 1998/99 the trust had assets of £393,000 and an income of £18,700. It gave 29 grants totalling £16,000, ranging from £30 to £1,000. Six grants of £1,000 were given to: Penumbra, a mental health charity in Aberdeen; Pillar Aberdeen; VSA/St Aubins Project; Christian Aid/Hurricane Mitch; Aberdeen Cyrennians and Instant Neighbour.

Smaller grants, mostly between £200 and £500, included those to Aberdeen Arts Centre, Aberdeen District Organist's Association, Aberdeen International Youth Festival, Prison Fellowship/Scotland – Aberdeen Centre, Strathbogie/Dunblane Church Youth Group, St Machar Cathedral/Junior Church, St Nicholas Congrational Church – Help the Aged and Visible Fictions Theatre. Four individuals were supported receiving a total of £1,400.

Exclusions Applications from the Aberdeen area only. Normally only registered charities are supported.

Applications An application form is available from the correspondent. The trust is looking for the following details:

- objectives of the organisation
- structure and management
- method for meeting goals
- funding and budgeting.

Where additional information is included this should be restricted to one side of A4. Audited accounts should be included when available. Trustees meet three times a year in February, June and November. Applications should be submitted by the second week of the preceding month.

The Arthur & Margaret Thompson Charitable Trust

General

£67,000 (2000/01)

Beneficial area The town or burgh of Kinross

Miller Hendry, 10 Blackfriars Street, Perth PH1 5NS

Tel. 01738 637311 **Fax** 01738 638685

e-mail info@miller-hendry.co.uk

Correspondent Alastair Dorwood

Inland Revenue no. SC012103

Information available Information was provided by the trust.

General This trust only gives to causes within the town or burgh of Kinross. In 2000/01 it had assets of over £2 million and an income of £155,000. Grants made during the year totalled £67,000. A wide range of causes within the beneficial area are supported.

Applications The trustees meet to consider applications about every four months.

D C Thomson Charitable Trust

General

£21,000 (1993/94)

Beneficial area Dundee and Tayside

William Thomson & Sons, 22 Meadowside, Dundee DD1 1LN

Tel. 01382 201534

Correspondent Irene Douglas

Trustees *D C Thomson & Co. Ltd; W D C & F Thomson Ltd.*

Inland Revenue no. SC018413

Information available Accounts are available from the trust for £10.

General This trust is connected to the Northwood Charitable Trust and was founded by D C Thomson & Company.

In 1993/94 it made grants ranging from £100 to £6,000, mainly to organisations working in social welfare, the arts, youth and disability. Beneficiaries included Operation Shipshape – RRS Discovery Appeal (£6,000), Talking Newspaper Association (£2,000) and £500 each to British Blind Sport – Have a go day, Scottish Fisheries Museum Trust and Scottish Commonwealth Games Youth Trust.

Applications The trust states that no applications will be considered or acknowledged.

The A F Wallace Charity Trust

General, welfare – see below

£37,000 to individuals and organisations (1999/2000)

Beneficial area UK, with a preference for Aberdeenshire

Enfield Investments Ltd, Bartlett House, 9–12 Basinghall Street, London EC2V 5NS

Tel. 020 7726 0835

Correspondent S J Thornton

Trustees *Falconer Alexander Wallace;*
Alistair James Wishart Falconer Wallace.

Charity Commission no. 207110

Information available Full accounts were on file
at the Charity Commission.

General This trust has general charitable
purposes, particularly supporting older people in
the Upper Donside area of West Aberdeenshire.
The Wallace family lived in Aberdeenshire and
the trustees try to reflect this in their
grantmaking.

In 1999/2000 the trust had assets of £855,000 and
an income of £47,000. It gave grants totalling
about £36,000. Grants were divided as follows:

- assistance to senior citizens in the Upper
  Donside area of west Aberdeenshire (seven
  grants totalling £23,000)

- former employees of Bombay Burmah Trading
  Corporation (totalling £7,300)

- registered charities (£400)

- other charitable donations (£6,000).

Applications In writing to the correspondent.

Central Scotland

The Appletree Trust

Disability, sickness, poverty

£41,000 (1998/99)

Beneficial area UK and overseas, with a preference for the north east Fife district

Royal Bank of Scotland plc, Private Trust & Taxation, 2 Festival Square, Edinburgh EH3 9SU

Tel. 0131 523 2648 **Fax** 0131 228 9889

Correspondent Don Henderson

Trustees *The Royal Bank of Scotland plc; Revd W McKane; Revd Dr J D Martin; Revd L R Brown.*

Inland Revenue no. SC004851

Information available Information was provided by the trust.

General This trust was established in the will of the late William Brown Moncour in 1982 to relieve disability, sickness and poverty. The settlor recommended that Action Research for the Crippled Child, British Heart Foundation and National Society for Cancer Relief should receive funding from his trust, particularly for their work in the north east Fife district.

In 1998/99 the trust had assets of £1.3 million. It had an income of £41,000, all of which was given in 11 grants ranging from £700 to £7,500. The largest went to Rymonth Housing Society Ltd (£7,500), Children's Hospice Association Scotland (£7,000) and Home Start North East Fife and Macmillan Cancer Relief Fife Project (£5,000 each). The other grants were £3,000 each to Imperial Cancer Research, Riding for the Disabled Association and Sight Savers International, £2,500 to Epilepsy Association of Scotland, £2,000 each to Enable and Marie Curie Cancer Care and £720 to Fife Society for the Blind.

Applications In writing to the correspondent. Trustees meet to consider grants in October and November. Applications should be received from July to September.

The Bruce Charitable Trust

Community work

£10,000 (2000/01)

Beneficial area Cupar, Fife

James Murray & Co., Chartered Accountants, 58 Bonnygate, Cupar, Fife KY15 4LD

Tel. 01334 654044

Correspondent G Lindsay, Trustee

Trustees *P W Hutchison; G Lindsay; Ms Elizabeth L Calderwood; Ms S A Clark.*

Inland Revenue no. SC014927

Information available Information was provided by the trust.

General The trust's purposes (confined to the borough of Cupar) are to support:

- Poor, aged, infirm or distressed people and charities or organisations providing assistance to, or facilities for such people.

- The creation or maintenance of youth organisations which provide cultural or recreational facilities for young people and creation and maintenence of other organisations which exist for the welfare of young people.

- Holidays or convalescing facilities at home or abroad for people who are suffering from or recovering from illness or disability and whose circumstances are such that they are unable to meet the cost of holidays or periods of convalescence.

• Cultural, educational and recreational facilities and any project which the trustees may consider for the benefit of the community.

Applications In writing to the correspondent.

Falkirk Temperance Trust

Alcohol, drug-related projects

About £10,000 to £15,000

Beneficial area The former burgh of Falkirk

Falkirk Council, Municipal Buildings, Falkirk FK1 5RS

Tel. 01324 506070 **Fax** 01324 506363

Correspondent A Jannetta, Director of Finance

Trustees *Three elected members are appointed to the trust.*

Inland Revenue no. SC001904

Information available Information was provided by the trust.

General The trust gives grants to address alcohol and drug-related problems. Organisations and individuals are supported in the former burgh of Falkirk. The grant total is about £5,000 to £10,000 each year. Grants usually range from £1,000 to £2,000 each. Most grants are given to organisations.

Applications In writing to the correspondent. Apply at any time.

Fife Council Charitable Trusts

General

Not known

Beneficial area Fife area

Corporate Policy, Fife Council, Fife House, Glenrothes KY7 5LT

Tel. 01592 416164

Correspondent Nicola Buchanan

Inland Revenue no. SC025078

Information available Brief information was provided by the trust.

General There are 17 grants schemes the council distributes funds through. These cover arts and heritage, community involvement, environmental grants, local economic development, social work projects, youth work, sports, community organisations, tenants grants, transport, community safety, start-up costs, community capital grants, floral enhancement, international women's week and childcare. Grants are given to voluntary organisations in the Fife area only.

Exclusions No grants to political organisations.

Applications In writing to the correspondent. Organisations applying must have a constitution, bank account, provision for accounts and a clear link to the trust's aims and objectives.

Fife Council – Common Good Funds and Trusts (East)

Individuals in need, community groups

£45,000 (2000/01)

Beneficial area East Fife

Fife Council, County Buildings, St Catherine Street, Cupar, Fife KY15 4TA

Tel. 01334 412200 **Fax** 01334 412940

Correspondent The Area Law & Administration Manager (East)

Inland Revenue no. SC019393

Information available Information was provided by the trust.

General The Common Good Funds and Trusts (East) administered by Fife Council is a collection of about 100 small trusts. Both individuals in need and local community groups can be supported, for example community councils, sports clubs etc. The following types of causes will be considered:

- arts
- buildings
- conservation/environment
- disability
- education/training
- heritage
- hospitals/hospices
- social welfare, people of all ages
- sports/recreation.

Most towns and large villages in East Fife feature in the beneficial areas of this collection of trusts, details of which can be obtained from the correspondent.

In 2000/01 the combined funds and trusts had assets of £170,000 and an income of £116,000. Grants totalled £45,000, leaving a large surplus of £71,000. The size of the grant depends on the individual trusts.

Exclusions The following causes are not supported:

- animal welfare
- medical/health and medical research
- overseas projects
- political appeals
- religious appeals.

Applications Contact the correspondent for further details. An application form and guidelines are available for the Common Good Funds but not for the trusts. Trustees meet monthly to consider applications.

New St Andrews Japan Golf Trust

Sport, recreation

£9,900 (1999/2000)

Beneficial area The county of Fife

Chestney House, 149 Market Street, St Andrews, Fife KY16 9PF

Tel. 01334 472255 **Fax** 01334 475792

Correspondent David S D Robertson, Secretary

Trustees *Sir Michael Bonallack; John Philp; Michael L Joy; David S D Robertson.*

Inland Revenue no. SC005668

Information available Information was supplied by the trust.

General This intriguingly named trust supports both individuals and groups associated with younger people for sports and recreational purposes. It mainly makes one-off grants within the county of Fife.

In 1999/2000 the trust had assets of £103,000 and an income of £7,000. Grants totalled almost £10,000, ranging from £100 to £1,500.

Applications In writing to the correspondent.

Paul Charitable Trust

Community work

£40,000 (1999)

Beneficial area Balfron and Kilearn and the surrounding area

c/o Morrison Bishop, 2 Blythswood Square, Glasgow G2 4AD

Tel. 0141 248 4672 **Fax** 0141 221 9270

Correspondent Miss Helen Stirling

Trustees *W G Davidson; G A Murray; J N P Ford; J F Bisset.*

Inland Revenue no. SC023880

Information available Information was confirmed by the trust.

General The trust makes grants for the provision of sports and recreation facilites, adult education and drama and music or other recreational activities. It gives grants to people in need and also to voluntary organisations or clubs with similar objects. The trust's work is for the benefit of people in the Balfron and Kilearn area.

In 1999 the trust had an income of £30,000 and gave grants totalling £40,000.

Applications In writing to the correspondent. The trustees meet quarterly.

Stirling Council Charitable Trusts

General

Not known

Beneficial area Stirling

Stirling Council, Viewforth, Stirling FK8 2ET

Correspondent Bob Jack, Director of Finance & Information Services

Inland Revenue no. SC025090

Information available Limited information was available on this trust.

General A number of local trusts are administered by the council. Grants are made to a range of organisations in Stirling. No further information was available.

Applications In writing to the correspondent.

Edinburgh, the Lothians & the Borders

The Benfield Motors Charitable Trust

Poverty, sickness, older people, general

£44,000 (1999/2000)

Beneficial area Worldwide with preferences for north east England, Leeds and Edinburgh

Benfield Motor Group, Asama Court, Newcastle Business Park, Newcastle upon Tyne NE4 7YD

Tel. 0191 226 1700 **Fax** 0191 272 4855

Correspondent Mrs Lynn Squires, Hon. Secretary

Trustees *John Squires, Chair; Malcolm Squires; Stephen Squires; Mrs Lynn Squires.*

Charity Commission no. 328149

Information available Full accounts were on file at the Charity Commission.

General This trust is financed by annual donations of £50,000 from Addison Motors and has general charitable purposes, with a preference for the north east of England.

In 1999/2000 it had assets of £30,000 and an income of £50,000. Grants to 75 organisations totalled £44,000.

The largest grants were £10,000 to Community Foundation (which also received three other grants totalling £480), £7,600 to St Oswald's Hospice, £6,700 to Tyneside Foyer, £3,000 in three grants each to British Red Cross and Christian Aid and £1,000 each to Acorn Centre Youth Project and The Church of St Thomas the Martyr.

Applications In writing to the correspondent.

The Bruce Bequest

Young people with learning difficulties

About £2,500

Beneficial area Edinburgh City

c/o Verandah Club, Royal Edinburgh Hospital, Morningside Terrace, Edinburgh EH10 5HF

Tel. 0131 313 6716

Correspondent Mrs Alison Goodwin

Trustees *Mrs M K Watt; J Briggs.*

Inland Revenue no. SC000354

Information available Information was supplied by the trust.

General The trust makes grants totalling about £2,500 a year, to young people with learning difficulties.

The committee has supported adult training centres and respite homes to enhance the leisure activities of the trainees, and other organisations offering social activities and group leisure for people with learning difficulties. Small grants are available between £50 and £100.

Exclusions Carers' expenses/salaries are not covered.

Applications Application forms are available from the correspondent.

The Courant Fund for Children

Children in need

£4,500 (1999/2000)

Beneficial area Edinburgh and district

41 Buckstone Loan, Edinburgh EH10 6UJ

Tel. 0131 445 3043

Correspondent David A G Taylor, Honorary Secretary

Inland Revenue no. SC017462

Information available Information was provided by the trust.

General The trust supports children in need. Grants are awarded to organisations working with children and cover the costs of holidays, outings, clothing, equipment and entertainment. In 1999/2000 it had an income of £5,000 and gave grants totalling £4,500. Grants ranged from £50 to £200. Beneficiaries have included children's hospitals, police aid, schools, Salvation Army and University of Edinburgh Children's Holiday Project.

Applications In writing to the correspondent. Trustess meet to consider grants in February and September. Applications must be received by January and August respectively.

East Lothian Educational Trust

Education, recreation

£31,000 (1998/99)

Beneficial area East Lothian council area, excluding Wallyford, Whitecraig and Musselburgh

John Muir House, Council Buildings, Haddington, East Lothian EH41 3HA

Tel. 01620 827436

Correspondent Kim Stirrat, Clerk

Inland Revenue no. SC010587

Information available Information was supplied by the trust.

General The trust supports education, sports and recreation and the arts. It supports schools and individuals. In 1998/99 it had assets of £1.1 million and an income of £46,000. Grants totalled £31,000. Grants are not usually more than £400. It supported university undergraduate and postgraduate students, schools, athletics and visits abroad by young people.

Applications On a form available from the correspondent. Trustees meet to consider grants in September. Applications should be sent by August 15th.

Edinburgh Children's Holiday Fund

Organisations providing holidays for children or helping with children's welfare

£59,000 (2000)

Beneficial area Edinburgh and the Lothians

Bryce, Wilson & Co., Chartered Accountants, 13a Manor Place, Edinburgh EH3 7DH

Tel. 0131 225 5111 **Fax** 0131 220 0283

Correspondent The Secretaries

Trustees *W G Waterson, Chair; Lady Clerk; Mrs P Balfour.*

Inland Revenue no. SC010312

Information available Information was provided by the trust.

General The trust supports organisations and charities which are concerned with the welfare of children and the provision of holidays for them.

In 2000 it had assets of £1.7 million and an income of £68,000. Grants allocated to 30 organisations totalled £59,000, 13 grants were recurrent from the previous year. This included grants to the councils of city of Edinburgh, Mid Lothian and West Lothian for the benefit individuals. Other grants ranged from £250 to £10,000. The largest grants were given to Children 1st (£10,000), Roses Charitable Trust

(£4,500), Sense Scotland (£3,200), Greendykes Primary School (£2,000), and Stepping Stones (£1,800).

Five grants were for £1,500 including those to Craigroyston Community High School, Craigmuir Primary School and Hopscotch. Smaller grants included those to Edinburgh Family Service Unit, Midlothian Women's Aid, and Scottish Down's Syndrome Association (all £1,000).

Applications On a form available from the correspondent. Trustees meet to consider grants in January and May. Applications should be sent in mid-December and mid-April respectively.

City of Edinburgh Charitable Trusts

General – see below
£295,000 to organisations (2000/01)
Beneficial area Edinburgh

Investment and Treasury Department, Edinburgh City Council, 12 St Giles Street, Edinburgh EH1 1PT

Tel. 0131 469 3895 **Fax** 0131 225 6356

Correspondent Susan Sharkie

Inland Revenue no. SC006504

Information available Information was provided by the trust.

General The City of Edinburgh Charitable Trusts is a collection of about 130 trusts which support both individuals and organisations in Edinburgh. They will support the following causes:

- arts
- children and young people
- education/training
- hospitals/hospices
- older people
- religious appeals
- social welfare
- sports/recreation.

In 2000/01 the individual trusts had assets ranging from £5 to £6.4 million. The combined assets were £14 million and the income was £582,000. Grants totalled £434,000, of which £295,000 was given to organisations and schools. Grants can be one-off or recurrent and usually range from £10 to £100. Grants to individuals were made in the form of pensions.

Exclusions The trust does not support:

- animal welfare
- buildings
- disability
- environment/conservation
- heritage
- medical/health, including medical research
- overseas projects
- political appeals.

Applications The application procedure varies with each individual trust. Contact the correspondent for further details.

Edinburgh Merchant Company Charitable Trust

Schools
Not known
Beneficial area City of Edinburgh and county of Midlothian

Edinburgh Merchant Company, 22 Hanover Street, Edinburgh EH2 2EP

Correspondent R H Wilson, Secretary

Inland Revenue no. SC022283

Information available Brief information was supplied by the trust.

General The trustees for this trust administer a number of other trusts, which are concerned with education provision at Edinburgh Merchant Company schools and in the care of the elderly.

Applications In writing to the correspondent.

The Edinburgh Old Town Charitable Trust

Education, social welfare

£2,900 (2000/01)

Beneficial area Edinburgh Old Town and South Side

Southbridge Resource Centre, 6 Infirmary Street, Edinburgh EH1 1LT

Tel. 0131 477 2910 **Fax** 0131 477 2907

e-mail neighbourhoodsproject@yahoo.co.uk

Correspondent Ms Margaret Allan, Administrator

Trustees *Ms Anja Amsel, Chair; Ian Begg; Mrs Linda Bettles; Robert Cairns; Lady Dunpark; John Ellis; Richard Ewing; Andrew Holmes; Cllr Sheila Kennedy; Andrew Kerr; Dr Derek Lyddon; Dr Harold Mills; Revd Charles Robertson; Graham T Ross; Revd Dr Duncan Shaw; Stewart Skirving; Dr Donald Smith; Robert Smith; James Thomson; Mrs Mary Whitfield; Lt Col. D J Wickes; Mrs Margaret Wilson; Andrew Wilson.*

Inland Revenue no. SC015514

Information available Information was provided by the trust.

General This trust was set up in 1987 to provide a channel for private funding to social welfare projects in Edinburgh Old Town and now includes the South Side. As a fundraising trust its income varies considerably from year to year. Grants usually range from £100 to £4,000.

In 2000/2001 it gave £2,900 in grants, including £300 to South Side Association towards the creation of a new community facility, £300 to Nelson Hall Steering Group for the development of a disused local hall and £1,000 to Canongate Youth Project towards a new minibus.

Exclusions Profit-making organisations, organisations without charitable status and individuals are excluded.

Applications Application forms are available from the correspondent.

Edinburgh Voluntary Organisations' Trust Funds

Social welfare, local community

£141,000 (2000)

Beneficial area Edinburgh and the Lothians

14 Ashley Place, Edinburgh EH6 5PL

Tel. 0131 555 9100 **Fax** 0131 555 9101

e-mail dianne.evoc@ukonline.co.uk

Correspondent Janette Scappaticcio, Trust Fund Administrator

Trustees *Maureen O'Neill; Jayne Fisher; Graeme Thom; Geoffrey Lord; Monica Langa.*

Information available Information was provided by the trust.

General At present the Edinburgh Voluntary Organisations Council is the administrative structure for the following trusts: Thomas Barclay Bequest; Miss A Beveridge's Trust; Buccleuch Place Trust; Christie Bequest; Edinburgh Coal Fund; Edinburgh Night Shelter Trust; New Town Dispensary; Quiller Bequest; James Richardson Trust; Scougall Bequest; William Thyne Trust; Kenneth Young Bequest and the Key Fund.

In addition, the Miss Anderson of Moredun Bequest and the Children in Need funds are reserved.

It now administers these together and there is one application form for organisations. The trustees then decide which fund is most appropriate.

Criteria and priorities

The trustees have revised their grant-making policy with effect from April 2001 in recognition of the difficulty that local voluntary organisations face in attaining regular funding for their main activites. During the period 2001 to 2005 the trust is looking to support social welfare causes, especially local initiatives which benefit people in Edinburgh and the Lothians. Applicant organsiations must:

- be properly constituted and registered charities

- be solvent and not have any debts

- have an imaginative and 'sound' plan

* have a turnover of less than £250,000

* show that they have made progress in the past or formative year, by providing accounts and report and particular examples of activity and tasks undertaken.

Priority is given to:

* local organisations – national organisations must indicate need in Edinburgh and the Lothians and have an independent local committee and accounts so the responsibiltiy is with the local initiative (financial restrictions above will apply only to the local unit)

* organisations that are not eligible for large sums of statutory or lottery funding

* organisations providing social service activties that assist people most in need

* organisations involving appropriate participation of volunteers.

Examples of activities that will be considered include: support groups for carers, older people, single parents, homeless young people, young people's clubs and work with and by people who are disabled. Arts or environmental tasks will only be considered when a social service or therapeutic is the main aim.

Types of grants

Grants are given for core funding to cover any main administrative or developmental need including salaries. They can be to:

* assist initial progress in any new local charitable organisations in its initial three-year period, grants can be up to £2,000 a year

* assist further progress in any local charitable organisation or its local project, grants can be up to £3,000 a year.

Grants for a genuine new development, after the first three years may also be provided to a local organisation, up to an amount of £3,000 and excluding salaries.

Grants to individuals

Grants will also be considered on behalf of individuals who are in serious need of assistance. Organisations must be recognised agencies in the City of Edinburgh and the Lothians. These grants are normally under £200. For further details see *A Guide to Grants to Individuals in Need.*

In 1999/2000 the trusts had assets of £3.7 million, an income of £242,000 and gave £141,000 in grants. The trust gave 31 grants of £1,000 or more to organisations, totalling £73,000, and a further £15,000 in smaller grants. The largest grant of £4,000 went to Edinburgh Family Service Unit. Grants of £1,000 each included those to Drake Music Project, Dosti Muslim Group, Out of the Blue Trust and YWCA (Roundabout Centre). Other grants included those to Edinburgh Association of Mental Health, Volunteer Tutor Organisation, Edinburgh Development Group, Positive Help and Shelter. In addition, 286 grants totalling £14,000 were given via BBC Children in Need and grants were given to 513 individuals totalling £39,000.

Exclusions No grants are given to or for:

* non-registered charities

* general appeals

* statutory agencies or to replace statutory funding

* commercial organisations or purposes

* private schools and colleges

* distribution by other agencies

* repairs, extensions and alterations for property or for new buildings (grants can be given for essential equipment as part of a project).

During 2001 to 2005 the trust regrets that applications will not be available for schools and related centres for any purpose, including educational and adventure projects, holidays or day visits.

Applications On a form available from the correspondent. Applications must be submitted to Edinburgh Voluntary Organisations Trust (EVOT) and not to the individual trusts. (If an applicant wishes to prepare an application by computer, the headings and respective information should be entered in the order and style of the application form.) A copy of the latest annual report and audited accounts must be included otherwise the application will not be considered (if not available a copy of the most recent unaudited accounts with an explanation). Only one application for a particular project will be considered in a twelve-month period, whether successful or not. Deadlines for applications are the end of February, May, August or November. Guidelines and application forms are available in large print and on tape.

The Edinvar Trust

Community welfare, housing research

£22,000 (1999/2000)

Beneficial area Edinburgh, the Lothians and areas in which Edinvar works

Wellgate House, 200 Cowgate, Edinburgh EH1 1NQ

Tel. 0131 225 2299 **Fax** 0131 225 4400

e-mail helenforsyth@edinvar.co.uk

Correspondent Helen Forsyth, Trustee

Trustees *Garry Watson; Norma Jones; Derek Munn; Helen Forsyth; Angela Yih.*

Inland Revenue no. SC011638

Information available Accounts were available from the trust.

General The trust was founded by Edinvar Housing Association to benefit its charitable activities.

The objects of the trust are:

* The provision of housing and associated amenities for people who old, infirm and otherwise in need.

* Research into housing and related matters.

The trust normally considers grants for housing, supported living and community activities which will assist the charitable work of Edinvar Housing Association, its subsidiaries, associated bodies and the communities in which they work.

Grants totalled £22,000 for the year, £7,700 of which was paid from the unrestricted reserve, the other £14,000 being paid out from the restricted funds and going to Dedridge Community Council. From the unrestricted £7,700, eight donations were made. These were £2,000 each to Connections user Group and Edinburgh Volunteer Tutors Organisation, £1,000 each to Positive Action in Housing and Edinburgh Sitters, £650 to ECC Millennium Celebrations, £500 to Scottish Housing and Support Conference, £350 to Edinburgh & Lothian Council on Alcohol and £200 to Wester Hailes Children's Play Project.

Exclusions Grants are not normally made to grant-giving trusts, for revenue funding beyond one year, or to individuals.

Applications On a form available from the correspondent. Trustees meet in February, May, August and November. Applications should be received by the preceding month.

The Alice Hamilton Trust

Preservation and improvement of the environment of the village of West Linton, recreational facilities for residents

About £5,000 to individuals and organisations

Beneficial area West Linton and surrounding areas

c/o West Linton Community Council, West Linton, Peebleshire EH46

Correspondent The Chair

Inland Revenue no. SC018803

Information available Information was provided the trust.

General The trust makes grants totalling about £5,000 a year to individuals, clubs and societies. It supports the preservation and improvement of the environment of the village of West Linton, and also makes grants towards recreational facilities and education for residents.

Applications In writing to the correspondent.

R S Hayward Trust

Education and training, community, older people, ex-services, health

Not known

Beneficial area Mainly Galashiels

c/o Pike & Chapman, Solicitors, Bank Street, Galashiels, Selkirkshire TD1 1ER

Tel. 01896 752379   **Fax** 01896 754439

Inland Revenue no. SC015427

Information available Limited information was available on this trust.

General The trust supports the following causes in Galashiels:

- educational organisations or clubs concerned with arts and crafts or culture
- the improvement of amenities in the burgh
- general welfare and accommodation of retired people
- the training in a trade or profession of anyone who has been incapacitated while in the armed forces
- Scottish organisations concerned with the care of people who are elderly, sick or blind.

No financial information was available.

Applications In writing to the correspondent.

Jewel Miners Welfare Charitable Society

Recreation, leisure

Not known

Beneficial area Jewel area of Edinburgh

56 Duddingston Park South, Edinburgh EH15 3LJ

Tel. 0131 669 5955

Correspondent The Secretary

Inland Revenue no. SC015240

Information available Limited information was available on this trust.

General The society makes grants to organisations working to improve the Jewel area of Edinburgh generally and the living conditions of the community.

Applications In writing to the correspondent.

Kenneth Paul Trust

General

£4,100 (1998)

Beneficial area West Linton

23 Bogsbank Road, West Linton, Peeblesshire EH46 7EN

Correspondent G L H Barlee

Inland Revenue no. SC019967

Information available Information was provided by the trust.

General The trust supports St Andrews' Church and various local groups in West Linton. In 1998 it had assets of £72,000 and an income of £9,500. It gave grants totalling £4,100. Grants usually range from £25 to £5,000.

Applications In writing to the correspondent at any time.

The Pleasance Trust

Disadvantaged young people

£27,000 (2000)

Beneficial area Edinburgh

23 St Andrew Square, Edinburgh EH2 1BB

Tel. 0131 226 3271

Correspondent Jacqueline Anderson, Secretary

Trustees *N Campbell; Barry McCorkell; David Thomson.*

Inland Revenue no. SC000309

Information available Information was provided by the trust.

General The trust gives grants to voluntary organisations such as youth clubs working with disadvantaged young people in Edinburgh and also to schools. In 2000, it had an income of

£23,000 and gave grants totalling £27,000. Grants usually range from £100 to £1,000. Of the 61 grants made, five were for £1,000. These were to Craigroyston Community High School, Edinburgh Family Service Unit, Edinburgh University Children's Holiday Venture, Granton Primary School and Kingsinch School.

Smaller grants went to youth groups and schools, and a variety of other young people's organisations and projects.

Exclusions No grants to individuals or to national organisations (except occasionally for specific local projects).

Applications In writing to the correspondent. Trustees distribute grants quarterly in January, April, July and October.

The Ponton House Trust

Young people, disadvantaged groups, older people, disability

£32,000 (2000)

Beneficial area Lothians

11 Atholl Crescent, Edinburgh EH3 8HE

Tel. 0131 477 8708 **Fax** 0131 229 5611

Correspondent David S Reith, Secretary

Trustees *G Gemmell; Hon. Lord Grieve; Mrs G Russell; Mrs J Gilliat; Revd J Munro; Mrs F Meikle; A Dobson.*

Inland Revenue no. SC021716

Information available Information was supplied by the trust.

General Grants are given to charities working with people aged 16 to 25, particularly to disadvantaged groups as well as those providing training. The trustees are also keen to support charities where help would make all the difference to their financial viability. Grants usually range between £300 and £2,000.

The trust also operates a 'Donate-a-Duvet' scheme providing free bedding to people, on referrals from medical practices or social workers. It has assets of about £1 million and an income of about £36,000. Grants totalled £32,000 in 2000.

Applications In writing to the correspondent. Trustees usually meet in January, April, July and October. Applications should include a full explanation of the project for which funding is sought plus annual reports and accounts.

The Red House Home Trust

Education and training, young people

£12,000 to organisations (2000)

Beneficial area East Lothian

c/o Scott-Moncrieff, 17 Melville Street, Edinburgh EH3 7PH

Tel. 0131 473 3500

e-mail graeme.thom@scott-moncrieff.com

Trustees *Dr R E J George, Chair; R Graeme Thom; Revd R H Brown; M Mavor; A Devlin; Mrs M McBride; Ms A McKinlay; Revd A J Roundhill.*

Inland Revenue no. SC015748

Information available Information was provided by the trust.

General The trust promotes the education and training of disadvantaged young people under the age of 22, to help them into independent living.

In 2000 the trust's assets totalled £537,000, it had an income of £25,000 and it gave grants totalling £17,000, including £5,800 to individuals and almost £12,000 to organisations.

Grants of £1,000 or over were: £2,400 to NCH Action for Children, for the 'young East Lothian homeless project'; £1,800 to Bridge Centre Management Committee for a training scheme 'via music'; £1,700 East Lothian Yacht Club for new training equipment; and £1,000 each to Red School Youth Centre for its summer programme and Prestonpans Partnership Breakfast Club, for setting up two breakfast clubs. A further eight grants were made to organisations, ranging from £350 to £700.

Applications In writing to the correspondent.

Lord Rosebery Charitable Settlement

General

About £5,000

Beneficial area Mainly Edinburgh and the Lothians

PricewaterhouseCoopers, Erskine House, 68 Queen Street, Edinburgh EH2 4NH

Tel. 0131 226 4488

Correspondent Mrs Jane Clark

Trustees *Rt Hon. Seventh Earl of Rosebery; Countess of Rosebery; D M Henderson.*

Inland Revenue no. SC008740

Information available Information was provided by the trust.

General The trust supports general charitable purposes mainly in Edinburgh and the Lothians. It has a preference for children's organisations and organisations working with disadvantaged people. It has about £5,000 to give away in grants. The maximum grant is normally £1,000. Examples of beneficiaries were not available.

Exclusions No grants to individuals.

Applications In writing to the correspondent. Trustees meet in February to consider grants.

The Russell Bequest

Sport

£102,000 (2000/01)

Beneficial area North Berwick

Lyle Crawford & Co., 15 Glenorchy Road, North Berwick EH39 4PE

Tel. 01620 892090 **Fax** 01620 892091

e-mail lyle.crawford@btinternet.com

Correspondent Mr Crawford

Trustees *J B Macnair; Cllr P O'Brien; Cllr Diana Kinnear.*

Inland Revenue no. SC001207

Information available Information is available from the correspondent above.

General The trust gives grants to sports organisations in North Berwick. Schools can be supported. No further information was given by the trust.

Exclusions Grants are only awarded for sports in North Berwick and are not available for private clubs.

Applications In writing to the correspondent. Apply at any time.

W J Underwood's Testamentary Trust

Medical research

About £5,000 a year

Beneficial area Edinburgh

Messrs Lindsays, 11 Atholl Crescent, Edinburgh EH3 8HE

Tel. 0131 229 1212

Correspondent C S Kennedy

Inland Revenue no. SC001625

Information available Information was confirmed by the trust.

General The trust supports medical research projects in Edinburgh. Grants total about £5,000 a year.

Applications In writing to the correspondent.

John Watson's Trust

Children and young people

£158,000 (2000)

Beneficial area Scotland, with a preference for Lothian

Signet Library, Parliament Square, Edinburgh EH1 1RF

Tel. 0131 220 1640

e-mail jwatson@signet.fsnet.co.uk

Correspondent Iola Wilson, Administrator

Trustees *Six representatives of the Society of Writers to Her Majesty's Signet: two from Lothian Regional Council – Councillor Ewan Aitken, Glen Rodger; one from the Lothian Association of Youth Clubs – Nancy L G Ovens; co-opted trustees – Fraser D Falconer; Dr David C Drummond; Pippa Snell; John Kerr; R Shaun Pringle.*

Inland Revenue no. SC014004

Information available Information was provided by the trust. Background notes were available from the trust.

General This trust makes grants to children and young people under 21 who are physically or mentally disabled or socially disadvantaged, for education and training, equipment, travel, recreational and cultural activities. Grants are given both to individuals and charitable organisations. There is a preference for Lothian residents. There is also provision for a limited number of boarding school grants, for residents in Scotland only.

The trust's assets in 2000 were valued at £4 million, and generated an income of £195,000. After expenses, donations totalled £158,000. The grants committee met seven times during 2000 and grants were distributed as follows:

Individuals
166 individual grants were made for education and 'advancement in life'.

Grants to individuals included equipment for people who are disabled, in-school special expenses, tutoring for children who are dyslexic, fees for special schools, post-school education for disadvantaged people, apprentice tools and equipment and other grants to encourage educational, sporting, cultural and social opportunities. Grants ranged from £30 to £2,500.

Organisations
There were 94 grants to organisations, including mainstream schools serving people who are socially disadvantaged and disabled. Almost all the beneficiaries were based in the Lothians. The trust stated that there was a wide range of specific grants. Grants ranged from £50 to £2,500, but most were for £500 or £1,000 for youth activities or equipment. The trust continued to support the setting up of after school clubs and summer schemes for children who are disabled.

Boarding education
Grants of £400 to £5,500 were given to 21 young people.

For the trust's future development it is 'continuing a long-term search for funds to increase the trust's capital with the aim of providing more income to further the education of underprivileged young people'.

Exclusions No grants to people over 21, nor for overseas causes or medical purposes. Grants are not available for day school fees.

Applications On a form available from the correspondent for individual applicants. By form or letter for organisations. Trustees meet five times a year (early February, late March, early June, middle of August, and late October). The trust is happy to receive telephone enquiries.

West Lothian Educational Trust

Education

£9,800 to individuals and organisations (2000/01)

Beneficial area West Lothian

Scott-Moncrieff, Chartered Accountants, 17 Melville Street, Edinburgh EH3 7PH

Tel. 0131 473 3500 **Fax** 0131 473 3535

Correspondent Mary Jaffery-Smith, Secretary

Trustees *W Cochrane, Chair; W D Stewart; A J Pirie; W Scoular; F James; Dr D R Fairbairn; M Walker; Mrs N A Watson; Cllr T Kerr; Cllr D McGrouther; Cllr W Russell; Cllr A Miller; Cllr T Smith; Cllr J McGinty; Miss A Neate.*

Inland Revenue no. SC015454

Information available Full accounts were provided by the trust.

General The trust mainly makes grants for educational purposes to schools, organisations and individuals, particularly those who cannot obtain grants from the Scottish Education Department. Recipients of grants must be from, or live in, West Lothian. The largest grants given are of £500, and grants are usually one-off. Interests supported by the trust include postgraduate studies, student apprentices, scholarships to study outside Scotland, the provision of sports and other equipment for schools and colleges, clubs with activities of an educational nature, adult education and promoting education in the visual arts/drama/music field.

In 2000/01 it had assets of £224,000 and an income of £19,000. Educational awards, prizes and bursaries totalled £9,800, broken down as follows: special payment for prize money (£130); additional prize money to schools (20 awards totalling £1,600); John Newland bursaries (4 grants totalling £1,000); Anderson bursaries (4 grants totalling £1,200); postgraduate scholarships (4 grants totalling £550); supplementary bursaries (18 awards totalling £3,200); travel scholarship (£200); 5 travel grants (£950 in total); an educational excursion (£100); educational travel (£250); sports facilities (£150); adult education (2 grants totalling £300); and promoting education in music (£150).

Applications Application forms are available from the correspondent. Applications must be received by 1 February, 1 May and 1 September each year.

The John Wilson Bequest Fund

Health, welfare, women

£28,000 to organisations (1999)

Beneficial area Mainly Edinburgh

Messrs J & R A Robertson, 15 Great Stuart Street, Edinburgh EH3 7TS

Tel. 0131 225 5095

Correspondent A D Sheperd

Information available Limited information was available from the trust.

General The trust supports charities which are concerned with people who are poor or unwell living in Edinburgh, especially those which make special provision for women. It also supports individuals in need in Edinburgh and foreign missionaries of any protestant church in Scotland while they are at home (for further information

on grants to individuals, see *A Guide to Grants for Individuals in Need*).

In 1999 the trust had assets of £1.6 million and an income of £70,000. Grants totalled £63,000, of which £28,000 went to organisations.

Applications In writing to the correspondent.

Miss Hazel M Wood Charitable Trust

The arts, architecture, national heritage, social welfare, medical

£35,000 (2000/01)

Beneficial area UK, with possible preferences for Edinburgh, London and the south east of England

Messrs Lindsays, 11 Atholl Crescent, Edinburgh EH3 8HE

Tel. 0131 229 1212

Correspondent W B Robertson

Trustees *Miss Hazel M Wood; Ian N MacDonald; Mrs Vanessa J Vasey.*

Inland Revenue no. SC003658

Information available Full accounts and guidelines were provided by the trust.

General The trust stated: 'The trustees have a wide remit but they have adopted the following guidelines:

- 'Applications from individuals are not entertained and, in particular, those individuals seeking funding for postgraduate study.

- 'The trustees do not give grants to charities based in the UK which undertake most of their work overseas.

- 'The trustees do not restrict themselves geographically within the UK although London, south east of England and Edinburgh tended to receive the bulk of the income distributed.

- 'The trustees like to strike a balance between social services and the environment.

'(a) In the case of social services, the trustees have helped the homeless, children and the elderly. The trustees tend to support the smaller less well-known charities and, where possible, the trustees prefer to contribute towards some specific project or item of equipment.

'(b) The environment: the trustees help charities working in the "great outdoors" and they also help with the renovation of historic buildings.'

In 2000/01 it had an income of £19,000 and gave grants to 36 organisations totalling £35,000.

The largest grants were £2,500 each to National Trust for Scotland for the Newhailes Appeal and Whizz-Kidz towards a regional mobility scheme (third of four payments), and £2,000 each to Amber Foundation towards a double decker bus, New Horizon Youth Centre, Princess Royal Trust for Carers and Sycamore Project for equipment.

Other beneficiaries included The Hebridean Trust towards lighthouse keepers' cottages and Scottish Down's Syndrome Association towards information service costs (£1,000 each), Campberwell Pocket Opera (£500), Prison Phoenix Trust (£200) and John Muir Birthplace Trust (£100).

Applications In writing to the correspondent no later than May or November for consideration in June/July and December for payments in July and January.

The John K Young Endowment Fund

Research, medical research, health, young people

£30,000 (1997/98)

Beneficial area Edinburgh

Skene Edwards WS, 5 Albyn Place, Edinburgh EH2 4NJ
Tel. 0131 225 6665 **Fax** 0131 220 1015

Correspondent Robin Morton, Partner/Trust Administrator

Trustees T C Foggo; A J R Ferguson; R J S Morton; R I F Macdonald.

Inland Revenue no. SC002264

Information available Information was provided by the trust.

General The trust supports medical and surgical research and also research into chemistry to aid UK industry. It also supports young people in Edinburgh and health organisations.

In 1997/98 the trust had an income of £40,000 and gave grants totalling £30,000. Grants are one-off and range from £500 to £2,000. Beneficiaries have included Barnardos, Edinburgh and Leith Age Concern, Marie Curie Cancer Care, Shelter and Waverley Care.

Exclusions No grants to individuals or non-registered charities.

Applications In writing to the correspondent. Trustees meet to consider grants in the spring and autumn.

Glasgow & the West of Scotland

Argyll and Bute Council Charitable Trusts

General
Not known

Beneficial area Argyll and Bute

Finance Department, Council Headquarters, Argyll and Bute Council, Lochgilphead PA31 8RT

Tel. 01546 602127 **Fax** 01546 604411

Correspondent Tommy Armour

Inland Revenue no. SC025066

Information available Information was provided by the trust.

General The council is responsible for a number of trusts. Areas of interest include older people, people experiencing poverty and residents of the former boroughs of Argyll and Bute. It also provides funds for educational purposes, in particular grants and prizes for pupils and ex-pupils of schools in the area.

Applications In writing to the correspondent. Some of the trusts do not accept unsolicited applications; many of those which do advertise in the local press when funds are available.

Argyll and Bute Trust

Young people
About £5,000

Beneficial area Argyll and Bute area

c/o Bank of Scotland Buildings, Oban, Argyll PA34 4LN

Tel. 01546 602524

Correspondent James Kirk, Hon. Secretary

Inland Revenue no. SC010534

Information available Information was provided by the trust.

General The trust aims to encourage young people up to the age of 25 to work together to provide charitable help for people of all ages in the community. It will support the work of young people in small, charitable projects. Both individuals and voluntary groups are supported, with emphasis on funds being used to put something back into the community. About £5,000 is available for distribution each year. Grants usually range from £100 to £500. The amount given to groups varies according to the applications received. It also administers funds on behalf of Argyll & Bute Council for the purpose of cleaning the shores/roadside blackspots. The funds are given to voluntary groups (of any age group) which are paid per mile or blackspot which they work on. About £10,000 is available for these grants.

Applications In writing to the correspondent, at 'Duntislai', Wilson Road, Lochgilphead, Argyll PA31 8RT. Apply at any time.

The Balmore Trust

Third world, social welfare, young people, women's projects
£25,000 (1999)

Beneficial area Third world and UK with a preference for Strathclyde

Viewfield, Balmore, Torrance, Glasgow G64 4AE

Tel. & Fax 01360 620742

Correspondent The Secretary

Trustees *J Riches; Ms R Jarvis; Ms O Beauvoisin; C Brown; Ms J Brown; J Eldridge; Ms R Riches; B Holman.*

Inland Revenue no. SC008930

Information available The trust produces a newsletter available free in its shop, The Coach House Charity Craft Shop in Balmore, or by sending an sae to the company secretary at the above address.

General The trust's assets consist of the stock of its shop, The Coach House Charity Craft Shop and a small investment. The figure for the trust's total income for 1999 was £27,000.

Two-thirds of the trust's grant total is awarded to projects overseas, with the remainder given in the UK. The trust favours schemes which are in areas of greatest social need and with which the trust has a personal link. Projects are also supported by importing greetings cards and high-quality crafts from cooperatives and women's groups in the third world through the trust's trading arm, 'Greeting the World'. Projects in the third world are also supported in kind.

Grants during the year totalled £25,000 with £7,000 home grants and £18,000 overseas. Grants usually range from £50 to £4,000.

Overseas grants included specific donations given to the trust which increased the amount disbursed.

Major grants to UK projects have continued to be with Women's Aid and youth projects, and this year to Glasgow Braendam Link which works with Glasgow families who have used the holiday facilities at Braendam House.

Major grants to overseas projects have been to the Amajuba Educational Trust which makes grants to students in South Africa, Child in Need Institute – Calcutta, various projects supervised by the Baptist Chuch in Burma and Rufiji Leprosy Trust.

The trust states that it is continuing to look for new partnerships and reduce the number of smaller projects with which it works.

Exclusions No grants to individuals.

Applications The trust is run entirely voluntarily and unless the applicant is known to the trust or has a connection with The Coach House and could be categorised as being in great social need, applications are unlikely to succeed.

Applications should be made in writing to the correspondent at the above address at the very beginning of the year (main disbursement is made annually in February or March). The following information should be provided:

- details of the project for which funding is sought
- the amount requested
- details of past and current funders
- an outline of the background and experience of key staff
- a copy of the organisation's recent accounts
- references
- details of other funders the organisation is approaching
- any other relevant information.

Applications are only acknowledged if an sae is enclosed.

The Bellahouston Bequest Fund

Religion, social welfare, health, education, restoration

£127,000 (1999/2000)

Beneficial area Glasgow and district

George House, 36 North Hanover Street, Glasgow G1 2 AD

Tel. 0141 552 3422 **Fax** 0141 552 2935

e-mail JAMC@Mitchells-Roberton.co.uk

Correspondent J A M Cuthbert, Administrator

Trustees *B G Hardie; D H Galbraith; J Forbes MacPhearson; N W McMillan; E H Webster; Peter C Paisley; Peter L Fairley.*

Inland Revenue no. SC011781

Information available Information, including accounts and report, was provided by the trust.

General The fund supports a wide variety of causes. Its objectives are to help build, expand and repair Protestant evangelical churches or places of religious worship, as well as supporting the clergy of these churches. It further states that it is set up to give grants to charities for the relief of poverty or disease and to organisations concerned with promotion of the Protestant and evangelical religion, education and conservation of places of historical and artistic significance. It will consider social welfare causes generally and also animal welfare and sport and recreation. All organisations should be within the parliamentary boundaries of the city of Glasgow or within a five mile radius of this area. In 1999/2000 the trust had assets of £3.9 million and an income of £147,000. It gave grants totalling £127,000. Grants are one-off and ranged from £150 to £5,500.

Exclusions No grants to organisations or churches whose work does not fall within the geographical remit of the fund. Overseas projects and political appeals are not supported.

Applications On a form available from the trust. The trustees meet to consider grants in March, July, October and December.

The Geoff Brown Charitable Trust

General

About £2,500 (1999/2000)

Beneficial area Cumbria and south west Scotland

Albert Cottage, Harker, Carlisle CA6 4HW

Tel. 01228 537149

Website http://freespace.virgin.net/iain.r/charity.htm

Correspondent Geoff Brown

Charity Commission no. 1044019

Information available Information was taken from the trust's website.

General Geoff Brown's fundraising began in 1989 when he staged a dance in Burgh-By-Sands which raised £110 that was donated to a local person in need. His fundraising efforts continued and in 1997 the trust was registered with the Charity Commission. It raises its funds by

sponsorships from local businesses as well as conducting its own fundraising in Cumbria and south west Scotland, donating the income back to the local community. Grants range from £500 to £2,500 and are mostly given to individuals to create a memorable moment for people who are experiencing a particular hardship, although grants are also available to organisations, with beneficiaries including older people's homes and special needs schools. In 1999/2000 the trust had an income of £3,000 and an expenditure of £2,700. However, in previous years the income has been around £10,000.

Applications In writing to the correspondent.

The D W T Cargill Fund

General

£288,000 (1999/2000)

Beneficial area UK, with a preference for the West of Scotland

190 St Vincent Street, Glasgow G2 5SP

Tel. 0141 204 2833

Correspondent Norman A Fyfe, Trustee

Trustees A C Fyfe; W G Peacock; N A Fyfe; Mrs M E Graham.

Inland Revenue no. SC012703

Information available Accounts were provided by the trust at the cost of £23.

General This trust has the same address and trustees as two other trusts, WA Cargill Charitable Trust and WA Cargill Fund, although they all operate independently.

This trust supports 'any hospitals, institutions, societies or others whose work in the opinion of the trustees is likely to be beneficial to the community'.

In 1999/2000 it had assets of £7.1 million which generated an income of £199,000. Grants totalled £288,000, broken down into annual grants and appeals.

Annual – 35 grants totalling £162,000
The largest grant was £35,000 to Ardgowan
Hospice. Other sizeable grants were £15,000 to
RUKBA, £9,000 to Marie Curie Cancer Care –
Hunter's Hill, £8,000 to Greenock Medical Aid
Society, £7,000 each to City of Glasgow Society of
Social Service and RNLI – Glasgow and £6,000 to
Glasgow and West of Scotland Society for the
Blind.

Other beneficiaries included Scottish Maritime
Museum – Irvine (£5,000), Ocean Youth Trust
Scotland and The Thistle Foundation (£4,000
each), YWCA Glasgow (£2,500), Glasgow City
Mission and Scottish Motor Neurone Disease
Association (£2,000 each) and Bethesda Nursing
Home and Hospice – Stornoway and Earl Haig
Fund (£1,000 each).

Appeals – 14 grants totalling £126,000
David Cargill House received five grants, £59,000
for a payment to Glasgow City Council, £15,000
for operating deficits, £1,900 for residents'
outings, £380 for residents' Christmas outings
and an unclassified £20,000. Other large grants
were £10,000 each to Greenock Medical Aid
Society for an extension to Bagatelle and
St Columba School for new classrooms. Other
recipients included University of Glasgow for a
summer project for an undergraduate student
(£2,200), The Bridge Community Project
(£2,000), Arthritis Care in Scotland and Trees for
Life (£1,000 each) and Bridge of Weir Elderly
Forum and Durness Village Hall Committee
(£500 each).

Exclusions No grants are made to individuals.

Applications In writing to the correspondent,
supported by up-to-date accounts. Trustees meet
quarterly.

The W A Cargill Fund

General

£230,000 (1999/2000)

Beneficial area Glasgow and the West of
Scotland

190 St Vincent Street, Glasgow G2 5SP

Tel. 0141 204 2833

Correspondent Norman A Fyfe, Trustee

Trustees *Alexander Campbell Fyfe;
William Graham Peacock; Norman Alexander Fyfe;
Mirren Elizabeth Graham.*

Inland Revenue no. SC008456

Information available Accounts were provided
by the trust at the cost of £23.

General This trust has the same address and
trustees as two other trusts, The DWT Cargill
Fund and The WA Cargill Charitable Trust,
although they all operate independently.

This trust supports a wide remit of causes in the
West of Scotland, particularly in Glasgow. It gives
a large number of grants generally ranging from
£1,000 to £3,000, although a few larger grants are
given.

In 1999/2000 it had assets of £10 million,
generating an income of £380,000. Grants totalled
£230,000, broken down as follows:

Medical research – 7 grants totalling £14,000
Beneficiaries included Imperial Cancer Research
Fund (£5,000), Leukaemia Research and Tenovus
– Scotland (£2,000 each) and Dyslexia Scotwest
– Glasgow and Dystonia Society (£1,000 each).

Medical care – 12 grants totalling £50,000
The largest grant was £18,000 to Erskine Hospital.
Other grants ranged from £1,000 to £6,000.
Recipients included Deaf Connections (£6,000),
Sense in Scotland (£5,000), Capability Scotland
(£3,000), Riding for the Disabled – Glasgow
(£2,000) and Glasgow Benevolent Society
(£1,000).

Care of children – 4 grants totalling £9,000
Beneficiaries were Children 1st and Sargent
Cancer Care for Children (£3,000 each), Hansel
Village – Symington (£2,000) and Scottish Society
for Autistic Children (£1,000).

Care of the elderly – 5 grants totalling £15,000
Recipients were Church of Scotland Baxter House
Eventide Home (£6,000), Glasgow Old People's
Welfare Association (£5,000), Glasgow Simon
Community (£2,000) and Community Central
Hall – Maryhill and Friends of Glasgow Humane
Society (£1,000 each).

Youth organisations – 9 grants totalling £20,000
Beneficiaries included Strathclyde Youth Club
Association (£3,000), Greater Glasgow Scout
Council and Glasgow YMCA (£2,500 each) and
Glasgow and South West Scotland Federation of

Boys' and Girls' Club and Scottish Schoolboys' Club – Glasgow (£1,000 each).

Heritage, arts – 9 grants totalling £27,000
The largest grants were £10,000 to National Trust for Scotland and £5,000 to Royal Scottish National Orchestra. Other grants were for £1,000 or £2,000 and recipients included Children's Classic Concerts, Hesilhead Wildlife Rescue Trust, Scottish Ballet and Scottish Opera.

Educational – 5 grants totalling £26,000
These were £7,500 each to Glasgow Academy Millennium Appeal (third of four grants) and High School of Glasgow Development Campaign (second of four grants), £5,000 each to Glasgow Academy and High School of Glasgow, both for bursaries, and £500 to Bridge of Weir School for its library.

Religious organisations – 2 grants totalling £18,000
Scottish Episcopal Church received £10,000 for widows and orphans whilst The Salvation Army received £8,000.

Ex-servicemen, sailors, police, fire services etc. – 6 grants totalling £15,000
Beneficiaries included King George's Fund for Sailors (£3,000), Army Benevolent Fund and Royal Naval Benevolent Fund (£2,500 each) and Strathclyde Fire Brigade Widows and Orphans Fund (£2,000).

Miscellaneous – 6 grants totalling £6,500
Recipients included PDSA Glasgow (£2,000), Renfrewshire Care & Repair Group and Scottish Council on Alcohol (£1,000 each) and Glasgow Phoenix Choir (£500).

Additional miscellaneous donations – 23 grants totalling £30,000
Beneficiaries included The Wynd Centre (£4,000), Starlight Children's Foundation for fun centres at Yorkhill Hospital (£3,000), Broomlea School Adventure Playground Fund and RSPB (£2,000 each), Dance School of Scotland and Ruchill Furniture Project (£1,000 each), Govan Youth Programme and Music Makers Ltd (£500 each) and Brittle Bone Society (£250).

Exclusions Individuals are not supported.

Applications In writing to the correspondent, including a copy of the charity's latest accounts or details of its financial position.

Castlemilk Environment Trust

Conservation

£10,000 (2000)

Beneficial area Castlemilk

Glenwood Business Centre, 21 Glenwood Place, Glasgow G45 9UH

Tel. 0141 630 1919 **Fax** 0141 630 2422

e-mail matthewfinkle@netscapeonline.co.uk

Correspondent Matthew J Finkle, Project Officer

Trustees *Lewis MacSween; Gordon Barbour; Deirdre Harte.*

Inland Revenue no. SC024420

Information available Information was provided by the trust.

General The trust works in Castlemilk to improve the environment of Castlemilk, conserve local woodlands, train and employ local people, and fund groups involved in improving the environment. Funds are only given in support of projects which are of benefit to Castlemilk. Participation by the local people is encouraged in projects, which will themselves be for public benefit.

The trust was given grant aid of £1.8 billion to £2 billion from 1996 to 2001. It has given £10,000 to Castlemilk Business Environment, Training and Audit.

Exclusions No grants to profit-making organisations.

Applications In writing to the correspondent.

Clyde Cruising Club Seamanship and Pilotage Trust

Young people, disabled

About £3,000

Beneficial area Glasgow

Suite 101, The Pentagon Centre,
36 Washington Street, Glasgow G3 8AZ

Tel. 0141 221 2774 **Fax** 0141 221 2775

Correspondent J Baird

Inland Revenue no. SC009099

Information available Limited information was available on this trust.

General This trust provides courses for people who are disabled and assists in the preservation of craft. It also aims to: educate the public in the knowledge and practice of seamanship; provide recreational sailing facilities for young people, especially from deprived areas; and to generally improve safety at sea. About £3,000 is available each year in grants. No further information was available on beneficiaries.

Applications On a form available from the correspondent.

Cumberland Building Society Charitable Foundation

General

£24,000 (1999/2000)

Beneficial area Cumbria, Dumfriesshire, Lancashire and Northumberland

Cumberland House, Castle Street,
Carlisle CA3 8RX

Tel. 01228 541341

Correspondent The Secretary

Charity Commission no. 1072435

Information available Information was provided by the trust.

General This trust has general charitable purposes in Cumbria, Dumfriesshire, Lancashire and Northumberland, giving grants of up to £1,000. In 1999/2000 grants totalled £24,000. The society's 1999/2000 annual report stated: 'Mainly in conjunction with Cumbria County Council's Educational Service, the society is supporting a number of initiatives to help children throughout Cumbria, including sponsorship of Cumbria Youth Orchestra, Work Scholarship Schemes, Big Book Competition for infant and junior schools, West Cumbria Schools Choir and National Trust's mini-bus education tours. Further sponsorship of education initiatives is proposed for 2000 and 2001.'

Applications In writing to the correspondent for consideration quarterly.

Dalrymple Donaldson Fund

Building restoration

Not known

Beneficial area Dalrymple

Banklug Farm, Neilston,
East Renfrewshire G78 3AY

Correspondent Mrs Hughson

Inland Revenue no. SC014803

Information available Limited information was available on this trust.

General The fund gives grants towards the repair and restoration of historically significant buildings. No further information was available.

Applications In writing to the correspondent. Trustees meet yearly to allocate funds.

Darroch Charitable Trust

General

About £22,000

Beneficial area UK, with a preference for the West of Scotland

c/o Bird Semple, 249 West George Street, Glasgow G2 4RB

Correspondent Norman Alexander

Inland Revenue no. SC018378

Information available Information was provided by the trust.

General The trust has general charitable purposes, with a preference for the West of Scotland. It gives about £22,000 a year to organisations. Grants ranged from £100 to £5,000. Beneficiaries have included Ayrshire Dementia Support Association, Ayrshire Hospice, East Kilbride Befriending Project, Oxfam, Visual Impairment Services Scotland and West Kilbride Out of School Care Group.

Exclusions No support to individuals.

Applications In writing to the correspondent. Trustees meet once a year in October. Applications are considered throughout the year.

Dumfries and Galloway Council Charitable Trusts

General

£70,000 (2000/01)

Beneficial area Dumfries and Galloway

Dumfries and Galloway Council, English Street, Dumfries DG1 2DD

Tel. 01387 260000 **Fax** 01387 260034

Trustees *The Members of the Council.*

Inland Revenue no. SC025071

Information available Information was provided by the trust.

General In 20/2001 the trusts administered by the council had an income of £103,000 and assets of £864,000. Of this £70,000 was spent on a range of things according to the purposes of individual trusts. Most expenditure related to grants to individuals and local organisations.

Grants were broken down as follows:

Social welfare	1%
Charitable	63%
Education	36%

The educational trusts are used to provide educational grants, school equipment and prizes. The welfare trusts are used for the well-being of residents of children's homes and the users of adult resource centres and family centres. Grants can range from £10 to £15,000. Organisations supported included Dumfries Academy and Dalbeattie Day Centre.

Exclusions No support for arts, religious appeals, health/medical appeals, animal welfare or environment/heritage.

Applications In writing to the correspondent.

The Dumfriesshire Educational Trust

Education

£18,000 to individuals and organisations

Beneficial area The former county of Dumfriesshire

Council Offices, English Street, Dumfries DG1 2DD

Tel. 01387 260000 **Fax** 01387 260034

Correspondent James M Smith, Clerk

Inland Revenue no. SC003411

Information available Information was supplied by the trust.

General The trust gives educational grants to individuals and organisations. It will support arts, training, sports and recreation, overseas projects and school excursions. Grants are one-off and usually range from £60 to about £300. Beneficiaries include schools, students (including mature students), local clubs and societies and adult education. The trust gives about £18,000 a year in grants.

Exclusions No grants to organisations or individuals based outside Dumfriesshire.

Applications On a form available from the correspondent. The trustees meet to consider grants in March, June, September and December. Applications should be sent by February, May, August and November.

East Ayrshire Council Charitable Trusts

General

See below

Beneficial area East Ayrshire

East Ayrshire Council, Council Headquarters, London Road, Kilmarnock KA3 7BU

Tel. 01563 576000 **Fax** 01563 576500

Correspondent Gillian Hamilton

Inland Revenue no. SC025073

Information available Information was supplied by the trust.

General The council is the administrative body for a number of trusts which serve different aspects of the community. The trusts and their objects are listed below, preceded by a table showing the capital and revenue for the first six trusts. Some of these trusts and guidelines suggest preferences for individuals, however they appear to be flexible in their approach to grantmaking. It is likely that support may be given to organisations helping such individuals.

	2000/01	
	Capital	Revenue
The Bessie C Roxburgh Bequest	£11,000	£12,000
Robert Cummings Bequest	£3,100	£22,000
Miss Annie Smith Mair Bequest	£15,000	£125,000
Matthew L Cochrane Bequest	£1,900	(£45)
John Fulton Soup Kitchen Trust	£1,400	£39,000
Archibald Taylor Trust	£18,000	£323,000

The Bessie C Roxburgh Bequest
Established to benefit the former burgh of Darvel, this trust meets annually in August to consider applications from clubs and organisations. Preference is given to proposals or projects which wholly or mainly benefit residents of Darvel. The trust is particularly keen that its funds encourage 'self-help' where appropriate, for example, by raising matching funding or providing voluntary labour. The trust prefers proposals which benefit large numbers of people, either directly or indirectly. Applications should be for single payments and not for continuing support beyond any one financial year.

The Robert Cummings Bequest
This trust was established to provide assistance and support to orphaned children who are natives of Kilmarnock. Assistance and support includes: granting weekly, monthly, quarterly, half-yearly or yearly allowances to the orphaned child or their guardian on their behalf; clothing costs; medical fees; educational fees; and modest holidays.

Miss Annie Smith Mair Bequest
This trust was established to provide assistance to needy individuals, especially spinsters and orphans, who are natives of, or residents in, the former burgh of Newmilns and Greenholm. The trustees meet three times a year in February, June and November, although applications can be considered between meetings.

The Matthew Cochrane Bequest
This trust was established for the provision of holidays for people who are older or in need, living in Kilmarnock. The trustees meet on an ad-hoc basis as necessary.

The John Fulton Soup Kitchen Trust
This was established to provide a soup kitchen for the poor of Kilmarnock, the food from which must be sold at no more than half the cost of the price of the ingredients. While the trust does not provide a soup kitchen, it has provided financial assistance to similar organisations such as the

Salvation Army. The trustees meet on an ad-hoc basis when required.

The Archibald Taylor Trust

The trust cares for unmarried women aged 45 or over who are native and living in Kilmarnock. It does this by providing special nursing or convalescent treatment and holidays of up to three weeks. Beneficiaries should be recommended by a specialist and be unable to afford the care themselves. The trustees meet on an ad-hoc basis.

Ayrshire Educational Trust

There are six sections of this trust currently in use. These are:

Section 28 – first scheduled payments paid to three churches in November of each year. The churches involved are Beith, Girvan and Kilbirmie.

Section 36 – travel grants are made to inhabitants of Ayrshire to enable them to travel either in the UK or abroad for any purpose of an educational nature.

Section 38 – special equipment grants are available for the purchase of special equipment, in supplement of that which is provided by a local authority, to improve the efficiency of education for schoolchildren with mental disabilities. Equipment for pilot projects or of an experimental nature will be considered.

Section 41 – support to clubs. Grants to assist in the formation, maintenance and encouragement of clubs, societies and organisations for the educational benefit of children and young people in Ayrshire. Equipment which is classed as 'personal' e.g. uniforms, musical instruments etc. are not considered under this section.

Section 43 – grants are awarded to defray or assist in defraying the expenses of organised school excursions for the benefit of children or young persons attending schools in Aryshire. The excursion must be outside the boundaries of the former county of Ayr and include an overnight stay.

Section 45 – grants are awarded towards the cost of expenses incurred in organised parties, approved by the governing body, for visits abroad which are of an educational nature.

Applications Further details and application forms are available from the administration manager at the council offices.

Easterhouse Community Trust

General

Not known

Beneficial area Easterhouse

c/o Bosco Juniors, The Billy Rafferty Centre, Glasgow G39 9DW

Correspondent Bob Gabner

Inland Revenue no. SC000779

Information available Limited information was available on this trust.

General This trust serves the community and people of Easterhouse, to help where organisations are unable to raise sufficient funds for a project from other sources. The trust will also, unusually, apply for funds to other trusts on behalf of organisations which are not in a position to do so themselves. Further information was not available.

Applications In writing to the trustees, giving information on the organisation applying and a project outline.

This entry was not confirmed by the trust.

The Gemmell Bequest Fund

General

£5,800 (1998)

Beneficial area Glasgow and the parish of Sorn, Ayrshire

Morison Bishop Solicitors, 2 Blythswood Square, Glasgow G2 4AD

Tel. 0141 248 4672

Correspondent The Secretary

Trustees *I L Dunsmore; H E Stirling.*

Inland Revenue no. SC001344

Information available Information was provided by the trust.

General The trust's assets totalled £270,000 in 1998, generating an income of £11,000. Grants totalled £5,800 and were awarded for general charitable purposes. Many grants are awarded on an annual recurrent basis, but one-off grants ranging between £50 and £100 can be made.

Exclusions No grants to individuals nor to charities outside the stated beneficial area.

Applications In writing to the correspondent at the above address.

The City of Glasgow Society of Social Service

General

£18,000 to organisations (1999/2000)

Beneficial area Glasgow

30 George Square, Glasgow G2 1EG

Tel. 0141 248 3535

Correspondent James Smillie, Secretary

Trustees *Daniel J Brewster; Ronald G Fulton; Alexander C Fyfe; Ian Jonstone; Mrs Grace Keele; John Keith; Donald J M Marshall; William McInnes; Dr Sarah Orr; James Smillie; Mrs Joyce Stevenson; Franco Rebecchi; Graeme Whyte.*

Inland Revenue no. SC000906

Information available Accounts were provided by the trust

General The 1999/2000 accounts state: 'The society exists to offer relief to Glasgow citizens who are in financial distress and whose situation cannot be assisted by any other agency. As well as administering its own funds, the society acts as a trustee for a number of other charitable foundations.'

The society operates a large number of funds, most of which give to individuals although a few give grants to organisations.

In 1999/2000 the society had assets of £3.2 million and an income of £328,000, mostly from subscriptions, donations and legacies. Grants totalled £233,000. There were 675 grants to individuals which ranged from £20 to £360 and

totalled £215,000. Grants to organisations totalled £18,000.

The largest grants were £4,000 to Glasgow Children's Holiday Scheme, £2,000 each to Boys Brigade Glasgow Battalion, Church House, Govan Youth Programme and Shakespeare Street Youth Club and £1,500 to Salvation Army.

Applications In writing to the correspondent.

Glasgow Conservation Trust – West

Conservation/heritage

£179,000 (2000/01)

Beneficial area The west end of Glasgow

30 Cranworth Street, Glasgow G12 8AG

Tel. & Fax 0141 339 0092

e-mail glasgowwest@cqm.co.uk

Website http://users.colloquium.co.uk/ ~glasgowwest/home.htm

Correspondent Dr John Russell, Technical Director

Trustees *Mrs Jean Charsley; Eric Curtis; Joseph Logan; Russell Logan; Dr James Macaulay; David Martin; Prof. Michael Moss; Brian Park.*

Inland Revenue no. SC012183

Information available Accounts and newsletters were provided by the trust.

General Established in 1990, this trust's principle aim is to conserve and improve the physical environment of the west end of Glasgow, thus promoting wider interest and confidence in the area. Its objectives stating as being to:

- coordinate investment in the improvement and renewal of the area through public and private agencies
- pool and extend knowledge and experience of methods of conserving the townscape and architectural heritage of the area
- set new and higher standards of maintenance, decoration and preservation of the buildings of the west end

- encourage the conservation and re-use of existing vacant buildings

- generate employment by the wider use of local specialised tradesmen in conservation works

- publicise the quality of the west end and its potential as a major tourist attraction

- show by example the possibility of regenerating other parts of the city.

Its autumn 2001 newsletter provided the following description of its grant programme:

'The Glasgow Conservation Trust West provides a range of grants for the repair and restoration of historic buildings in the west end. The purpose of the trust's conservation grant programme is threefold: to return the built heritage to its original condition and appearance; to promote the proper care and maintenance of the west end's built heritage; and to encourage the best practice through the use of traditional materials and craft skills. The primary responsibility for maintenance and repair lies with the property owner, and grants are made available to help meet the additional repair costs normally associated with the use of traditional materials and craftsmanship for the conservation of original features. The type of grant provided depends on the cost and scope of the work proposed:

'Small Scheme grants are designed for repairs to both listed and unlisted buildings within the trust's remit area. These grants usually involve the repair or restoration of architectural features such as decorative glass, ironwork or stonework details, and cost less than £5,000 (including professional fees and VAT).

'Building Repair Scheme grants provide financial assistance to owners where the grant-eligible cost of external repairs is more than £5,000 (including professional fees and VAT). These grants are restricted to listed buildings within the Glasgow West Conservation Area.

'Townscape Enhancement Scheme grants apply to conservation projects which preserve or restore the setting of an individual listed building or a group of listed buildings. These grants usually involve formal gardens, historic lighting or architectural features in common ownership.

'Demand for grants is high, and each application has to be assessed not only in terms of the merit of the property, but also the nature, urgency and financial viability of the works proposed. Grant assistance from the trust is not designed as an emergency source of funding for repairs to buildings which have deteriorated through neglect. Evidence of a maintenance history will therefore be an important factor in the assessment of eligibility for grant and the level of grant awarded. The final decision on whether an application is awarded a grant lies solely with the trust and its funding partners.'

The 2000/01 annual report and accounts contained the following grant levels for 2001/02:

Council tax band	Minor/limited repairs (%)	Comprehensive repairs (%)
A	50	75
B	50	75
C	50	75
D	50	75
E	45	70
F	35	60
G	25	40
H	25	35

'Grant levels may be adjusted up or down 10% depending on the individual merit of the scheme and funding available.

'Enhancement schemes

Grants for Enhancement schemes are not subject to the council tax banding. Approved grants will normally be in the range 65 to 80% of grant eligible cost depending on the individual merit of the scheme and funding available.

'Note: The above figures are for guidance only and may be varied by the board of trustees. Up-to-date information should always be sought from the trust.'

In 2000/01 the trust had assets of £89,000 and an income of £234,000, including grants received of £148,000 from Historic Scotland and £70,000 from Glasgow City Council. From a total expenditure of £262,000, grants totalled £179,000.

Exclusions Grants are only given for external repairs.

Applications Applications are subject to detailed technical approval. The trust recommends that potential applicants contact the trust to discuss eligibility and the availability of funds before submitting an application.

The Glendoune Charitable Trust

Armed forces charities

Not known

Beneficial area Ayrshire

Messrs A J & A Graham, 105 West George Street, Glasgow G2 1QA

Tel. 0141 204 4225 **Fax** 0141 204 4511

Correspondent J A Aitkenhead

Inland Revenue no. SC016249

Information available Information was provided by the trust.

General The trust supports armed forces charities and similar causes, e.g. ex-service charities. The majority of the grants are recurrent. Recent beneficiaries have included Erskine Hospital, The Ghurka Welfare Trust and South Ayrshire Forces Association. Unfortunately financial information was not available but the trust stated that donations are usually each for £500 or more. The trust also indicated that the removal of the Advance Corporation Tax Credit will lead to a reduction in the trust's income of about 20%.

Exclusions No grants to individuals and not generally to non-registered charities.

Applications In writing to the correspondent. Applications should be received in December or January.

The Dora Hay Charitable Trust

General

£2,200 (2000)

Beneficial area Moffat

Bannerman, Johnstone Maclay, Tara House, 46 Bath Street, Glasgow G2 1HG

Tel. 0141 332 2999 **Fax** 0141 333 0171

Correspondent G J Johnstone, Trustee

Trustees *J G L Robinson; G J Johnstone.*

Inland Revenue no. SC008886

Information available Information was provided by the trust.

General In 2000 the trust had net assets totalling £84,000, generating an income of £2,900. Grants totalled £2,200. Organisations based in Moffat are given preference. No further information was available.

Applications Contact the correspondent for further details.

The M V Hillhouse Trust

General

About £50,000

Beneficial area Ayrshire and Gloucestershire

Bowldown, Tetbury, Gloucestershire GL8 8UD

Trustees *G E M Vernon; H R M Vernon.*

Inland Revenue no. SC012904

Information available Information was provided by the trust.

General The trust supports only local organisations that are known personally to the trustees. It gives grants local to Hillhouse Estate in Ayrshire and in Gloucestershire. The trust anticipated that in the year 2000 about £50,000 would be available for distribution. The removal of the Advance Corporation Tax Credit has unfortunately led to a reduction in the trust's income. The trust would otherwise have had approximately £70,000 available for grants. The grant total is divided equally between England and Scotland.

Applications The trust states that unsolicited applications are not welcome and cannot be responded to. All available funds are allocated each year to organisations previously supported.

The Holywood Trust

Disadvantaged young people between 15 and 25 years

£326,000 (1999/2000)

Beneficial area Dumfries and Galloway

Mount St Michael, Craigs Road,
Dumfries DG1 4UT

Tel. 01387 269176 **Fax** 01387 269175

e-mail funds@holywood-trust.org.uk

Website www.holywood-trust.org.uk

Correspondent Peter O Robertson, Director

Trustees *C A Jencks; J J G Brown; A M Macleod; A D Scott; Mrs E Nelson.*

Inland Revenue no. SC009942

Information available Information was provided by the trust.

General The trust supports young people, aged 15 to 25 who live in Dumfries and Galloway, particularly those experiencing mental, physical or social disadvantage. It does this through grant awards to young people and by actively seeking opportunities to support others working directly with or for young people, by means of secondment of staff, management, clerical or administration support and fundraising activity.

It is involved with projects or organisations concerned with:

- homeless young people (Nithsdale Trust)
- youth work (YMCA, Youth Clubs Scotland)
- personal development of young people
- detached youth work
- drop in centres for young people
- counselling support of young people involved with drug and solvent abuse
- other trusts supporting young people (BBC Children in Need, Rank Foundation).

Grants are provided to both individuals and groups/organisations. These generally range from £50 to £500 for individuals and up to £3,000 for groups/organisations; exceptionally, higher amounts may be available where group/organisation proposals address a need of special interest to the trustees.

In 1999/2000 the trust had assets of £6.9 million and an income of £559,000. Direct charitable expenditure totalled £326,000.

Exclusions Grants are not given: to political parties; as a substitute for statutory funding; for landlord's deposits; or for retrospective applications.

Applications On a form available from the correspondent. Applications are considered by the trustees at least four time a year.

The Hoover Foundation

Education, health, welfare

About £150,000

Beneficial area UK, but with a special interest in South Wales, Glasgow and Bolton

Pentrebach, Merthyr Tydfil,
Mid Glamorgan CF48 4TU

Tel. 01685 721222 **Fax** 01685 332946

Correspondent Mrs Marion Heaffey

Trustees *D J Lunt; A Bertali; C Jones.*

Charity Commission no. 200274

Information available Information was supplied by the trust.

General This trust supports strategic UK charities and provides small grants to local organisations working in South Wales, Glasgow and Bolton. In 1998/99 the trust had an income of £121,000. Grants total around £150,000 each year.

Exclusions No grants to individuals.

Applications In writing to the correspondent.

The George Hunter Trust

General – see below

£11,000 (1998/99)

Beneficial area Lochmaben

Dumfries & Galloway Council, Council Offices, High Street, Annan DG12 6AQ

Tel. 01461 203311 **Fax** 01461 205876

Correspondent Alex Haswell, Clerk to the Trust

Trustees *James Gordon; Revd Jack Owen; Ian Pennie; John Dinwoodie.*

Inland Revenue no. SC004898

Information available Information was provided by the trust.

General The trust supports organisations in Lochmaben in Dumfries and Galloway. It supports community groups and voluntary organisations promoting the well-being of the local community of Lochmaben. It will consider the following types of causes: arts, children and young people, disability, education/training, environment/conservation, heritage, older people, social welfare and sports/recreation.

In 1998/99 it had an income of only £690 and gave grants totalling £11,000. Grants are one-off and range from £50 to £400. Beneficiaries have included Lochmaben AFC and Castle Rovers AFC which received £500 to establish a football pitch, Lochmaben in Bloom (£250), Lochmaben Cub, Scouts and Brownie Association (£200) and Lochmaben After School Club (£150).

Applications On a form available from the correspondent.

The Inverclyde Bequest Fund

Sailors' charities

£55,000 (1999)

Beneficial area UK and USA with a preference for Glasgow and the West of Scotland

Merchants House of Glasgow, 7 West George Street, Glasgow G2 1BA

Tel. 0141 221 8272

Correspondent Jimmy Dykes, Assistant Collector

Trustees *The Directors of the Merchants House of Glasgow.*

Information available Information was supplied by the trust.

General The trust supports seamen's missions. Two-thirds of the fund's income is distributed in Glasgow and the West of Scotland. Due to the decline in the shipping industry there are fewer missions and the trust states that most grants are recurrent. It prefers to support long-established missions. In 1999 it gave grants totalling £55,000. Grants range from £300 to £4,000.

Exclusions The fund does not give grants to individuals.

Applications In writing to the correspondent, including your annual report and audited accounts.

The Kennyhill Bequest Fund

People who are disadvantaged

£10,000 (1998/99)

Beneficial area Glasgow only

Messrs Mitchells Roberton, George House, 36 North Hanover Street, Glasgow G1 2AD

Tel. 0141 552 3422 **Fax** 0141 552 2935

Correspondent J A M Cuthbert, Trustee

Trustees *P C Paisley; Mrs Gillian Weir; J A M Cuthbert; Peter Forrester.*

Inland Revenue no. SC000122

Information available Information was provided by the trust.

General The trust supports charitable organisations in Glasgow working for people who are disadvantaged. In 1998/99 it had assets of £421,000, an income of £15,000 and made grants to 14 organisations totalling £10,000, of which nine were for £800 each and five for £500 each. Recipients included ACET Scotland, Centre for Project Ability, Fairbridge in Strathclyde, Glasgow Council on Alcohol, Glasgow Veterans Seafarers Society and SYCA.

Exclusions No grants to organisations outside the stated beneficial area.

Applications In writing to the correspondent at the above address. The trustees meet annually in December.

Lamb, Middleton and MacGregor Bequest Funds

Relief of poverty and suffering

About £8,600 (2000/01)

Beneficial area Glasgow

Glasgow City Council, City Chambers, 285 George Street, Glasgow G2 1DU

Tel. 0141 227 4042/4044/4068

Correspondent The Director of Finance

Trustees *Glasgow District Council Finance Committee.*

Information available Information was provided by the trust.

General The trust is an amalgamation of three funds, now administered together. It gives grants to charities in Glasgow for the relief of poverty and suffering. Local branches of national organisations will be supported. In 1999/2000 it made grants totalling £7,000. Grants ranged from £300 to £500. Beneficiaries included The Big

Issue, Children 1st, Glasgow Council on Alcohol, Shelter and Marie Curie Cancer Care.

Exclusions No grants to individuals.

Applications In writing to the correspondent. Trustees meet once a year in December to consider grants.

Duncan Campbell Leggat's Charitable Trust

General

£19,000 (2000/01)

Beneficial area The West of Scotland

Miller, Beckett & Jackson, 190 St Vincent Street, Glasgow G2 5SP

Tel. 0141 204 2833

Correspondent G A Maguire, Trustee

Trustees *G A Maguire; N A Fyfe; H C Leggat.*

Inland Revenue no. SC011512

Information available Information was provided by the trust.

General The trust had assets valued at £413,000 in 2000/01, with a total income of £20,000. Grants totalled £19,000, with all the grants for £500 each with the exception of £2,000 given to Moral Re-Armament. Beneficiaries included Alzheimer Scotland, Barcaple Christian Outdoor Centre, Glasgow Zoo, Howwood Playgroup, Princess Louise Scottish Hospital, Shelter Scotland and Tak Tent.

Applications In writing to the correspondent.

Lethbridge – Abell Charitable Bequest

Welfare

Not known

Beneficial area Glasgow

Glasgow City Council, City Chambers, Glasgow G2 1DU

Tel. 0141 287 4002

Correspondent The Private Secretary to the Lord Provost

Inland Revenue no. SC019203

Information available Limited information was available on this trust.

General The fund assists poor people in Glasgow. Most grants are given to people in need, however, small, local community groups can also be supported. Grants to both individuals and community groups can be for up to £300 each.

Applications In writing to the correspondent.

The Andrew & Mary Elizabeth Little Charitable Trust

Disadvantaged people

£56,000 to individuals and organisations (1998)

Beneficial area Mainly Glasgow and the surrounding area

Low Beaton Richmond, Solicitors, Sterling House, 20 Renfield Street, Glasgow G2 5AP

Correspondent R Munton

Inland Revenue no. SC011185

Information available Information was supplied by the trust.

General The trust mainly supports individuals whose sole income is income support, disability benefit or a state pension and who live in Glasgow or the surrounding area. About 20% of the trust's income is given to welfare organisations in the benefical area.

In 1998 it gave grants totalling £56,000. Most of the grants were recurrent. Local Glasgow charities and some national charities were supported. Beneficiaries have included Ayrshire Hospice, Glasgow City Mission, Glasgow Marriage Guidance Council, Glasgow Old Peoples Welfare Committee, St Margaret's of Scotland Adoption Society and Strathclyde Youth Club Association.

Most grants to individuals are given through the Strathclyde Regional Council Social Work Department.

Applications In writing to the correspondent. Trustees meet to consider grants once a month. Individuals should provide financial details of income support.

Loaningdale School Company

Children and young people

£18,000 (2000/01)

Beneficial area Lanarkshire

Scott-Moncrieff, 17 Melville Street, Edinburgh EH3 7PH

Tel. 0131 473 3500 **Fax** 0131 473 3535

e-mail graemethom@scott-moncrieff.com

Correspondent R Graeme Thom

Inland Revenue no. SC001065

Information available Information for this entry was provided by the trust.

General The trust was established to benefit children and young people in need, and where appropriate, gives preference to those living within the Clydesdale local area of South Lanarkshire. Both individuals and organisations are supported.

Priority is given to:

- young people aged 12 to 20 years inclusive
- creative and outdoor pursuits for young people
- young unemployed people

- post-school education and training of young people.

In 2000/01 it had assets of £350,000 and an income of £20,000. Grants totalled £18,000, are one-off and usually range from £100 to £1,000. Examples of grants include: sports equipment for a community centre; uniforms and instruments for a pipe band; and equipment for a newly formed brownie group.

Applications On a form available from the correspondent, including a copy of the constitution and latest audited accounts. Trustees meet in March, June, September and December, applications should be received by the preceding month.

Lockerbie Trust

General

£28,000 (1998/99)

Beneficial area Lockerbie

Dumfries and Galloway Council, Council Offices, High Street, Annan, Dumfriesshire DG12 6AQ

Tel. 01461 207012 **Fax** 01461 207013

Correspondent Alex Haswell, Clerk

Trustees *Local MP; Chair of Lockerbie and District Community Council; two Lockerbie Councillors.*

Inland Revenue no. SC019796

Information available Information was provided by the trust.

General In 1998/99 the trust had assets of £402,000 and an income of £27,000. It gave grants totalling £28,000. The trust supports projects for the community in Lockerbie. It will consider the following causes: arts, children/young people, conservation, disability, education/training, heritage, social welfare and sports/recreation.

It makes grants of up to 50% of the cost and for pump-priming only. The largest grant in the year was £18,000 given for Lockerbie Christmas Lights, it is not clear how this grant meets the funding criteria mentioned above. Other grants included South of Scotland Ice Rink Club (£7,000), Lockerbie Jazz Festival (£1,000) and Lockerbie Scout Group (£500).

Applications On a form available from the correspondent. Trustees meet to consider grants in February, July and December. Applications should be sent in the month prior to the meetings.

The Lord Margadale Charitable Trust

Health and welfare, general

£4,000 (2000/01)

Beneficial area Wiltshire and the Scottish Island of Islay

The Old Rectory, Fonthill Bishop, Salisbury, Wiltshire SP3 5SF

Tel. 01747 820231

Correspondent Mrs V Meeker, Secretary

Trustees *2nd Lord Margadale; Hon. Alastair Morrison; Hon. Mary Morrison.*

Charity Commission no. 276410

Information available Information was provided by the trust.

General In 2000/01 the trust had an income of around £4,000, all of which was given in donations. Grants were made to 20 organisations in the range of £50 to £500. Those supported were health and welfare related charities.

Beneficiaries included Islay and Jura Enterprise Trust (£250), Kilarrow PCC Round Church – Bowmore and Museum of Islay Life (£200 each) and Islay and Jura Guides and RNLI Islay Branch (£100 each).

Exclusions Only applications for Wiltshire and Island of Islay are considered. No applications from individuals considered.

Applications In writing to the correspondent. Applications are considered at trustees' meetings twice a year.

Lord Provost's Charities Fund

Welfare

Not known

Beneficial area Glasgow

Glasgow City Council, City Chambers, Glasgow G2 1DU

Tel. 0141 287 4003

Correspondent The Private Secretary to the Lord Provost

Inland Revenue no. SC019204

Information available Limited information was available from the trust.

General The fund assists poor people in Glasgow. Most grants are given to people in need, however, small, local community groups can also be supported. Grants to both individuals and community groups can be for up to £300 each.

Applications In writing to the correspondent.

Dr J N Marshall – Island of Bute Memorial

General

About £3,000

Beneficial area Preference for Isle of Bute

Messrs Mitchells Roberton, George House, 36 North Hanover Street, Glasgow G1 2AD

Tel. 0141 552 3422

Correspondent D B Reid

Inland Revenue no. SC008765

Information available Information was provided by the trust.

General This trust has general charitable purposes, favouring appeals from the Isle of Bute. Grants are usually for 'a few hundred' pounds each and total 'a few thousand' pounds each year.

Applications Application forms are available from the correspondent. Applications should be received by 1 March or 1 October.

The McCallum Bequest Fund

Relief of poverty and illness

£14,000 (2001/02)

Beneficial area Greater Glasgow

MacDonalds, Solicitors, 1 Claremont Terrace, Glasgow G3 7UQ

Tel. 0141 248 6221

Correspondent T McNeil

Trustees *G G Morris; Mrs G E Morris.*

Inland Revenue no. SC007713

Information available Information was provided by the trust.

General The trust supports the relief of poverty and illness, preferring to give grants to established organisations and for specific projects. Where grants are not for specific projects, the money must be used to benefit the people of Glasgow. In 2001/02 the trust gave grants totalling £14,000 to nine organisations. Beneficiaries of £2,000 each were Alzheimer Scotland Action on Dementia for the Glasgow welfare benefits project, Glasgow City Mission, The Maxie Richards Foundation for the drug rehabilitation programme, Queen's Cross Housing Association and Enable. Parkhead Housing Association, Hopscotch Holidays, Action on Addiction for the Easterhouse Drugs Initiative and The Big Issue Foundation Scotland received £1,000 each.

Exclusions Grants are not normally given to individuals, or to organisations of a purely religious, educational or sporting nature.

Applications In writing to the correspondent. It is helpful if the application is backed up by a copy of accounts. Applications should received by October. Trustees distribute grants in December/January.

The McCrone Charitable Trust

Relief of poverty, education, religion, general

£15,000 (1999/2000)

Beneficial area Glasgow and the West of Scotland

13 Glasgow Road, Paisley PA1 3QS

Tel. 0141 842 1205 **Fax** 0141 848 5670

Correspondent Mary McTaggart

Trustees *G A Maguire; Charles Jackson; Mrs E K F Hudson; Dr H E M McCrone.*

Inland Revenue no. SC015385

Information available Information was provided by the trust.

General The trust was established in 1977 by the McCrone family and an annual award of £3,500 is given to Strathclyde University in memory of the late R W McCrone. Other grants are smaller, ranging between £50 and £1,000. It will support the relief of poverty, education and religion as well as general charitable purposes. Grants are mostly recurrent but new applications will be considered.

In 1999/2000 the trust gave grants totalling £15,000. Beneficiaries included British Deaf Association, Breadline Africa, RNLI, RSPB, RSPCA, Glasgow High School, Help the Aged, Red Cross – Glasgow branch and Save the Children.

Applications In writing to the correspondent. Applications should be received before August each year.

The Merchants House of Glasgow

Seamen's missions, general

£125,000 to organisations (1998/99)

Beneficial area Glasgow and the West of Scotland

7 West George Street, Glasgow G2 1BA

Tel. 0141 221 8272

Correspondent Jimmy Dykes, Assistant Collector

Inland Revenue no. SC008900

Information available Information was provided by the trust.

General The trust supports seamen's missions, general charitable purposes and grants to pensioners. The Merchants House of Glasgow is one of a number of Merchants Houses found in the major Scottish cities. In 1998/99 the trust gave grants totalling £259,000. Grants were divided as follows:

* about 100 grants to pensioners were given totalling £102,000

* education grants and bursaries totalled £33,000

* grants to seamen's missions in Inverclyde totalled £55,000

* grants to organisations for general charitable purposes totalled £70,000.

Educational grants were probably given to individuals. Grants to general organisations ranged from £500 to £5,000. Beneficiaries included Alexander Gibson Opera School, Glasgow Polio Association and Riding for the Disabled.

Applications In writing to the correspondent at any time, supported by a copy of accounts.

James and John Napier's Trust

Disabled young people, older people, maritime, medical research

£15,000 (1999/2000)

Beneficial area Glasgow and the West of Scotland

Headrick Inglis Glen & Co.,
48 West Regent Street, Glasgow G2 2QR

Tel. 0141 332 3341 **Fax** 0141 331 2517

Correspondent Neil M Headrick, Trustee

Trustees *A S Headrick; N M Headrick; I Bruce.*

Inland Revenue no. SC002114

Information available Accounts are available from the correspondent.

General The trust had a total capital of £223,000 in the year 1999/2000. The income for the year was £14,300 and grants totalled £14,500.

The trust states that grants are awarded to smaller local organisations and charities in Glasgow and the West of Scotland. Grants are awarded to a wide range of organisations and in 1999/2000 ranged between £500 and £1,000. Beneficiaries included Beaston Oncology Centre, Glasgow Children's Holiday Scheme, Maggies Centre, Reality at Work in Scotland and RNLI – Troon.

Applications In writing to the correspondent. Trustees meet in November, applications should be received by October.

New Templar Halls Trust

Temperance

About £10,000

Beneficial area Paisley

48 Causeyside Street, Paisley PA1 1YJ

Tel. 0141 889 7531 **Fax** 0141 887 3380

e-mail mail@reidlaw.co.uk

Correspondent W M Reid, Secretary/Treasurer

Trustees *W Fulton, Chair.*

Inland Revenue no. SC000615

Information available Information was provided by the trust.

General The trust gives to temperance organisations operating in Paisley. The trust will also give to individuals working in this field. Grants total about £10,000 a year.

Applications In writing to the correspondent.

Charitable Trusts of North Ayrshire Council

Local community

About £20,000

Beneficial area North Ayrshire district

North Ayrshire Council, Cunninghame House, Irvine KA12 8EE

Tel. 01294 324100

Correspondent The Chief Executive's Department

Inland Revenue no. SC008443

Information available Information was provided by the trust.

General The trusts support community projects which benefit people in the North Ayrshire district. It gives about £20,000 each year in total. Further information was not available.

Applications In writing to the correspondent.

Pastoral Care Trust

Welfare

£86,000 (1999/2000)

Beneficial area Glasgow

196 Clyde Street, Glasgow G1 4JY

Tel. 0141 226 5898 **Fax** 0141 225 2600

e-mail pctrust@rcag.org.uk

Website www.rcag.org.uk

Correspondent Elizabeth M McQuade, Development Officer

Trustees *Monsignor Maguire; Mrs Kathleen McConville; Frank McCormick; Miss Angus Malone.*

Inland Revenue no. SC029832

Information available Information was provided by the trust.

General The 1999/2000 annual report stated: 'The Pastoral Care Trust was set up in 1992 to mark the 500th anniversary of the Archdiocese of Glasgow. It was founded to establish in a modern context the traditions of five centuries of Christian life and action here in Scotland. In particular it was established to offer small grants to groups, agencies and projects working for the common good of all Glasgow's people.'

The trust also provided the following information: 'The trust exists to provide help in Christ's name to those most at need in our society regardless of their race, colour or creed. The trust encourages shared social action, so empowering local communities to combat identified social need. The trust gives preference to groups and organisations which operate on a self-help basis; where there is considerable involvement of local people as volunteers; where funds are limited.'

In 1999/2000 grants to 41 organisations totalled £86,000. The largest grant was £25,000 to Scottish Churches Community Trust. All of the other grants were for £5,500 or less, but were mostly of £1,000 or below. Beneficiaries included Milton Volunteer and Care Project (£5,500); 1 in 100 Theatre Company and St Matthew's Centre (£5,000 each), Spinal Injuries Scotland (£3,500); Govan Churches Elderpark Project (£3,000); Pathway (£2,900); Ruchill Summer Outreach and Wee Care Group (£2,000); St Pius X Church (£1,300); Our Lady of Fatima Family Resource Centre to develop a community resource for young people and families (£1,200); and Glasgow YWCA Family Centre and Starters Packs Glasgow (£1,000 each).

Exclusions No grants to individuals.

Applications On a form available from the correspondent.

The John Primrose Trust

Young people

About £10,000 a year

Beneficial area Dumfries

Primrose & Gordon, 92 Irish Street, Dumfries DG1 2PF

Tel. 01387 267316

Correspondent The Trustees

Inland Revenue no. SC009173

Information available Information was provided by the trust.

General This trust gives grants to young people 'to give them a start in life', supporting organisations and individuals. Some grants are also given to older people. About £10,000 is given in total each year.

Applications On a form available by writing to the correspondent. The trustees meet in May/ June and December.

Radio Clyde – Cash for Kids at Christmas

Children

£507,000 (2000/01)

Beneficial area Radio Clyde transmission area i.e. west central Scotland

Clyde Action, 236 Clyde Street, Glasgow G1 4JH

Tel. 0141 566 2827 **Fax** 0141 248 2148

Correspondent Yvonne Wyper, Finance Officer

Trustees *Paul Cooney; John R Bowman; Robert F Caldwell.*

Inland Revenue no. SC003334

Information available Accounts were provided by the trust.

General Established in 1984, this trust supports the relief of poverty of children who are in need, deprived or disabled in west central Scotland, particularly at Christmas. The trustees meet regularly throughout the year to plan fundraising in the run-up to Christmas and then distribute these funds to 'reach those children who might otherwise face a bleaker Christmas'.

In 2000/01 it had assets of £167,000 and an income of £588,000, of which £580,000 came from donations received. After fundraising expenses of £66,000, grants totalled £507,000.

The accounts stated: 'All grants and donations made were payments for the benefit of needy children. These were predominately channelled as group applications but the amounts were generally calculated on the basis of payments per child in the range of £3 to £15. In the most needy cases, the payments made were generally £20 (2000: £18).

'The number of children who benefited from the payments was approximately 70,000 (2000: 75,000).'

Only grants of £2,000 or over were listed in the accounts. These were £10,000 to Make a Wish Foundation, £7,000 to Hamish Allan Centre Childrens' Fund, £4,400 each to Langlands School, Locherbie Primary School, Millflats Playgroup Fund and Stranraer Summer Respite Scheme, £3,500 to Money Matters, £3,300 to Castlemilk Health Centre, £2,600 to Queens Cross Housing Association and £2,000 to Festive Lights.

Exclusions The trust does not fund trips in the summer or at Easter, equipment or salaries. Children benefiting must be aged 16 or under.

Applications On a form available from the correspondent. 'To ensure proper stewardship of the funds raised, all nominations from those who believe the funds should be destined to a particular family or group have to be accompanied by a recommendation from an accredited body such as social work departments, Children 1st, headteachers, members of the clergy and community workers.'

Rutherglen Old Parish Church Of Scotland Benevolent Fund

General

Not known

Beneficial area Glasgow

304 Inverleith Street, Glasgow G32 6DZ

Correspondent Donald G Galbraith

Inland Revenue no. SC004093

Information available Limited information was available on this trust.

General The trust makes grants to a range of local organisations. Further information was not available.

Applications In writing to the correspondent.

The Rosemary Scanlan Charitable Trust

Roman Catholic Archdiocese of Glasgow, religion

£19,000 to organisations (1999/2000)

Beneficial area Glasgow

Grant Thornton, 95 Bodwell Street, Glasgow G2 7JZ

Tel. 0141 223 0000 **Fax** 0141 223 0001

Correspondent The Trustees

Trustees *Archbishop of Glasgow; K Sweeny.*

Inland Revenue no. SC000360

Information available Information was provided by the trust.

General The trust's main objects are to support the office of the Roman Catholic Archbishop of Glasgow and the advancement of religion. It makes grants to both individuals and Roman

Catholic schools, to promote Roman Catholic education.

In 1999/2000 the trust's income was £38,000 and it gave grants totalling £55,000, including £36,000 to individuals.

Previous beneficiaries have included various projects run by the archdiocese, including Catholic Education Commission, Glasgow University Catholic Chaplaincy and a research project.

Applications In writing to the correspondent. The trust stated that most funds are fully committed.

Mrs Elizabeth Scott's Charitable Trust

General
About £10,000

Beneficial area Unrestricted, but with a preference for the West of Scotland

c/o Neill Clerk & Murray, Solicitors, 3 Ardgowan Square, Greenock PA16 8NW

Correspondent D I Banner, Trustee

Trustees *Miss J K Edgar; D I Banner; D R Macdonald.*

Inland Revenue no. SC015420

Information available No recent information was available on this trust.

General Unfortunately this trust was unwilling to provide information on its activities. The following information is repeated from the 1996 edition of *The Scottish Trusts Guide.*

The trust had assets totalling £135,000 in 1993/94. Grants, ranging between £250 and £1,000, totalled £10,000 and were awarded to 15 organisations. These included £1,000 each to Alzheimer's Scotland, Intermediate Technology and Oxfam Indian Appeal; £500 each to The Ark, Borderline, Scottish Society for the Prevention of Cruelty to Animals, Simon Community and Victim Support; and Francis Gay Sunday Post Coal Fund (£250).

Applications In writing to the correspondent. Distributions are made in June and December of each year and rarely at other times.

South Ayrshire Council Charitable Trusts

General
£176,000 to organisations (2000/01)

Beneficial area South Ayrshire

Support Services, South Ayrshire Council, County Buildings, Wellington Square, Ayr KA7 1DR

Tel. 01292 612463 **Fax** 01292 612367

e-mail marion.young@south-ayrshire.gov.uk

Correspondent Marion Young, Grants Officer

Inland Revenue no. SC025088

Information available Grants list, guidelines and an application form were provided by the trust.

General This trust supports organisations and individuals. The following is taken from the detailed guidance notes for voluntary and community organisations available to potential applicants:

'South Ayrshire Council will consider applications from community and voluntary organisations which are consistent with the information given below. Applicants should note that no guarantee of funding should be assumed by any organisation.

Who can apply?
'Financial support may be available to national or local voluntary organisations and locally based community groups which are properly constituted and can assure the council that they operate for the benefit of the wider community.

'Organisations may apply more than once in any financial year but it should be noted that as demand increases careful consideration will be given to individual applications and no guarantees can be given that any specific application will be approved.

'In considering applications the council will take into account the extent to which groups are prepared and able to make a financial contribution towards their project/activities.

What can groups/organisations apply for?
'Financial support may be available to support voluntary organisations and community groups which provide and promote social, cultural, economic, environmental and recreational facilities, or support projects which are in the interest of people living in South Ayrshire.'

Financial support will broadly be considered in three categories:

* grants up to £1,500

* grants over £1,500

* grants to playschemes (available for Easter, Summer and October activities).

'In all cases no financial support will be provided retrospectively and all applications must be in advance of any project/activity being started.

How to apply
'The enclosed form should be completed and returned to the address printed at the end of the form. All sections must be completed and all additional information e.g. constitution, financial details, included. Incomplete applications will not be considered by the council.

'Wherever possible please detail costs of any equipment requested and, in the case of refurbishment or building projects attach copy plans or drawings.

'Your application will be acknowledged and a member of staff from an appropriate council department will contact your organisation/group if required to discuss your application and compile an assessment report for the council.

'You should note that it is the responsibility of all organisations to arrange appropriate insurance cover for any equipment purchased with financial support provided by the council.'

The general criteria for financial assistance states:
'The following general criteria are applied by the council for funding voluntary bodies. These criteria are independent of conditions applied in existing standard contracts or service agreements.

* 'Voluntary bodies applying for council support either in kind or financial should be able to clearly demonstrate their contribution towards the council's overall objectives and specific objectives.

* 'Voluntary bodies should demonstrate that they consult on an ongoing basis and have the support of the local communities and/or the groups intended to benefit from the service provided.

* 'Voluntary bodies should seek to provide a service or activity that is based upon best practice and which makes the most effective and efficient use of available resources.

* 'Voluntary bodies funded by the council are expected to demonstrate that they will incorporate equal opportunities principles and legislation into their policy and practices.

* 'Voluntary bodies are required to set out expectations for the use of the award or resource and to specify clear outcomes with timescales, methods of monitoring and evaluation, and clarify the appropriate reporting requirements.

* 'The council will state clearly its criteria for making the award or resource available and its financial relationship with that organisation.

* 'The council will confirm the role, responsibilities and obligations of its officers' and/or members' representatives on the management committee or board of initiative (as appropriate).

* 'The council will provide the voluntary board with a copy of the "Standard Conditions for Grant Assistance", and will attach any additional conditions required, relevant to the specific grant, loan or service requirement.'

In 2000/01 grants totalled £185,000, of which £176,000 was given in 184 grants to organisations and £8,900 to 61 individuals.

The largest grants were £16,000 to North Ayr Resource Centre, £14,000 to SALVO – South Ayrshire Local Volunteer Organisation, £8,200 to Ayrshire Fiddle Orchestra, £6,000 to Council for Voluntary Organisations, £5,500 to Waverley Steam Navigation Co./Waverley Excursions Ltd., £5,100 to One Plus: One Parent Families, £5,000 each to Carrick Community Transport Group and South Ayrshire Sports Council, £4,600 to

Arthritis Care in Scotland and £4,000 to Girvan Traditional Folk Festival.

Other beneficiaries included Keynote Trust Limited (£3,000), Ayr Arts Guild (£2,300), West Of Scotland Community Relations Council (£1,800), Couple Counselling Ayrshire (£1,600), Scottish Cricket Union (£1,500), Deafblind UK (£1,000), Council for Music in Hospitals (£750), Monkton Community Council (£550), Jolly Dollies (£500), Kyle Resource Centre Parents and Careers Group (£480), Troon Blind Club (£400), Barnaby's Playscheme (£340), HM Deep Sea Rescue Tugs Association (£300), Sunshine Summer Playgroup (£290), Dailly Community Council (£280), Prestwick Elderly Forum (£250), Troon Senior Mens Dayroom (£200), Annbank Over 60s Club (£100) and Tiny Tots Playgroup (£80).

Applications On a form available from the correspondent with guidelines.

South Lanarkshire Council Charitable Trusts

General
Not available
Beneficial area South Lanarkshire

Council Offices, Almada Street, Hamilton ML3 0AA

Tel. 01698 454530 **Fax** 01698 454682

Correspondent Archie Strang, Executive Director of Finance and IT Resources

Inland Revenue no. SC025089

Information available Information was provided by the trust.

General 117 trust funds are administered by the council. Grants are made to a range of organisations in South Lanarkshire. Many of the funds primarily support individuals. Further information was not available.

Applications In writing to the correspondent

Strathclyde Police Benevolent Fund

Police, general
About £150,000 to individuals and organisations
Beneficial area Strathclyde

Strathclyde Police Federation, 151 Merrylee Road, Glasgow G44 3DL

Tel. 0141 633 2020

Correspondent Robert Waterston, Secretary

Inland Revenue no. SC009899

Information available Information was provided by the trust.

General Funds are mainly available for members of Strathclyde police, retired members, and widows or other dependants who may be in need. The trust may also donate to other registered charities for general charitable purposes. Grants total about £150,000 a year.

Applications In writing to the correspondent. Applications to be received by the end of March for consideration in the annual meeting held in April.

The Talbot-Crosbie Bequest

General
Est. £15,000 a year
Beneficial area Bearsden

Community Support Services, The Triangle, Kirkintilloch, Glasgow G64 2TR

Tel. 0141 578 8563

Correspondent Maifie McCrae

Inland Revenue no. SC018494

Information available Limited information was available on this fund.

General The fund gives grants towards the costs of work undertaken by organisations based in Bearsden. The trust estimated that grants total about £15,000 a year. Grants are not awarded to organisations which raise money through house-to-house collections or flag days.

Applications Contact the correspondent at the above address for an application form which must be returned by 31 December of each year. Applications are considered annually in January.

The Templeton Goodwill Trust

General
About £100,000 (1998/99)

Beneficial area Glasgow and the West of Scotland

12 Doon Street, Motherwell ML1 2BN

Tel. 01698 262202

Correspondent W T P Barnstaple, Trustee and Administrator

Trustees *A D Montgomery; J H Millar; B Bannerman; W T P Barnstaple.*

Inland Revenue no. SC004177

Information available Information was supplied by the trust.

General The trust supports a wide range of charities in Glasgow and the West of Scotland. It is interested in supporting organisations which help others. Types of beneficiaries include: youth organisations, medical research charities, churches, ex-services organisations and other organisations concerned with social work and providing caring services for all age groups. In 1998/99 the trust gave about £100,000 in grants. Grants ranged from £250 to £4,000 and about 65 to 70 organisations received support. Beneficiaries included Boys' Brigade in Glasgow, Glasgow Girl Guides and Glasgow Council on Alcohol.

Exclusions Support is given to Scottish registered charities only. Individuals are not supported and grants are generally not given to arts or cultural organisations.

Applications In writing to the correspondent, preferably including a copy of accounts. Applications should be received by April as the trustees meet once a year, at the end of April or in May.

Donald Thomson Memorial Educational Trust

Gaelic education
About £1,000 a year

Beneficial area Particular interest in Argyll

Sannox, Crannaig-A-Mhinister, Oban PA34 4LU

Tel. 01631 563977

Correspondent R Macintyre

Inland Revenue no. SC013598

Information available Information was provided by the trust.

General The trust makes grants towards the advancement of Gaelic education in Argyll. Grants total about £1,000 a year.

Exclusions No grants to individuals.

Applications In writing to the correspondent.

The Trades House of Glasgow – Commonweal Fund

Social welfare, general
About £100,000

Beneficial area Glasgow

310 St Vincent Street, Glasgow G2 5QR

Tel. 0141 228 8000

Correspondent The Clerk

Inland Revenue no. SC012507

Information available A booklet about the various trusts comprising this charity, its report and accounts were available. These do not include lists of grants.

General The Trades House of Glasgow was first established in 1605. It manages a number of trust funds, each bound to their separate trust deeds. Most of the trusts are tied to specific causes and locations. The majority are concerned with various aspects of social welfare and individual need, particularly in Glasgow. Only one of the funds, the Commonweal Fund, is able to respond to applications from organisations. All the others can only support those organisations named in their trust deeds.

The Commonweal Fund makes grants to projects totalling about £100,000 each year. Grants are made to a range of charitable causes and can be for up to 'a few thousand pounds'. All grants are one-off and the vast majority of funds are donated within Glasgow.

Exclusions The funds are held primarily for the benefit of Glasgow and its citizens, if you fall outside those parameters you should not submit an application. Political, municipal, and ecclesiastical appeals cannot be entertained. Charities duplicating rather than complementing existing services and those with national purposes and/or large running surpluses normally cannot be helped.

Applicants receiving help one year will normally be refused the next.

Applications There is no set form of application for organisations seeking help. You should write a summary in your own words extending to not more than a single A4 sheet, backed as necessary by schedules and accompanied by your latest accounts and/or business plan. Evidence of need must be produced, as should evidence that client groups participate in decision making and that their quality of life and choice is enhanced. Where possible, costs and financial needs should be broken down, evidence of the difference which a grant would make be produced, and details given, with results, of other grants applied for.

Applications should include evidence of charitable status, current funding and the use you are making of that. Projects should be demonstrated to be practical and business-like. It is a condition of any grant that a report be made as to how the funds have been used. Grants not used for the purposes stated must be returned.

Tullochan Trust

Young people

About £25,000 a year

Beneficial area Dunbartonshire, Bearsden, Milngavie and Helensburgh

Tullochan, Gartocharn G83 8ND

Tel. 01389 830205 **Fax** 01389 830653

Correspondent Mrs Fiona Stuart, Chair

Inland Revenue no. SC025309

Information available Information was provided by the trust.

General This trust gives grants of up to £1,000 to youth organisations and individuals, totalling around £25,000 each year.

Applications In writing to the correspondent. Applications must be submitted before the end of April and the end of October each year.

The Walton Foundation

Medical, education, general

£76,000 (1998)

Beneficial area West of Scotland

Deloitte & Touche, 9 George Square, Glasgow G2 1QQ

Tel. 0141 204 2800

Correspondent Fiona Jamieson

Trustees *D Walton; Mrs C Walton; Prof. R A Lorimer; E Glen; Prof. L Blumgart; M Walton; J R Walton.*

Inland Revenue no. SC004005

Information available Accounts are available from the trust.

General The trust will support a wide variety of organisations, with a particular emphasis on education and medical causes. Grants can range from £100 to £25,000 and are usually recurrent.

In 1998 the trust had assets of £2.1 million and an income of £121,000. Grants totalled £76,000. During this year mainly medical charities appeared to benefit; some educational, heritage and Jewish charities also received support. The trust listed 13 of the beneficiaries in the accounts. One very large grant of £50,200 was given to Jewish Care Scotland. Other grants ranged from £250 to £6,000. Large grants included those to British Council of SZMC (£6,000), Lubavitch Foundation (£4,000), Glasgow Jewish Education Trust (£2,000), Jewish National Fund (£1,950), Queens Park Hebrew Congregation (£1,725) and Glasgow Maccabi (£1,240).

Smaller grants went to Glasgow Jewish Representative Council (£625), Scottish Jewish Archives (£500) and Glasgow Hebrew Burial Society (£250). 'Other' grants totalled £6,340.

Exclusions No grants to individuals. No grants for political causes.

Applications In writing to the correspondent. Trustees meet to consider grants in June; applications should be received by March.

Western Recreation Trust

Recreation

Between £20,000 and £25,000

Beneficial area West of Scotland

Scott-Moncrieff, 25 Bothwell Street, Glasgow G2 6NL

Tel. 0141 567 4500

Correspondent Ian Paterson

Inland Revenue no. SC002534

Information available Information was provided by the trust.

General The trust supports organisations in the West of Scotland working to improve recreational facilities for young people, older people and those who are unemployed. Grants are given towards the costs of equipment and are mostly of £200, although they can be up to £1,000 in exceptional cases. Between £20,000 and £25,000 is given in grants each year.

Exclusions Grants are not normally given to individuals.

Applications In writing to the correspondent at any time.

James Thomas Yuillie's Trust

General

About £4,000 a year

Beneficial area The burgh of Rothesay

34 Castle Street, Rothesay PA20 9HD

Tel. 01700 503157

Correspondent Ian Maclagan, Trustee

Trustees *Ian Maclagan; Mrs W C C Mackay; Revd R R Samuel; Mrs Marjorie J Bullock.*

Inland Revenue no. SC015388

Information available Information was provided by the trust.

General The trust donates to charitable organisations that operate within Rothesay. Grants total about £4,000 a year.

Applications On an application form available from the correspondent. Applications should be submitted by mid-June each year.

Highlands & Islands

The Brownies Taing Pier Trust

Community groups

£31,000 (2000)

Beneficial area Sandwick and Levenwick

Tait & Peterson, Bank of Scotland Buildings, Lerwick, Shetland Islands ZE1 OEB

Tel. 01595 693010

Correspondent George S Peterson

Information available No financial information was available.

General Grants are given to community projects in Sandwick and Levenwick. Projects which receive part of their funding from the local community are given preference.

In 2000 a total of £31,000 was given in grants. No further information was available about recent beneficiaries or the size of grants.

Applications Contact the correspondent at the above address for further information.

The Cromarty Trust

Preservation of buildings, conservation, education

£19,000 (2000)

Beneficial area UK, with a preference for the Parish of Cromarty, Ross and Cromarty

Wormshill Court, Sittingbourne, Kent ME9 0TS

Correspondent J Nightingale, Trustee

Trustees *Miss E V de B Murray; J B W Nightingale; A P Mc Nightingale; Mrs R Homfray.*

Charity Commission no. 272843

Information available Information was provided by the trust.

General In 2000 the trust had an income of £26,000 and gave grants totalling £19,000. It supports organisations mainly in the parish of Cromarty concerned with: preservation of buildings of historical or architectural interest; conservation of landscape; and education of the public in the history, character and wildlife of the parish.

Applications Applications are not invited and the trustees take a proactive approach to grantmaking and the development of projects which they wish to support. Unsolicited appeals other than those from the parish of Cromarty will not receive a response.

The Culra Charitable Trust

General

£26,000 (1999)

Beneficial area Scottish Highlands and Kent

c/o The Hedley Foundation, 9 Dowgate Hill, London EC4R 2SU

Tel. 020 7489 8076

Correspondent P T Dunkelley

Trustees *C Byam-Cook; P J Sienesi; G Needham.*

Charity Commission no. 274612

Information available Full accounts were on file at the Charity Commission.

General This trust has general charitable purposes, giving grants in the Scottish Highlands and Kent.

In 1999 it had assets of £483,000 and an income of £26,000, all of which was given in grants.

The largest grants were £3,000 to Sons of Clergy, £1,800 to Bedford School Trust, £1,300 to Hospices in the Weald and £1,000 each to Help our Hospices and Talbat Hospice Trust.

Exclusions Grants are not given to non-registered charities or individuals.

Applications In writing to the correspondent.

The Davidson (Nairn) Charitable Trust

Social welfare

Not known

Beneficial area Nairn area

Messrs Macgregor & Co., Royal Bank of Scotland Buildings, 20 High Street, Nairn IV12 4AX

Tel. 01667 453278 **Fax** 01667 453499

e-mail macgregorco@btinternet.com

Correspondent Ian A Macgregor, Solicitor

Trustees *Ian A Macgregor and others.*

Inland Revenue no. SC024273

Information available Information was provided by the trust.

General The trust gives grants in the Nairn area for social welfare causes. This includes making grants towards the provision of leisure and recreation facilities, relieving poverty, assisting elderly people, and educational concerns. Since its formation in November 1995, total grants paid amounted to £373,000 by August 2001.

Exclusions Only recognised charities are supported.

Applications Write to the correspondent for an application form.

The Garnett Charitable Settlement Dated 15 August 1973

Medical, education, environment

£22,000 (1999/2000)

Beneficial area Newtonmore area

c/o Chiene & Tait, 61 Dublin Street, Edinburgh EH3 6NL

Tel. 0131 558 5800

Correspondent James G Morton

Trustees *Eira Drysdale; Debbie Findlay; J A Findlay.*

Inland Revenue no. SC043705

Information available Accounts were on file at the Charity Commission.

General The trust supports medical, educational and environmental charities in the Newtonmore area. In 1999/2000 the trust had assets of £475,000, an income of £23,000 and gave £22,000 in grants. Grants are usually in the range of £500 to £2,000. The largest grant was for £2,000 to the Game Conservancy Trust. Others include Alzheimer Scotland and Highland Primary Care (£1,000 each). There were 38 beneficiaries in total, with 25 receiving less than £1,000 including Shelter Scotland and North Scotland Kosovo Appeal (£500 each), and Scottish Garden Appeal (£200).

Exclusions Grants are not given to individuals.

Applications In writing to the correspondent.

Highland Council Charities

General

Not known

Beneficial area The Highland Council area

The Highland Council, Glenurquhart Road, Inverness IV3 5NX

Tel. 01463 702000

Correspondent Gavin Gilray, Principal Accountant

Inland Revenue no. SC025079

Information available Information was provided by the trust.

General The council runs a number of common good and trust funds, which can award grants to support local community projects. These funds are administered through local offices as shown below:

Inverness Common Good Fund
Area Manager, Town House, Inverness IV1 1JJ (01463 724235)

Cromarty, Dingwall, Fortrose, Invergordon amd Tain Common Good Funds
Area Manager, Council Offices, High Street, Dingwall IV15 9QN (01349 868500)

Nairn Common Good Fund
Area Manager, The Court House, High Street, Nairn IV12 4AU (01667 458569)

Caithness Educational Trust Scheme
Area Education Manager, Rhind House, West Banks Avenue, Wick KW1 5LZ (01995 602812)

Iverness-shire Educational Trust Scheme
Area Education Manager, 13 Ardross Street, Inverness IV3 5NS (01463 663812).

Applications Contact the appropriate division for further information.

Orkney Arts Society

Arts
About £5,000
Beneficial area Orkney

Claireholm, Glaitness Road, Kirkwall, Orkney
Tel. 01856 873781
Correspondent Lydia Campbell, Secretary
Inland Revenue no. SC004819
Information available Information was provided by the trust.

General The society receives a covenant each year of £5,000 from Elf Consortium to distribute in grants. It gives grants to organisations for the promotion of the study or the practice of the arts

in Orkney. The society says that most relevant applications are successful. Grants range from £100 to £1,500. It is not known whether the Elf Consortium covenant will continue as the company has been taken over.

Exclusions Organisations must be constituted bodies based in Orkney. Individuals are not supported.

Applications On a form available from the correspondent. The trust advertises in December and the closing date is the end of February every year. Please note, the future of this trust is uncertain; contact the correspondent for further details.

James Paton's Charitable Trust

General
About £15,000
Beneficial area Inverness

7 Muirfield Road, Inverness IV2 4AY
Tel. 01463 231025
Correspondent R M Murray, Trustee
Trustees *R M Murray; Hugh Hutchison.*
Inland Revenue no. SC000496
Information available Information was provided by the trust.

General The trust supports a wide variety of local charities in Inverness. It has about £15,000 to give in grants each year. Past beneficiaries have included Highland Regional Council's Social Work Department, Isobel Fraser Home of Rest and Highland Society for the Blind.

Exclusions The trust does not normally fund national charities.

Applications Applications are not encouraged as the trustees do their own research.

Ross and Cromarty Educational Trust

Education and training, children and young people

£10,000 (1998/99)

Beneficial area Isle of Lewis

Comhairle nan Eilean, Education Department,
Sandwick Road, Stornoway,
Isle of Lewis HS1 2BW

Tel. 01851 709498

Correspondent The Director of Education
& Leisure Services

Information available Information was provided
by the trust.

General The trust supports children and young
people and education and training on the Isle of
Lewis. Individuals are supported for educational
purposes. Organisations are also supported. The
amount given to individuals and organisations
varies each year. In 1998/99 the trust had an
income of £10,000, all of which was given in
grants. The usual maximum grant is £200.

Exclusions The trust only supports people
living on the Isle of Lewis.

Applications In writing to the correspondent.

Shetland Amenity Trust

Conservation, heritage

£102,000 (2000/01)

Beneficial area Shetland

22-24 North Road, Lerwick, Shetland ZE1 ONQ

Tel. 01595 694688 **Fax** 01595 693956

e-mail shetamenity.trust@zetnet.co.uk

Website www.shetland-news.co.uk/website/
amenity

Correspondent The Trustees

Trustees Andrew Blackadder;
William A Cumming; Cecil Eunson;
Florence Grains; Brian Gregson; Martin Heubeck;
Roger Riddington; Frank Robertson;
Douglas Sinclair; John Scott; P Brian Smith.

Inland Revenue no. SC017505

Information available Accounts were provided
by the trust.

General The trust's objectives are:

- 'the protection, improvement and
  enhancement of buildings and artefacts of
  architectural, historical, educational or other
  interest in Shetland with a view to securing
  public access to such buildings and the
  permanent display for the benefit of the public
  of such artefacts for the purposes of research,
  study or recreation

- the provision, development and improvement
  of facilities for the enjoyment by the public of
  the Shetland countryside and its flora and
  fauna, the conservation and enhancement for
  the benefit of the public of its natural beauty
  and amenity and the securing of public access
  to the Shetland countryside for the purposes of
  research, study or recreation

- such other purpose or purposes charitable in
  law as the trustees shall from time to time
  determine.'

In 2000/01 it had assets of £2.5 million and an
income of £2 million, including £1.7 million in
grants and donations received, mostly from
Shetland Islands Council Charitable Trust. Grants
were given to 27 projects totalling £102,000. The
total expenditure was £1.5 million, mostly spent
on its own initiatives.

Beneficiaries included Old Scatness Broch
(£34,000), Whalsay History Group (£7,500),
University of Glasgow (£7,300), Scottish
Conservation Volunteers (£4,800), Shetland
Ranger Service (£3,000), SAT Viking Legacy
(£2,200), SAT Delting Disaster Fund and
Scalloway Waterfront Trust (£2,000 each), Fetlar
Museum Trust (£1,500), Auld Skule Recycling
Centre (£1,000), Lunnasting History Group
(£840), Quarff Primary School (£750) and Unst
Heritage Centre (£420).

Applications In writing to the correspondent.

Shetland Arts Trust

Arts

£10,000 (2000)

Beneficial area Shetland

Pitt Lane, Lerwick, Shetland ZE1 0DW

Tel. 01595 694001 **Fax** 01595 692941

e-mail admin@shetland-arts-trust.co.uk

Correspondent Jacqueline Clark

Trustees *Dr Christine M Begg; Anne Dickie; J Hutton; Anne Halford-MacLeo; W H Manson; F A Robertson; Dorota Rychlik; B Stove; Marion Tarrant; Celia Smith; Jane Thomas.*

Inland Revenue no. SC003098

Information available An annual report and guidelines were provided by the trust.

General The trust promotes visual, performing and creative art in Shetland. It also assists in arranging a widespread service of performances, exhibitions and lectures about any artistic-related pursuits. It coordinates the efforts of government agencies, local authorities, societies, trade unions and local people. It operates an arts development grant scheme, the guidelines for which are as follows:

Who can apply?
'Individuals who have practiced in their particular art form for two years or more. Individuals must submit a portfolio/examples of their work with their application and have a bank account. References may be requested.

'Groups who are planning an arts based project/event. Groups must submit a constitution with their application and have a bank account. Groups must submit examples of their work and previous publicity material with their application. Office bearers should be 18 years old or over.

'Groups/individuals undertaking a commercial venture may apply for a "Guarantee Against Loss". Further information on this aspect of the scheme is available through your grant contact.

How do you apply?
'By completing the scheme's application form and submitting a project report (see page two of the application form). Each applicant is allocated a grant contact who will provide assistance and advice.

'The majority of applications are considered by Arts Trust officials. On occasions the advice of our grants panel, sub-committees or board of trustees may be sought.

When can you apply?
'Applications are considered throughout the year. However, our budget is limited and we would advise that you apply in the initial project planning stage of your project.

What do SAT look for?
• 'originality within an arts project
• 'benefits to the wider Shetland community and the project participants
• 'developmental potential
• 'quality
• 'increased access to and awareness of the arts
• 'advancement of artistic skills.

'Financial assistance for equipment purchase will not be provided.

'Financial assistance for framing costs will not be provided unless it is part of a larger development project.

'Educational bursaries/grants are not currently provided.

Funding will not be awarded retrospectively.

What happens if you are successful?
'Funding will not exceed 50% of the total project cost. The grant amount will not exceed £750 (£1,000 if travelling outside Shetland). The grant amount for individuals will not normally exceed £500.

'Grants under £500 will be paid in full prior to the project start date. For grants of £500 or over a 10% retention will be withheld. 90% of your grant will be payable prior to the project start date, the 10% retention once all conditions of grant aid have been complied with.

'The trust reserves the right to consider an "Interest Free Loan" or a "Guarantee Against Loss" as a more appropriate method of support on certain projects. Please ask your grant contact for further information.

What is matched funding?
'Funding will not normally exceed 50% of the total project costs. The remaining 50% project shortfall must be covered from other sources,

e.g. box office takings, Shetland Enterprise, Scottish Arts Council etc.

'The trust stores information on funding agencies and general arts information. Please ask your grant contact for further information.

'You will be required to vouch for the total cost of your project.

What is retrospective funding?
'Retrospective funding is when an applicant submits a bid for funding for a project which has already been paid for in part or in full.

'You are required to inform the trust of the project start and finish dates. If the money has been spent prior to these dates your project may be deemed to be retrospective.

'Any bid which is submitted too near to the project start date runs the risk of being classified as retrospective. The trust advises all applicants to submit bids at least four weeks in advance of the project start date.

Is there anything else you need to know?
- 'each application will be considered on its merit

- 'the Development Grant Scheme is a discretionary one

- 'Shetland Arts Trust reserves the right to reject an application

- 'any award will depend on the availability of funds

- 'it can take between four and seven weeks to process any application

- 'the trust encourages applicants to investigate other funding options

- 'the trust operates an appeals procedure.

- 'only one application can be submitted in any financial year (1 April to 31 March).

- 'Shetland Arts Trust funding must be acknowledged on all publicity material.'

In 2000 the trust had an income of £540,000, it had direct charitable expenditure of £300,000 and gave £10,000 in grants.

Applications On a form available from the correspondent, to be returned with recent accounts and publicity material.

The Shetland Islands Council Charitable Trust

General

£12 million to organisations (1999/2000)

Beneficial area Shetland

Breiwick House, 15 South Road, Lerwick, Shetland ZE1 0TD

Tel. 01595 744681 **Fax** 01595 744667

Correspondent Jeff Goddard, Finance Department

Trustees *24 trustees, being the elected Shetland councillors (acting as individuals), the Lord Lieutenant and the Headmaster of Anderson High School. The Chair is Robert Irvine Black.*

Inland Revenue no. SC016192

Information available Model reports and accounts, available from the trust for £2.

General The original trust was established in 1976 with 'disturbance receipts' from the operators of the Sullom Voe oil terminal. As a clause in the trust deed prevented it from accumulating income beyond 21 years from its inception, in 1997 most of its assets were transferred to a newly established Shetland Islands Council Charitable Trust, which is identical to the old trust except for the omission of the prohibition on accumulating income. The trust is run by the Shetland Islands council, which receives around £650,000 a year for this service.

The 1999/2000 annual report states:

'The Shetland Islands Charitable Trust seeks to benefit Shetland and its inhabitants. In particular the trustees set out to:

- improve the quality of life for the inhabitants of Shetland, especially in the areas of: social need, leisure, environment, education

- build on the energy and initiatives of local self-help groups and assist them to achieve their objectives, without destroying the independence and enterprise which brought them into being

- utilise the funds in order to provide large-scale facilities which would be of long-term benefit to the inhabitants of Shetland

- support traditional industries and assist in the introduction of new ones, in ways where a charity and a trust might usefully assist, particularly: agriculture, fishing, knitwear, aquaculture

- maintain flexibility for the trust's funds; in order to be able to meet new situations and priorities, but to do so against the background of a published framework of plans.'

Applications are through the appropriate Shetland Islands council department and in practice the trust operates much as a council funding programme.

In 1999/2000 the trust had assets of £327 million and an income of £15 million. Grants totalled £13 million, including £1.3 million to individuals. The largest grant was £5 million to Isleburgh Trust, although there was no analysis of this in the accounts.

A number of larger grants were given to charitable trusts connected to the council. These were £2.1 million to Shetland Recreational Trust, £1.9 million to Shetland Welfare Trust, £767,000 to Shetland Amenity Trust and £319,000 to Shetland Arts Trust.

Other beneficiaries included Independence at Home Scheme grants (£162,000), Walter and John Gray Eventide Home for construction and running costs (£123,000), Shetland Alcohol Trust (£99,000), Shetland Islands Citizens Advice Bureau (£84,000), Community Opportunities for Participation in Enterprise for infrastructure (£74,000) and Shetland Churches Council Trust (£52,000).

Exclusions Funds can only be used to benefit the inhabitants of Shetland.

Applications Applications from the general public are not considered. Projects are recommended by the various committees of Shetland Islands Council.

The trustees meet every six to eight weeks.

Shetland Wildlife Fund

Conservation

Up to £2,000 a year

Beneficial area Shetland Islands

c/o East House, Sumburgh Head Lighthouse, Virkie, Shetland ZE3 9JN

Tel. 01950 460760

Correspondent Martin Heubeck

Inland Revenue no. SC021306

Information available Information was provided by the fund.

General The fund was set up in 1993 following the Braer oil spill off the coast of the Shetland Islands. In the aftermath of the crisis, various donations were given to assist wildlife in the area and it was decided that the best thing to do with any unspent donations was to set up a trust.

Since 1993 the fund has supported a range of environmental and wildlife projects in the Shetland Islands. These have included: a rehabilitation sanctuary for seals; a tree-planting scheme; environmental survey work; and educational work with an environmental feel. It aims to make the Shetland Islands beneficial to the public. It will not usually fund all of a project's costs.

The trust has no income and in 2001 had roughly £13,000 to £15,000 held as capital for it to distribute in grants. Up to about £2,000 is usually donated each year. When all capital is spent, the trust will wind up.

Applications In writing to the correspondent.

Index